5,000 WRITING PROMPTS

A MASTER LIST OF PLOT IDEAS, CREATIVE EXERCISES, AND MORE

BRYN DONOVAN

5,000 WRITING PROMPTS:
A Master List of Creative Exercises, Plot Ideas, and More

Copyright 2019 Stacey Donovan

First edition, March 2019

Print: 978-0-9967152-5-6
eBook: 978-0-9967152-6-3

This book is dedicated to Gill Donovan, my husband, soul mate, and best friend.

TABLE OF CONTENTS

INTRODUCTION

Welcome to *5,000 Writing Prompts!*

This book is for all kinds of writers and storytellers—novelists, short story writers, essayists, poets, screenwriters, playwrights, memoirists, bloggers, improv actors, fans of role-playing games, and more—as well as for teachers and anyone else who wants inspiration. Although I've broadly classified the prompts as "Fiction Prompts," "Poetry Exercises," and "Autobiographical and Blogging Prompts," they can all be used in many different ways.

Why I Wrote This Book

I'm a publishing professional and an author who also blogs about writing and teaches creative workshops. Because of this, I talk to a lot of writers and aspiring authors.

People often say things like:

"I want to write, but I don't know where to start."

"I haven't written in a long time. How can I get back into that creative mindset again?"

"I have a fictional world and characters I love, but I don't have a plot."

"I want to start a blog, but what if I can't think of enough things to write about?"

In all of these cases, people need a little extra spark of inspiration. I felt like I was in a unique position to help because I'm an inveterate list maker. I have journals and notebooks filled with creative idea starters, from master plots and essay subjects to character quirks and fascinating words. I have a particular obsession with identifying and compiling the smaller elements that can go into a script, short story, blog, personal essay, play, or novel. I'll never be able to use them all in my lifetime, so why keep them to myself?

I also wanted to write this book because I believe creative possibilities are limitless. When it doesn't seem that way to us, it's often because we've gotten bogged down with the demands, details, and sorrows of everyday life, and it's given us tunnel vision. I hope because this book has a *lot* of writing prompts, it reminds people of all the possible stories inside them...way, way more than five thousand!

Are Writing Prompts "Cheating"?

I thought I'd address this right up front, because some people worry about it! Using one of my writing prompts for a story, poem, or other original work absolutely isn't cheating, even if you get it published. We writers take inspiration from everywhere: magazine articles, the stories our friends and family tell us, observations of our neighbors or strangers, and yes, other books, TV shows, and movies. It's the way we treat that little spark of inspiration and what we do with it that makes it original and makes it ours.

I hope this book supports other people's success. If you purchased the book, checked it out of the library, or received a gift copy purchased by someone else, then if it inspires you to write a novel that makes you a million dollars, you don't owe me a dollar of those royalties. If your novel wins the Pulitzer, I'd love a shout-out in your acceptance speech...but you probably won't do that, and that's okay. I understand. I'll still be proud of you!

If you still don't feel comfortable using a specific prompt, just take a minute to ask yourself: "How can I make this different?" Then put your own spin on it.

You're likely to come up with new ideas of your own just from perusing the pages of this book. You're a creative person, after all, and that's just how creative brains work.

HOW TO USE THIS BOOK

How To Beat Writer's Block: The Two-Week Program

If you've suffered from writer's block for weeks, months, or even decades, try this.

Every day at roughly the same time, close your eyes, flip through this book, and point to something on a page. Whatever prompt you're touching, write about it for fifteen minutes.

Fifteen minutes! That's it! You can do almost anything for only fifteen minutes.

I don't care if you think it's a stupid prompt. Don't look for another one. You're stuck with it. If it's very different from anything you would ever imagine yourself writing, that's *good*. And if it's a prompt that makes you think, "I know nothing about this subject," I don't care. You might know more about it than you realize at first, and anyway, the point is to get your imagination going.

Write a description, a short scene, a conversation, a paragraph—whatever comes into your head is fine. For those fifteen minutes, write *fast*. Don't judge what you're writing. It doesn't have to be high quality. It just has to be writing. Get it out there.

Do this once a day for two weeks.

Now, while you're doing it, two weeks may seem like a long time. It's really not. How many weeks have you spent not writing at all?

You may not enjoy this process. Change is often uncomfortable, and it takes effort. Then again, you may have fun with it. You won't be under any pressure to create a finished, brilliant story—and that pressure may have been shutting you down in the first place.

Either way, if you do this exercise for two weeks, it'll switch on the part of your brain that enables you to do creative writing. I bet you'll be surprised at the new ideas that come to you.

A new journal dedicated to the two-week challenge might inspire you.

Using This Book to Begin a New Story

If you need a story idea, I recommend going to the section of plot prompts by genre first for inspiration. However, any one of the prompts might also kick off a new story for you.

Using This Book to Help You With Your Work in Progress

If you're feeling stuck in the middle of a story, flip through the fiction prompts and use one of them to spark some new writing. Lots of the fiction prompts will help you add conflict to the story, flesh out a subplot, or make a scene more memorable.

Many of the prompts in this book can help you get to know your characters better. Choose an autobiographical prompt and write out a response to it as your character. Alternately, go to the character prompts that are all about making your character angry, embarrassed, or guilty. Use one of those prompts with your specific character in mind.

Using This Book As a Teacher

In my experience, students of any age do better if they have in-class exercises and not just homework. You might want to try this: put one prompt on a piece of paper for each student in your class and put them in a bag. Have each student pick one of the prompts and write about it for fifteen or twenty minutes.

THANK YOU

Thanks for getting this book. I hope you enjoy it, and I hope it's a useful resource for you for years to come. Happy writing!

FICTION PROMPTS

Although I'm calling this section, which comprises the largest part of the book, "Fiction Prompts," they can also be used for screenwriting, role-playing games, improv troupes, and many other creative endeavors! Keep in mind that I use "he" and "she" more or less at random. You can always change the gender.

50 WAYS TO BEGIN A STORY

Even when you have a basic idea for your story, sometimes it's hard to know where to begin. I think one of the best things you can do with your first five or ten pages is get the readers to care about what happens to your main character (or to one of them.) Writers are often tempted to go into a lot of backstory at the beginning, telling readers about the world of the novel or about everything that happened before the story begins. It's usually better to weave that material into the story here and there, and begin with action. But there are exceptions to this rule (the Pixar movie Up, *for example), and exceptions to every rule.*

1. The arrival of a letter, email, or package.

   The Thirteenth Tale by Diane Setterfield opens in this way.

2. The text of a letter, email, or diary.

   You might want to dive right in with what it says, and let the reader learn later about the character reading it.

3. An invitation—to join a club, attend a dinner party, or do something shocking.

4. A main character is in a frustrating situation.

   This can also give the reader a feel for her everyday life, while making them empathize with her right away. Maybe her car has broken down, or her cat is puking.

5. A main character is in an awkward or embarrassing situation.

   This could be momentous. However, it could simply tell the reader about the character's everyday life, such as an odd private message on a dating site.

6. An escape—from a boring meeting, or prison.

7. Someone discovers a dead body.

    Countless mysteries and thrillers open in this way.

8. A funeral is held for someone in the family or the community.

    This is a popular one with authors, and understandably so, because an ending is a new beginning.

9. A birth.

10. The beginning or the middle of a disaster.

    It could be a bombing, a plane crash, or a tornado.

11. The aftermath of a disaster.

12. A character does something which will be discovered later: slips a love note in someone's purse, poisons the wine, or plants a bomb in a car.

13. A game or contest.

14. A kiss.

15. A performance, or the conclusion of one.

    Bel Canto by Ann Patchett is a wonderful example of this. It also has a kiss in it!

16. One character rescues another.

17. A main character declares that he is in big trouble.

    Andy Weir's *The Martian* is a terrific example of this.

18. A main character clearly *is* in big trouble.

19. A main character is in the hospital.

Olivia Butler's *Kindred* is an example of this.

20. A main character sees a house or a city for the first time.

21. A plane, ship, or train arrives.

    The character might be on board, or she might be watching it come in.

22. A plane, ship, or train departs.

    If the character is on board, you can take the reader on a journey.

23. Someone gets amazing news.

24. Someone gets devastating news.

25. Someone goes on a date.

26. The main character breaks up with someone or is dumped.

27. A scene at a party, a bar, or a nightclub.

    This is another popular one. Leo Tolstoy's *War and Peace*, which opens with a *soirée*, is an example.

28. A fight.

    This is a fairly popular opening for novels that are heavy in action. *Children of Blood and Bone* by Tomi Adeyemi begins in this way. The main character could be watching the fight instead of taking part in it.

29. An all-out battle scene.

30. A character moves in to a new place.

    I love this idea for an opening because I think it would really welcome the reader into the story.

31. A dramatic moment in the middle or the end of the story.

    Some stories begin here and then backtrack to show how

they got there. Donna Tartt's *The Secret History* is a good example of this approach.

32. Someone is arrested.

33. A courtroom trial.

34. A job interview.

    I really like this idea because you could get a lot of information across about your character naturally. She might be giving appropriate answers while her internal monologue tells you the rest of the story. Also, an applicant at a job interview is in a vulnerable position, which I think would create empathy for your heroine right away.

35. A main character gets fired from a job.

    This elicits immediate sympathy for a character while setting up a clear, relatable conflict.

36. A chase scene.

37. Characters wait for another character—maybe for an ambush, or maybe for a surprise party.

38. A visitor shows up at the door.

    A stray cat? A future love interest? Raymond Chandler's *The Big Sleep* is one example of this.

39. A busy street scene.

    Your character could be getting an errand done or going to visit somebody. For a novel that takes place in an historical, futuristic, or fantasy setting, this can be a good way to establish a sense of place as well as establish your character's normal life and priorities.

40. A character or characters get dressed, shave, put makeup on, or do their hair.

41. A character commits a crime.

42. A character or characters do a job.

    Two examples of this are *Our Mutual Friend* by Charles Dickens and *Farenheit 451* by Ray Bradbury.

43. One character teaches another how to do something.

    This one is a good way to establish your main character's personality and his everyday life.

44. Character or characters prepare or sit down to eat a meal.

45. A main character comes across a significant object.

46. Someone teaches or attends a class.

47. Someone attends a church service.

48. A main character is in a triumphant situation.

    Set her up before you knock her down. She could be giving a speech, winning a race, or accepting an award. It could also be a smaller personal triumph, such as successfully fixing a car or turning in her term paper on time.

49. Someone unwraps a gift.

50. A birthday party.

    The beginning of J.R.R. Tolkien's *Lord of the Rings* is probably my favorite example.

PLOT PROMPTS BY GENRE

Need a little push on your space opera screenplay or your romance novella? Feel like beginning a sweeping historical epic or a quirky young adult story? Need help on a subplot or an idea for what happens next?

Start right here. A lot of these prompts could also be described as "plot bunnies." No two writers would handle them in quite the same way.

150 FANTASY PROMPTS

1. She isn't happy about being left at home to run the castle when they go off to war... and she winds up leading the biggest battle of all.

2. Once every thousand years, the phoenixes catch fire, burn to ash, and are reborn again from their own ashes. Contrary to legend, they aren't birds, but humanoid creatures.

3. A fae, a giant, and a gnome walk into a tavern.

4. A woman survives being struck by lightning, but it left a map burned onto her back.

5. The mermaids are empaths who find it hard to resist the urge to sing about the desires of any human nearby.

6. This hideous monster is pretty nice when you get to know him.

7. The birth of twins was considered bad luck in their country, so his father ordered his twin sister to be killed at birth. Someone disobeyed the order, and she's still alive.

8. The magical spell turned the hoard of gold and jewels into a living, sparkling dragon.

9. A man is sent to kidnap the king's daughter, and things don't go according to plan.

10. The barbarian girl from the north arrives at the school for priests.

11. A royal birth is usually a happy occasion, but this time it leads to disaster.

12. He's the zookeeper at a zoo for magical and mythological beasts.

13. The playwright didn't realize at first that his plays predicted the future.

14. The king sent his son on the quest fully expecting that the young man would get killed.

15. She commands the fireflies.

16. This so-called school for wizards is a scam—no one can do magic. Until now.

17. Can he prevent civil war by betraying the man who's both his friend and his king?

18. She's looking for her brothers who were turned into wolves.

19. When one takes out the jewel, it absorbs all of the light within about a mile radius.

20. The fallen angel tries to get a second chance.

21. Two souls live within the same body.

22. Nobody wants to be the woman whose foot fits into that slipper.

23. They call him the King of Keys. Well, he calls himself that, anyway.

24. The potion poisons anyone who has just told the truth.

25. The hellhounds have been locked out of hell.

26. His only magic is being able to weaken other people's spells.

27. This library is also a kind of arsenal.

28. What good is a banshee who has been rendered mute?

29. A new virus with strange symptoms affects only one magical species.

30. His voice magically compels everyone else to obey. Only she is unaffected.

31. Because of his unique parentage, he travels easily between the land of the living and the land of the dead.

32. Entrusting the quest to a couple of non-warriors turned out to be a terrible idea.

33. Anyone who touches the cursed river will die of thirst, no matter how much they drink.

34. Although humans don't know it, a certain business or institution is run by a cadre of supernatural beings.

35. She was a minor goddess once, but now she's the only one left.

36. He can smell fear. Also jealousy. And embarrassment. All emotions have specific scents to him.

37. Two warriors fight. One of them desperately wishes to avoid hurting the other.

38. No one remembers it now, but the four suits in a deck of

playing cards or Tarot cards were based on four long-lost kingdoms.

39. The demon is in trouble for being disloyal.

40. The horses burst into flames.

41. This magical item erases the wearer's bad memories as soon as they are made.

42. They've got a good reason to bring the evil guy back to life.

43. Whoever he shoots with one of his arrows falls in love... with him.

44. Thunderstorms bring him power, which he loses gradually over long stretches of clear weather.

45. She believes a shocking act of bloodshed is needed to inspire the uprising.

46. The statue appeared in the middle of town and no one knows how it got there.

47. In this culture, one of the most profound bonds is between the steed and the rider.

48. The weapon makes its owner invincible for a time, but will also be the death of its owner.

49. They are the spirits of the waterfalls.

50. One bone in his body once belonged to someone else.

51. When the woodsman cut down a tree, he freed a sprite imprisoned there.

52. In this land, exchanging wedding vows causes the couple to be able to hear one another's thoughts for the rest of their lives.

53. Any person who kills her will inherit her power.

54. Giant peacocks stand guard at the gate.

55. These walls do talk if you touch them in the right places.

56. She wants to poison the sacred well.

57. A wizard's severed hand wields fearsome power, but only if it is willingly sacrificed to the owner.

58. Everyone thinks he's the Chosen One, but he's just a good liar.

59. This incense can mask any smell.

60. The only black market in the realm is on the open ocean.

61. She pretended to be dead to escape the seven men in the woods.

62. A chieftain must sacrifice one of his warriors without telling him why.

63. They are able to cross the desert by taking the form of sandstorms.

64. The queen decides her son is unworthy to inherit the throne because of one particular reason.

65. No one ventures here without a mask.

66. A so-called fool triumphs in a battle over her enemies.

67. This plan will both appease a monster and rid the city of its undesirable residents.

68. The waters of this river will make anybody drunk.

69. The local police force actually knows all about her "secret" supernatural activities.

70. He recruits new servants among souls yet to be born.

71. Reincarnation is real, and she remembers all her past lives...and her future ones, too.

72. The good witch had been under the impression that it was a good spell.

73. She breaks the oath. It was a stupid oath anyway.

74. Getting that particular ancient symbol tattooed on that particular place on her body has unforeseen consequences.

75. The hero's captors are surprisingly polite.

76. No human who has entered this cave has ever emerged alive again.

77. The angel is reluctant to deliver this message.

78. The problem with hobgoblin companions is that they love playing practical jokes.

79. A man offers to take his place at the executioner's block despite being a complete stranger.

80. Party in the catacombs!

81. In the middle of a duel, the most embarrassing thing happens.

82. He called for all witches to be punished by death, not realizing his wife was one.

83. The Biblical rod of Aaron, which turns into a snake when thrown on the ground, has survived to the present day.

84. She doesn't know why he can read the runes.

85. The curse was lifted from him, but he wants it back.

86. They are from two different, warring species, and they're falling in love.

87. She reveals her true identity: she's the princess. Nobody believes her.

88. As the two sit by the fire, he makes a shocking confession.

89. The gargoyles are no longer stone.

90. The servant of the cruel master accidentally murders him.

91. Why does this modern corporation have a necromancer on the payroll?

92. Oh, no. He forgot to take off the ring.

93. The myth of the Easter Bunny is based on a true story.

94. She's been indoctrinated in this magical cult from childhood, but now she has doubts.

95. His armor has one special opening.

96. The magical sword was melted down to make various objects that are now scattered across the world.

97. This path changes course as you walk on it.

98. Some astounding things are for sale at the goblin market.

99. He first suspects he is the incarnation of an ancient god.

100. A musician can kill, heal, or resurrect people with his or her songs.

101. People are committing surprising acts in their sleep.

102. This might cure the current plague...if it can be found.

103. A smuggler, mercenary, or thief takes down or helps take down an oppressive ruler or regime.

104. An attempt to rescue a friend, family member, or lover will put a larger mission or cause in jeopardy.

105. A peasant girl, who may be good or evil, believes that a divine figure in a vision told her to lead an army to victory.

106. The ones who live in the bottom of the ocean come to the surface.

107. Someone can bring a person back to life by taking his or her place in the underworld.

108. A counterfeiter's coins or a forger's fake works of art become more valuable than the real thing for this one reason.

109. A warrior defects to the other side in hopes of bringing a costly war to a quicker resolution.

110. Anything becomes true if enough people believe in it deeply enough.

111. A person has been turned into an object by magic.

112. To open the door, a person must use a key whittled out of one of his or her own bones.

113. A person doesn't know why he or she has stopped aging.

114. After an archaeologist digs up an ancient treasure, the original owner shows up to take it back.

115. Two allies or two factions of the same army are tricked into attacking one another.

116. Miners discover stone spheres with strange markings.

117. Soldiers take souvenirs from their fallen enemies, which proves to be their downfall.

118. A woman or a group of women plot an escape or revolt against a forced marriage or a whole system of forced marriage.

119. His magical powers don't work when he's drunk.

120. The flowers from this garden are the most precious commodities in the realm...for a very good reason.

121. A vending machine dispenses some very peculiar items instead of Coke.

122. For this race of beings, the sense of smell is more important than vision or hearing.

123. She made a noble sacrifice, and now, as a ghost, she resents it.

124. They live on an island in the middle of a lava lake. It has advantages and disadvantages.

125. For this society, battle is a religious observance.

126. This is the most pitiful excuse for a castle in all the land.

127. This so-called magical sword has turned out to be a piece of junk.

128. A beautiful unmanned ship sails itself into the harbor.

129. So many birds or butterflies migrate across this land that for days, it darkens the skies.

130. The land has been cursed to permanent darkness, daytime, fog, wind, or lightning strikes.

131. Sibling rivalry is intense when it's between twin demigods.

132. At this auction, people are bidding a lot more than money.

133. He's the keeper of a hive of sentient bees.

134. A worker learns that the tower they are building will serve a much different purpose than what they were all told.

135. Each person's spirit is connected to a particular tree in the forest.

136. He's been hiding in the catacombs for years.

137. They find the fossil or skeleton of a creature they'd assumed to be mythical.

138. The changeling thought she was human, but now she's been returned to her own kind.

139. A spirit possesses a human or animal body and is then unable to get out of it.

140. The river has a soul of its own.

141. The king ran away and is living under an assumed name.

142. They fought long and hard to bring this new king to the throne, and it turns out he's totally incompetent.

143. This muse inspires artists, writers, and musicians to great work, but when she leaves them, they become so despondent they sometimes die.

144. He's assigned to be a bodyguard to someone on whom the fate of the world depends. The tricky part is, she can never find out that's what he's really doing.

145. No one knows who made the Garden of Obelisks or what the stone pillars signify.

146. There are good things and bad things about having an invisible dog for a pet.

147. The leaves of this tree make great parachutes.

148. The evil ruler is forcing her to forge an ancient prophecy that foretells his glorious reign.

149. She finds a century-old catalog, attempts to place an order, and succeeds.

150. The hero is killed halfway through, and the sidekick takes over.

150 SCIENCE FICTION PROMPTS

Some of these may be more along the lines of "speculative fiction" than science fiction. They include prompts about the environment, artificial intelligence, genetics, medicine, time travel, space exploration, alien races, and alternative histories.

1. All citizens are temporarily neutered at birth. Would-be parents must prove to the government that they'll be suitable caretakers and providers before they are allowed to procreate.

2. All marriages must be approved by a department of the government, which analyzes massive amounts of data to predict the success of the union, its economic and social impact on society, the health and welfare of any children, and so on. It's such a hassle that many people opt for government-arranged marriages instead.

3. Global warming prompts rapid mutations in the human species.

4. The world's leaders broker a deal with the alien invaders that many see as unfair.

5. Humans have discovered a way to communicate directly with animals, and all the meat humans consume now is lab-created.

6. Extreme elective surgery is the societal norm, and humans undergo creative modifications that include extra limbs, cartoon-like features, and so on.

Bryn Donovan

7. Breeding modern humans with large amounts of Neanderthal DNA leads to interesting results.

8. In this world, Napoleon's army took over Australia, and he never lost at Waterloo. France took control of most of Europe, and World War I and World War II never happened.

9. An alien from a planet where no one else experiences empathy comes to live on Earth, believing s/he will fit in better there.

10. A drug that makes people non-confrontational has been added to the public water supply and to all beverages sold by major corporations.

11. The huge, thin sheets of material covering some trees and yards turn out to be discarded placentas.

12. A low-level employee in a bureaucratic government office realizes the paperwork he files every day contains codes that determine others' fates.

13. A human and alien fall in love, causing an interplanetary crisis.

14. An alien doesn't know how to tell the humans she's become intimately involved with that she's an alien, even though they will find out soon enough.

15. High-speed robotic horses become a trendy alternative to cars and weave through heavy traffic with ease.

16. Hunters track down fugitives who resisted vaccinations or implants.

17. Personal information, including patterns of behavior and psychological triggers, has never been easier to obtain. Corporations synthesize and sell algorithms about consumers that make it easier than ever before to get them to buy goods and services.

18. Mars has been terraformed by dropping nuclear bombs on its poles, and the first human colonists have been assured that almost all of the radiation has escaped the atmosphere.

19. An attempt to save the honeybees has surprising consequences.

20. Online bullying is made a felony, which leads to unforeseen complications.

21. At a new underwater amusement park and resort, built at a greater depth than any other construction before, the guests face an unforeseen threat.

22. Spies use tiny implants in the retina that record and transmit everything to the commanders in another country. The implants dissolve after a certain amount of time.

23. The first time travelers seem to have no ability to improve the course of human events. If they kill Hitler, for instance, some other person does exactly what he did. They search for a way to really alter the timeline.

24. Astronauts develop strange and unexpected symptoms in response to traveling at light speed.

25. It's easy to look up exactly where any person is at any given time.

26. New fitness devices track your movements and everything you eat automatically.

27. A new device automatically tracks your mood levels and emotions. This leads people to avoid more of what makes them unhappy and do more of what makes them feel good.

28. People become human mood rings: they get implants that make them change color along with their mood.

29. Criminals and dissidents undergo illegal genetic therapy to change their DNA so the government has no record of them.

30. Euthanasia is legal and painless means are widely available. A detective specializes in suspicious cases of euthanasia that may have been murder.

31. Books and videogames have both been replaced by interactive virtual worlds filled with fascinating characters.

32. Colonists on another planet want to be an independent country and lead a rebellion.

33. People from a civilization that mysteriously disappeared centuries ago, such as ancestral Puebloans in the U.S. Southwest, return.

34. An alien planet outsources city planning by creating a complex, engrossing city-building videogame popular with humans.

35. A time traveler from centuries in the future fails in their attempt to impersonate a person of the 21st century. They enlist someone's help to carry out a mission.

36. A virus can be transmitted from computers or other machines to humans with bionic upgrades.

37. Advertisements appear randomly in thin air in front of a person. Getting media without this advertising is prohibitively expensive.

38. Scientists attempt to genetically alter a human to adapt to another planet's terrain or outer space travel. They accidentally make him or her immortal.

39. Implants make telepathy possible between the humans who get them.

40. The Air Force uses invisibility technology for the first time, but the pilot realizes her mission is morally reprehensible.

41. People are nostalgic for snow, so they create artificial snowstorms.

42. In a world where pain and suffering have been eliminated, people pay to experience a variety of negative sensations under safe and controlled circumstances.

43. A secret society of scientists labors to make medical discoveries and to save the planet, even though a religious fundamentalist government has outlawed their activities.

44. Medical researchers are attempting to bring people back to life after they've been dead for thirty minutes or even an hour and give them a full recovery. Their experimentation is unethical and/or leads to strange alterations to people's brains.

45. Someone is shrunk to a tiny size to perform a life-saving

or planet-saving procedure impossible for a machine or an average-sized human.

46. His loved one died, but is alive in a parallel universe, and he is somehow getting messages or clues about her life there.

47. An international videogaming competition is more popular than the Olympics ever were, but cheating and foul play are rampant.

48. Because it's too hard to screen for performance-enhancing drugs, they are made legal and are an important component of sports.

49. The ability to make visual recordings of dreams has exhilarating and terrifying consequences.

50. Drugs and medical treatments can be tailored to a patient's specific body—their age, medical history, and genetic makeup.

51. Patients are woken up from hibernation when the cures to their diseases have been discovered.

52. One person begins to notice subliminal coded messages in media, books, public signs, and more.

53. At nursing homes for the elderly, robot workers have completely replaced the human ones, and cuddly robot kittens and puppies also keep the residents company.

54. A newly discovered old text contains a revolutionary formula.

55. AI is now capable of writing reasonably coherent books

and movie scripts, albeit with a surrealist bent that many people prefer.

56. An entertainment company synthesizes huge amounts of data they collected about viewers' responses to movies and shows, and they use it to create a TV show that's dangerously addictive.

57. Human biological processes, such as heartbeats and electrical activity in the brain, are harnessed as an energy source that powers cities.

58. It's now possible to implant memories, which can give people whole new abilities.

59. It's now possible to remove or rewrite traumatic memories with almost surgical precision, bringing better mental health to many.

60. Negative emotions such as sadness and rage can be removed quickly with this simple treatment.

61. Humankind finds a way to move the Earth further from the sun in order to counteract the threat of global warming.

62. Humankind finds a way to rapidly grow huge forests of mature trees to counteract the effects of global warming.

63. Pieces of an alien spacecraft crash to the earth.

64. Aliens explore earth, but humans aren't able to perceive them.

65. An alien is taken prisoner after destroying a town. It was a total accident and the alien feels terrible about it.

66. An engineered virus wipes out people who are physiologically prone to depression.

67. A woman is hunted by her clone, created when she was still a child.

68. A huge volcano has obviously erupted, spreading ash over the entire planet, but nobody saw the volcano erupt, and nobody can find it.

69. A glacier melts and the skeleton of a twelve-foot-tall humanoid is discovered.

70. Birds and butterflies are able to navigate on long migrations due to proteins in their bodies that align with the earth's magnetic fields. Scientists put these proteins to a new use.

71. Whales and dolphins can be underwater for long periods of time due to a protein called myoglobin. Scientists put this protein to a new use.

72. A once-extinct species is re-created in order to control the population of another one.

73. After a virus wipes out about ninety percent of the world's human population, it becomes socially acceptable to take over the property of wealthy dead people with no living heirs.

74. A sharp increase in the birth of intersex babies has led to a society in which the binary notion of gender has been erased.

75. Most intelligent species in the galaxy aren't equipped

for war, and humans conquer planets with ease. One commander turns traitor and helps an alien race resist.

76. A person gets an abstract tattoo of his own design. Strangers snatch him from his home in the middle of the night. The tattoo happens to be a symbol for the shadow world government that nobody knows about.

77. A person learns that another person or being is playing her life like a videogame, causing events to happen and seeing how she responds to them. All of the people she thought were real are simulations—characters controlled by the player.

78. Humans can rate each other in the same way they'd rate restaurants or movies. People with one-star and two-star average ratings have no luck in dating or finding work.

79. A person works as a designer of subliminal messages in visual signs, pop songs, and other entertainment that keep the population calm and law-abiding.

80. They made him into a super soldier, but unfortunately, his enhanced powers are susceptible to glitches and hacks.

81. In this world, China and the U.S.S.R. joined together to become one big Communist state in the 1950s.

82. A scientist learns the real reason why the trees in this grove grow in strange bent and crooked shapes.

83. They can't get any decent volunteers to colonize the planet, so they simply abduct people with a variety of skills and talents and ship them off.

84. Aliens raid a fertility clinic, make off with all the embryos, and raise humans of their own.

85. Scientists bore into the center of the earth to obtain and study the minerals in its very core.

86. One of the richest men in the world hires young women to undergo surgery and genetic therapy and become actual mermaids, just to liven up parties at his estate. The pay is very good.

87. On Ceres, a large asteroid, there's a fueling station for spaceships. Terrorists take over the station and disrupt space travel and trade.

88. New zoos are filled with genetically engineered marvels, such as tigers with translucent skin and birds that can sing Beethoven.

89. A person can partially manifest in another dimension, where she's a child's "imaginary friend."

90. After a massive hack, the technologically advanced planet is reduced to a bartering system in place of money.

91. Because robot "kids" have become so lifelike, amusing, and hassle-free, no one wants to have real ones.

92. A person heroically accepts the mission to go back in time and kill his past self for the good of humanity. But then, things get complicated.

93. A person learns for the first time that they are one of the living results of an attempted upgrade to the human race.

94. An entire population of one particular species of mammal dies, seemingly overnight.

95. People with the genetic predisposition to dislike cilantro have a latent superpower.

96. Advances in medicine have made it easy for the wealthy to appear to be any physical age from adolescence on up, even though their lifespan hasn't increased.

97. People can loan out their bodies to others; they go into an unconscious state while another consciousness uses the body.

98. A person's consciousness can be downloaded into an artificial body, making them effectively immortal, but one person suspects that her consciousness was tampered with during the procedure.

99. Metabolism can be safely adjusted to accommodate a higher caloric intake so that no one is ever overweight.

100. Facial recognition and ubiquitous video recording by the government have led to a much bigger business in secret, drastic plastic surgery.

101. It appears as though many people are beginning to recall their past lives—in startling detail.

102. A vaccine for the deadly flu pandemic was created but kept secret from the general public.

103. They were prepared for an alien invasion and for a pandemic, but not at the same time.

104. It's now legal in every country in the world to buy organs from living donors.

105. A corporation patents the process of 3D printing human organs for successful transplants. A humanitarian thief sets out to steal the secrets to the process and share them with the world.

106. Someone believes she's destroying an AI but murders a person by mistake.

107. It's now widely known that psychological trauma can be passed down genetically from generation to generation, and there are ways to fix it.

108. It's been years since any human has done any writing or drawing by hand, which has had a surprising effect on brain development and function.

109. A biologist discovers some scientific basis for the personality types described by zodiac signs.

110. A home security AI keeps warning there's a stranger in the house, but there doesn't seem to be anyone there.

111. When a person first gets a new AI, it uses many faces, many different voices, and a wide range of speech patterns. Over time, through analysis of the owner's facial expressions, tone of voice, and body language, it settles into the appearance and communication style that pleases the owner most.

112. He's an Empathy Instructor, helping people pass a series of tests to earn their Empathy Certificate.

113. Angels are real, but they're an alien species that hasn't visited Earth in quite a while.

114. A government program infiltrates people's dreams in order to control them in waking life.

115. Hitting the "unfriend" button is more dramatic now that people interact almost entirely in the virtual realm.

116. It's their most amazing weapon yet: the ability to rewrite the collective memory of an entire population.

117. The planet's main export: adorable pets.

118. It's a prison break…from the international maximum-security prison on the moon.

119. The asteroids are small, but three of them have hit Earth now, and it's a serious problem.

120. The humans at a research station in Antarctica take in an alien after her ship crashes.

121. They're refining their formula for retrocausality—the way that future events can change past ones.

122. The new religion is based on scientific discovery.

123. A person learns that in fact, he doesn't just have bad luck: his series of unfortunate circumstances is part of a large psychology experiment.

124. She's treating someone who was exposed to high levels of radiation during space travel.

125. They discover that the Earth is caught in a long time loop. It's about to go back to prehistoric times and repeat again.

126. After she becomes pregnant, no one believes her when she says she's a virgin. She gives birth to a surprising offspring.

127. Since none of the nearby planets were truly ideal for colonizing, they created this one.

128. In this environment, no one can touch another person without delivering and receiving a strong shock of static electricity.

129. He's one of many voluntary human subjects getting superpowered senses—hearing, eyesight, etc. They've all signed a nondisclosure agreement.

130. She thought she'd be in outer space alone for the rest of her natural life, and she's thrilled to encounter this new life form.

131. If he says yes to the space mission, he'll be working in close quarters with a bitter rival.

132. A person gets sucked into a black hole. In one reality, he's instantly shredded into little pieces, but in another reality, he enters the black hole unharmed.

133. Her resume includes adapting novels into interactive virtual worlds.

134. The newly engineered crop grows best in environments previously considered useless for farming.

135. The aliens on this planet are doing the best they can to make the human explorers believe the planet is deserted.

136. Time travelers frequently wind up at this specific, random

time and place by mistake, and they're trying to figure out why.

137. People with a genetic predisposition for resilience to sleep deprivation are recruited for this particular job or mission.

138. Tiny bots are used to deliver drugs directly to the site that they are needed in the body.

139. The village will reward the hero for slaying the dragon. Except it's not really a village—it's a settlement on a distant planet. And it's not really a dragon.

140. Her clone thinks she's the original. But she's wrong. Isn't she?

141. No one's going to believe him unless he uses himself as a test subject and documents the results.

142. Earth has one big democratic government. Aliens have hacked the latest election.

143. In this world, people were able to not only train but actually domesticate elephants, and the countries with elephants won all the wars and dominated the world.

144. Their job is to gather up trash that humans have put into Earth's orbit over the decades and haul it out further into outer space.

145. A method to reverse global warming worked too well, and now the planet is going through another Ice Age.

146. The spaceship is programmed to blow itself up if the pilot is about to use it for anything destructive.

147. The metamaterial suit is so thin you can't even feel it against your skin, but it renders you invisible.

148. The commuter spaceship has been hijacked.

149. Since cockroaches are nearly indestructible as a species, scientists put them to a special use.

150. A particle accelerator opens up a hole to an alternate universe.

150 HORROR PROMPTS

Some of these are skeletal (ha) plots, while others are images or suggestions. There's quite a bit of overlap between horror, mystery, and fantasy, so don't be surprised if you wind up writing a mystery or fantasy based on a horror prompt.

1. A musician practices. When she finishes a piece, she hears someone clapping for her, although she lives alone.

2. Frightening events in a small town lead its citizens to dig up the grave of a deceased inhabitant.

3. Someone gets on the elevator by himself and is never seen by his friends or family again.

4. The Furies—the vengeance deities of classic mythology—are back in business again.

5. A collector buys an unpublished manuscript by an obscure writer that describes a terrible historical event a year before it occurred. The collector learns the writer wrote many unpublished stories...

6. Creating a hybrid of a human and this particular animal turns out to be a bad idea.

7. A person has the ability to make other people very ill.

8. The dead walk out of the sea.

9. An individual begins seeing and hearing from someone who looks just like her – and learns she had a twin who died at birth.

10. A killer places an advertisement for a willing victim and finds one.

11. A basement contains jars filled with unusual specimens.

12. A person finds new photos of herself on her cell phone that she has no memory of.

13. The spirit of a brutalized slave or prisoner of war wants revenge on his tormentor's descendants.

14. A couple vacationing in a remote area begins having the same nightmares.

15. All the circus performers were killed in the train wreck.

16. The television switches to another station of its own accord and plays footage of something horrible that happened long before the technology existed to record it.

17. A spouse or sibling dies. He or she begins to take over the body of the surviving spouse or sibling.

18. Weekend adventurers explore a cave and can't find their way out again. Then they encounter something terrible…

19. Authorities go through the cluttered apartment of a deceased man who lived alone with no known friends or relatives for decades and find something disturbing.

20. A group of teenagers trolls everyone else in an online group by telling made-up stories about terrible things they've done. Things then get out of hand.

21. It's bad luck in the theater to mention the Shakespeare play *Macbeth* by name, but someone in the company keeps doing it anyway…and the superstition proves true.

22. Every exhibit in this carnival sideshow is fake. Except this one thing.

23. An individual develops a terror of water – drinking it, touching it, or even being near it. There's actually a good reason why.

24. The grandfather clock starts running backwards.

25. People in this neighborhood begin having freak accidents that involve normal appliances and machinery, such as blenders, weed whackers, and garage doors.

26. The cure for a new deadly epidemic is almost scarier than the disease.

27. He locked the doors and shuttered the windows; it came in through the roof.

28. A woman is happy when her dead loved one comes back to life…but he's changed.

29. This centuries-old beauty secret is effective but horrifying.

30. A killer toys with his victims by orchestrating a series of false hopes for them.

31. She wakes up in the middle of the night and runs out to a certain tree.

32. Tourists on a ghost tour, along with their guide, fall into the hands of an evil presence.

33. A young woman is impregnated by her handsome new boyfriend, who turns out to be something other than human.

34. The empty swing is swinging.

35. A bride on her honeymoon discovers she's not her new husband's first wife…not even close.

36. Long ago when he was a baby, a man's parents made an unwise deal in order to bring him back from the dead.

37. Members of a family or people in a town begin sleepwalking and doing strange things in their sleep.

38. A young man confesses to a killing that hasn't happened. The murder he describes takes place while he's in custody.

39. Grisly events happen after the arrival of a hypnotist in Victorian London.

40. An author's fictional villain stalks him.

41. Fraternity hazing goes way too far.

42. It always happens when he's alone in the car.

43. A patient in a mental hospital encounters a malevolent ghost, but nobody believes her.

44. A mother's young child may or may not be a changeling.

45. Swarms of insects appear in various places in a town, always followed by an untimely death.

46. The ghost at the movie theater wants everyone to watch one particular snippet of film.

47. A child's imaginary friend starts to cause real trouble.

48. When putting together a slide show for a wedding or

funeral, someone notices that for decades, the same man, dressed in the same fashion, has been appearing in the background of photographs taken in public places.

49. A politician, religious leader, or celebrity exerts mind control over the will of his or her followers.

50. The fairy godmother isn't the good kind of fairy.

51. Right before his wedding, a man's future in-laws try to welcome him into the family in a terrifying way.

52. An evil person outfits an ice cream truck for a nefarious purpose.

53. It's a ghost town because long ago, all of the inhabitants abandoned it on the same night, and no one's sure why.

54. From the time he was born, his family raised him in secret away from the rest of the world because of what he was.

55. No matter how many times she leaves the town, she always wakes up in it again.

56. When they drained the swamp, they found dozens of skeletons.

57. She gets texts from a dead loved one.

58. In the middle of the night, this church holds bizarre secret services.

59. A parent or spouse is descending into madness.

60. What is the dog barking at? There's nothing there...

61. Always a bridesmaid, even after death.

62. The home security camera records something alarming.

63. The toddler is using words that no one taught him.

64. When he woke up, he found a word carved into his arm.

65. From the bottom of the well, a face stares up.

66. This is no ordinary medical trial.

67. The weapon is a curse to its owner.

68. A graffiti symbol or image appearing in various places around the city turns out to have a ghastly significance.

69. She receives an unexpected package from another country. The contents freak her out.

70. For weeks, she felt like someone was watching her. Then she found out why.

71. A previously unknown sea creature emerges from the deep.

72. Halfway through the meal, he realizes he is actually eating.

73. Formations in the rocky cliffs look like faces. Out of the corner of her eye, one of them moves.

74. He knows he's a soldier, but doesn't know he's a ghost.

75. The hikers assumed that the name Devil's Canyon wasn't literal.

76. The dead manipulate her into taking care of their unfinished business.

77. It was stored in the freezer.

78. An evil spirit or demon causes several cases of spontaneous combustion.

79. She feels the hand of an invisible small child take hold of hers.

80. Victorian mourning jewelry incorporated hair from the deceased loved one. In this case, the dead person's soul is attached to the hair.

81. It keeps happening in that one particular room in the hotel.

82. Nobody knows that at this site, an instance of starvation and cannibalism happened centuries ago.

83. Brothers who communicate only with one another in a language only they understand (cryptophasia) behave in increasingly erratic ways.

84. At a remote filming location, the celebrated movie director insists on increasingly real special effects.

85. No one is on board the ship.

86. The ghost of her husband's late wife is insanely jealous of her.

87. In this city, always after nightfall, ordinary people begin committing shocking crimes.

88. He delivers pizza to what appears to be an abandoned mansion, and it turns out to be the strangest night of his life.

89. After what she saw, she never wants to look into a mirror again.

90. The minotaur is not just a myth.

91. The body goes missing from its coffin before they can bury it.

92. The plants in the greenhouse seem to have wills of their own.

93. It's not actually possible to upload a soul to a computer... or is it?

94. A study of old gravestones leads to an unfortunate discovery.

95. The painting looked different the last time she viewed it.

96. An up-and-coming executive at a successful corporation discovers their true source of income.

97. Two spirits fight for the possession of a child.

98. They're a classic posse in the Wild West, but the outlaw they want to bring to justice is a supernatural being.

99. The room had a door when she entered, but now there is no door by which to escape.

100. What happened in Vegas did not stay in Vegas.

101. The person she's exchanging letters or emails with is much different than she's been led to believe.

102. The entries in this old diary sometimes change.

103. It's surprisingly difficult to tell if she's really dead.

104. Turning the ghost town into a tourist destination was a terrible idea.

105. The doll's eyes aren't supposed to open when the doll is lying down.

106. The story he told around the campfire was more than a story.

107. A thief cracks the safe open and discovers something unexpected.

108. Sacred texts inspire a psychopath.

109. This B&B host seems incredibly nice.

110. The man she chatted with on the airplane shows up in her hotel room.

111. This object should've never been put in a museum.

112. After working late, he finds that he's been locked into the office building alone.

113. The feeling of being watched has become almost constant.

114. The plastic surgeon is renowned for achieving amazing results.

115. The dead body in the bed was surrounded by dozens of writhing venomous snakes.

116. The magician's secret goes far beyond smoke, mirrors, or sleight of hand.

117. She starts hearing everything, even the sound of an ant crawling across the floor.

118. The TV turns itself to a different channel.

119. The man was executed for a crime he didn't commit.

120. People's dreams come true after hearing this preacher or motivational speaker, but there's a high price to pay.

121. She finds a painting in a thrift store that appears to be a portrait of her.

122. This person seems like his long-lost soulmate, but other people who talk about her seem to be describing a completely different person.

123. The spider problem is only getting worse.

124. It doesn't have any eyes.

125. The monkeys are screeching at the zoo tonight.

126. This kid draws the creepiest things in crayon.

127. She keeps seeing a woman around town who looks exactly like a doll she owned as a child.

128. Random details and lines of dialogue from his nightmares show up in his everyday life.

129. The orphanage was the only safe place for them.

130. The building site has more than one freak accident.

131. Some people in town start loathing one another for no clear reason.

132. Every day, he notices that one or two small facts of his life have changed...or is he remembering things incorrectly?

133. The trapdoor leads to a small space where, apparently, someone's been living all along.

134. Ever since he played the videogame, things have been off.

135. Why did miners abandon the mine so long ago? There's still gold in it.

136. Doctors believe the parasites are a delusion.

137. This is the real story behind the "Bloody Mary" legend.

138. He predicted he would die and take everyone with him... and after his death, the disaster hit.

139. Who left this gift at the door, and how did they know it's something he wanted?

140. At first, everyone in the theater thought it was part of the act.

141. Blood drips and spatters on the lilies.

142. The roots break through the foundation; the branches break through the walls.

143. The amusement park's been abandoned for thirty years.

144. She can't remember anything about her dental appointment.

145. His fiancé swears that he visited last night. He didn't.

146. No one else remembers her friend being at the party.

147. He lives alone in a rural area, and the browser history on his computer is filled with websites he didn't visit.

148. Both doors to the room slam shut at the same time.

149. One by one, the stars wink out of the sky.

150. He's been isolated for decades and has lost his remaining shreds of humanity.

150 MYSTERY PROMPTS

The mystery genre is diverse, including kind-hearted amateur sleuths in adorable small-town settings, hardened private eyes with questionable morals, police procedurals, historical and literary stories, and more. Any good mystery, though, sprinkles enough clues and plausible false leads to guide the reader along in trying to solve the puzzle. This genre in particular tends to be published in series, rather than individual books, so a main character who readers can root for—or at least stay interested in—is key.

1.   A woman asks a writer to write the story of her life. Then she goes missing.

2.   Murder victims are found buried with some of their wordly goods, Viking style.

3.   Three people close to the murder victim have confessed. Each of them swears they acted alone.

4.   Notes and gifts from her "Secret Santa" at work take a strange turn.

5.   It's going to be a beautiful wedding at a beautiful destination, but two people in the wedding party have been murdered.

6.   The creator of a high-tech prototype that will change an industry has gone missing.

7.   Her parents believe her to be their biological child, but they all learn otherwise.

8. The dead woman's wedding ring is found in a ditch forty miles away.

9. A museum conservator is restoring an old painting, and an X-ray reveals something shocking or mysterious painted or written in the layer beneath.

10. A sorority sister who bullied prospective pledges is found dead.

11. As a man researches his genealogy, he finds that ancestors from a few different generations and a few different countries made visits to the same remote place.

12. Someone replaced the woman's contact lens solution with a damaging liquid.

13. He's always been a faithful husband, but someone has planted false evidence of his having an affair.

14. A detective is hired for a high price to find a thief who stole something that doesn't appear to have any real value.

15. Every unmarried lady at the ball wanted to dance with the duke, so it's too bad he was found stabbed in the garden.

16. In the middle of a wilderness, someone finds an abandoned bunker with security cameras, powered by a generator.

17. The graves of historic figures are being robbed.

18. Clues to the mystery come to him in dreams, but nobody believes him.

19. Serial murders in cities in two different countries are very similar.

20. A man she didn't know left her a valuable and unusual item in his will.

21. A writer researching his biography of a Golden Age movie star comes across something that makes him suspect that contrary to the official story, she was a murder victim.

22. The accidental death of this investigative reporter seems a little too convenient.

23. The murders all relate to common fears, such as public speaking, flying, and heights.

24. A woman wakes up with a headache and goes in to work, only to learn that she's been missing for a month.

25. Writers are being murdered at the mystery writers' convention.

26. The painting must have been stolen from the museum in broad daylight, but the security cameras malfunctioned and no witnesses have come forward.

27. Three different guests at the Air BnB died later under mysterious circumstances.

28. A practicing witch or voodoo priestess is accused of murder.

29. The murders are re-enactments of famous murders in novels or movies.

30. He claims to be the rich man who was lost at sea two decades ago.

31. The inspector's friend is murdered while he is talking on the phone to the inspector.

32. A dead body is found in an unclaimed piece of luggage at the airport.

33. He was murdered on his honeymoon on a cruise ship, and his new, much-younger bride was the only one on board who even knew him.

34. A woman who didn't know she was adopted meets her twin sister, who gives her a dire warning.

35. One of the pies submitted to the state fair contest was poisoned.

36. The report of a celebrity's death is false, but he dies soon after.

37. The murder victims all have the same tailor.

38. Who would kill the guest of honor at their 100th birthday party?

39. A woman accuses a maid of stealing valuable items from the attic. Her husband secretly sold the items, not wanting to tell his wife they were in difficult financial straits.

40. A wife arranges a romantic "scavenger hunt" for her husband, but someone else changes a few of the clues.

41. The thief who steals rare books always leaves a sonnet behind.

42. The wrong body is in the casket at the visitation. No one knows who it is, or where the other body is.

43. The murders were definitely committed by a human, but resemble the attacks of wild animals.

44. After the woman returned the lost wallet, someone began stalking her.

45. The book she's reading seems to be telling the story of her own life, though she doesn't think she's ever met the author.

46. A man who faked his own death must be found in time.

47. Someone in a villain costume and mask attempts to kill an actor at a fan convention. The actor is saved by a fan dressed as a superhero.

48. An Egyptian mummy, or what appears to be one, is found in an unlikely place.

49. The man is murdered following an argument with several people on social media.

50. A body is found in the organic vegetable garden at a hippie commune.

51. A woman finds notes in her apartment, in handwriting she doesn't recognize, reminding her of errands and appointments.

52. An Easter egg hunt leads to a startling discovery.

53. Someone goes missing after a city-wide blackout.

54. Someone begins investigating a suspicious death while she's on vacation, much to the annoyance of her partner or spouse.

55. A beauty pageant contestant is murdered, but not for a reason anyone expects.

56. Someone mistakes his spouse or family member for an intruder and shoots...but was it really a mistake?

57. The victim was seen getting onto an elevator, but nobody saw him exit it.

58. A tragic fire may have been started to kill just one person.

59. The murder victim made a video soon before she died that contains a clue to the identity of her killer.

60. The kidnapping was faked to cover up something else.

61. A priest at a church embroiled in scandal is found dead.

62. After her twin sister dies unexpectedly, she gets threatening notes.

63. Who would want to destroy his taco truck?

64. The mysterious attempt on the pop star's life actually revived his career.

65. The murderer has offered him a challenge: correctly solve the case in one week, or become the next victim.

66. A woman claims that a hypnotist forced her to commit the crime.

67. A cop who went undercover with a biker gang is the prime suspect.

68. A murdered gang member turns out to be an undercover cop.

69. The murder of a member of the royal family leads to accusations that throw the whole country into turmoil.

70. Wolves at the wolf sanctuary are turning up dead.

71. A movie reviewer who angered many people by criticizing sexism in popular movies has disappeared.

72. The bride didn't get cold feet—she was abducted on the way to her wedding.

73. The dead man dumped at the veterans' cemetery was not a veteran.

74. The famous motivational speaker is being blackmailed by an anonymous person.

75. Two senators who are political rivals are found dead in the same hotel room.

76. A photographer obsessed with abandoned tunnels beneath Chicago—freight tunnels, cable car tunnels, and more—goes missing.

77. A professor is murdered by a group of his students.

78. Somebody poured gasoline all over the pumpkin patch and set it on fire, ruining the farm's fall tourist season.

79. The railway "accident" benefitted several people in the city.

80. A baby is stolen from the hospital.

81. The symphony conductor was found murdered in an ironic fashion.

82. The prime murder suspect is a flighty, ditzy woman.

83. An ex-con tries to start a new life in a small town, but is soon suspected of a robbery.

84. The body of the woman found in a deep freezer matches no ID records.

85. Someone discovers that an abandoned warehouse or barn contains hundreds of homemade bombs and rocket-propelled grenades.

86. A self-proclaimed psychic and Tarot card reader is murdered.

87. A boy investigates the disappearance of two of his fellow students at a boarding school.

88. All of the bottled water in the company fridge was replaced with vodka. Who did it?

89. A man jumped from a cliff near the beach, hit his head on rocks, and drowned. More than one person in the village swears that they've seen a mermaid.

90. Someone is stealing priceless objects and then returning them without being caught.

91. The murder victim had recorded several odd phone conversations, but only his or her side of the conversation can be heard.

92. A multi-level marketing scheme, in which people try to sell products to their friends, turns deadly.

93. An entire family, except for one girl, is found murdered in their home.

94. She can talk to ghosts, but the ghost of the murder victim doesn't want to reveal the killer.

95. The security footage shows someone dressed as the actual Grim Reaper murdering someone with a scythe.

96. An outbreak of a deadly disease in a community did not happen by chance.

97. The three murders in the small town bear no resemblance to one another in terms of method or possible motive.

98. Someone detonated a bomb in the DMV office, fortunately killing no one.

99. The corporation said the executive was leaving his or her position "in order to pursue other interests," but one employee suspects this person was murdered.

100. Not only does the murder suspect lack a strong alibi, but s/he keeps getting even the most basic details about his or her life wrong.

101. Nobody called the police for quite a while because the kidnapped person was known for playing elaborate pranks.

102. The murder took place at the Burning Man festival, and none of the eyewitnesses seems particularly reliable.

103. The "private investigator" on this case just went into business this week and has no idea what he or she is doing.

104. When disposing of his friend's ashes according to his last wishes, he finds a message that seems to be from his friend, suggesting he is not dead after all.

105. The parade organizer is determined to find out who sabotaged all the floats.

106. At the scene of the crime, they find a tiny modern-day object trapped in amber.

107. He evaded the man in the toy store trying to kill him, but has no idea who the guy is.

108. The murder victim was found with a bite of poisoned apple in her mouth, like Snow White in the fairy tale.

109. The "Cinderella Killer" murders his attractive young female victims right around midnight.

110. Her beloved older brother was murdered as an adolescent, when she was a little girl. Lately, strange events and coincidences keep reminding her of his murder.

111. Three different times now, the police force has gotten clues from an apparent would-be killer about a murder he's going to commit, but he has yet to follow through.

112. The murderer left a note saying that the victim was too good for this world.

113. As he looks for clues, the detective falls in love with the dead murder victim.

114. Three coffee shop customers have been poisoned, and one barista begins her own investigation.

115. Cattle rustlers are common, but the sheriff can't figure out why or how someone would drive all of a man's cattle off of his ranch and leave them to roam around free.

116. A handwritten draft of the best-selling author's next novel was stolen.

117. The rich widow used a lot of money and influence to make it seem as though her husband was still alive. What really caused his death?

118. She got an eviction notice even though she owned her own home. Thirty days later, she came home to find most of her belongings tossed out in the yard.

119. The parent of a murder suspect believes that all of his teenager's creepy and bizarre behavior is totally normal and rational.

120. Two of the actors whose characters died on a TV show have now also died in real life.

121. The 19th-century killer sells the bodies of his victims to medical schools.

122. When a couple decides to have an addition built to their home, the contractors who dig a foundation find a skeleton buried on the property.

123. A man in need of a kidney transplant gets one from his dead friend or family member, who previously backed out of donating him one.

124. A drowned man is found in a pool hundreds of miles from the ocean. His lungs are filled with salt water.

125. She overheard her would-be killers discussing their plans. They didn't know that she understood their language.

126. The murdered therapist engaged in questionable or illegal practices.

127. No one has called about the necklace sitting at the lost and found, although it's worth over a million dollars.

128. A man in perfect health has an apparent heart attack at a spa.

129. The night after he throws a huge party, he discovers that his custom-painted purple pickup truck has been stolen.

130. A lottery winner's suicide is investigated.

131. A young woman who accused a college athlete of a crime is found dead, apparently by her own hand.

132. An old woman has uncovered fresh evidence about her husband's unsolved murder from half a century before.

133. The thief has developed a huge crush on the person s/he robbed.

134. The investigation turns up the fact that the missing person was a secret bigamist.

135. The investigation turns up the fact that the missing person was a good fifteen years younger than she claimed to be, and she changed her appearance to fit this claim as much as possible.

136. All of the bank robberies take place on the full moon.

137. The town's new community center has been defaced with offensive graffiti.

138. Several women in the city have woken up to find that their long red hair has been cut off.

139. A celebrated perfume designer disappears at a fragrance conference.

140. Someone replaces one of the fake swords with a real one, and one actor seriously injures another by accident during the onstage duel.

141. They got all of the horses out of the exclusive riding stables in time, but the place burned to the ground.

142. A serial killer only commits murder on major holidays.

143. A man behind leaks of classified government information turns up dead.

144. It seems as though someone might have deliberately goaded the elephant into stampeding.

145. At each of a string of robberies, scattered rose petals are left behind.

146. Someone is murdered at the top of the St. Louis Arch.

147. She begins to suspect that the nonprofit is a huge scam.

148. A murder takes place on the set of a movie or TV show about solving crime.

149. Professors at an elite university are being targeted.

150. The murder victim's social media account is repeatedly hacked with supposed new messages from the victim.

150 ROMANCE PROMPTS

Romance is one of the biggest fiction genres, and other genres regularly feature a romantic subplot. Some of these prompts are ideas for whole stories, while others are more images or suggestions. It also includes some ideas for how people can meet. Two other lists in this book, "50 "Meet Cute" Ideas" and "50 Cute Date Ideas," might also be helpful for a love story.

One of the few hard-and-fast rules about the romance genre is that it must have a happy ending—an HEA ("happy ever after") or at least an HFN ("happy for now.") Not all love stories belong in the romance genre, and if you want to write a love story with a sad or bittersweet ending, that's fine! It'll just go in another category— perhaps mainstream, upmarket, or literary fiction.

As with all of my fiction prompts, some of these are gender neutral, and in the cases where they're not, you can always switch the genders of one or both of the people, as you like.

1. One of them learns a shocking secret about the other.

2. One of her parents is getting married, and she's attracted to another guest.

3. They have a meaningful conversation in a bookstore or a library.

4. She recruits him to help plan a charity or community event.

5. They meet when a hotel catches on fire and they, like the rest of the guests, have to evacuate in their pajamas.

6. She finally learned to trust someone and fall in love

again…and now, it looks as though that person has betrayed her.

7. They broke up years ago, but now they're on the same long train or bus ride.

8. He decides to be the high school mascot and wear an animal costume so that he'll have more chances to talk to a cheerleader.

9. She helps a wounded man and then realizes he's on the enemy's side.

10. He quits his manager job so that he's free to ask this employee out.

11. She becomes interested in him after she fires him.

12. Someone donates their kidney to a stranger…and then meets and falls in love with the transplant recipient.

13. She models for her for a painting.

14. She sees his photo on a friend's social media account and finds a way to meet him in person.

15. He learns all of the words to the songs from her favorite musical. He doesn't even like musicals.

16. She adopted the dog from the shelter. Weeks later, the original owner tracked the runaway dog down.

17. One of them is the dog walker or dog sitter for the other.

18. He gives up on a goal that he's pursued for years because it will negatively impact her.

19. They agree to have a Thanksgiving or Christmas dinner together, just as friends, because a family holiday isn't going to happen and all of their other friends are already busy.

20. She finds out that he's lost all his money and has been keeping it a secret.

21. There's an immediate spark between the tourist and the tour guide.

22. He believes he's dying and he doesn't have descendants, so he marries a widow who's financially struggling so she and her son can benefit from his life insurance and his estate.

23. They kiss while watching a meteor shower.

24. They're both stuck in the air on a malfunctioning amusement park ride.

25. The person he was in love with turns out to be alive, after all...but now he's committed to somebody else.

26. He learns that she's actually from another century.

27. This has got to be one of the least romantic marriage proposals ever.

28. This has got to be the most unromantic place to first meet the love of your life.

29. He's just about to declare his love when he gets interrupted in a dramatic fashion.

30. She's just about to declare her love, and then chickens out.

31. One of them says "I love you" for the first time under unexpected circumstances.

32. One of them remembers the other from a past life.

33. She's being pursued by bad guys and accidentally drags somebody else into it.

34. Since they've been friends forever, he's getting her advice on how to get another woman to date him.

35. They build a bonfire on the beach.

36. They meet in Spanish class.

37. They meet when he accidentally rear-ends her car in traffic.

38. They meet as ghosts immediately after dying in the same accident.

39. The best man has a crush on the bride-to-be.

40. It's like Cinderella, but she left behind something very different from a glass slipper.

41. Apple or cherry blossoms rain down on them during a springtime walk.

42. She thought she was alone, and someone has overheard her singing.

43. Okay, yes, she broke into his house, but she has a good reason.

44. Well, sure, he hot-wired her car, but there are extenuating circumstances.

45. He's so surprised by being asked out that he says no, and then he regrets it.

46. She decides to turn him down, only to be jealous when she sees him with someone else.

47. They're the only two people in the movie theater.

48. They keep meeting in their dreams.

49. She has a dream about this woman before she meets her.

50. The detective is falling in love with the sister of the guilty man.

51. She looks up her ex to ask him if he still has an antique item she gave him, which she has since learned is worth a lot of money.

52. As they work together to find a girlfriend for their awkward friend, they wind up falling for each other.

53. They are next-door-neighbors, and a storm knocks a tree in her yard onto his roof.

54. This is the second year they've met at the same conference or convention.

55. They meet for the first time at a planetarium.

56. They are counselors at the same summer camp.

57. She would have a chance at romance with this person if she revealed her real identity, but that would ruin everything else.

58. One of them catches the other in a lie but doesn't tell anyone else.

59. One of them tells an outrageous lie in order to help the other one out.

60. Because his father murdered his mother in a rage and he himself has a hot temper, he's scared to get seriously involved with anyone.

61. They never expected to see each other again, and especially not at this spot halfway around the world.

62. She's showing her the ropes at a new job.

63. The day after she breaks up with him, she finds the handwritten love letter from him (or it arrives in the mail.)

64. He was always in love with his brother's wife, and now that his brother is dead he feels guilty even thinking about starting a relationship with her.

65. They get set up by friends and realize they shared a disastrous first date years before.

66. She's sure it can't work—she's fifteen years older than he is.

67. He returns an engagement ring to a jewelry store after his proposal is rejected and develops a crush on the sales associate.

68. She thought he forgot her birthday, and then he surprises her in a dramatic and unique way.

69. He likes her, but he's also intimidated by her—she's literally a genius.

70. He comes up with a cute and original pet name for her based on where she's from or something she likes.

71. They develop a code word or sign that only they know about.

72. They meet in person after knowing each other online for years.

73. A chef creates new recipes inspired by her beloved or milestones in their relationship.

74. Although they're strangers, they wind up sharing food or splitting a meal.

75. They're cast as romantic leads in the same theater production.

76. When he sees her for the first time, she's walking alone at night in the pouring rain.

77. They try to stay warm on a cold night.

78. They are both in their nineties, but magically get the chance to be younger again.

79. He has a late-night radio show and she falls for him before she ever sees him.

80. One of them gives the other a backrub.

81. One of them tickles the other.

82. She helps him look for something.

83. He helps her get rid of something.

84. Their first kiss is terribly awkward.

85. Their first kiss has surprising consequences.

86. At the office, she sets candy out on her desk, and her coworker comes by to get some candy more and more often.

87. They discover that they've both been hired to kill the same bad guy.

88. Well into the conversation, he realizes he knew this guy when they were teenagers. In fact, he had a crush on him back then.

89. They've been married for twenty-five years...and have suddenly fallen in mad, passionate love with each other all over again.

90. She accidentally left her diary in a public place, and a stranger found it and read it.

91. She accidentally sent an email *about* him...*to* him.

92. They discover that they have the same password.

93. When they were little children, they swore that they would get married someday.

94. They fall in love while they're both in the hospital.

95. She's fallen asleep with her head on his shoulder or his knee.

96. She's a corporate recruiter trying to persuade him to apply to a new company.

97. A high school or college reunion rekindles a romance.

98. They dated years before, and when he meets her again she's changed her looks and her lifestyle so much, it's like she's a different person.

99. He or she is ridiculous, but hard to resist.

100. He or she is stiff and formal, but still intriguing.

101. One of them wants to take their friendship to the next level, and the other isn't at all sure it's a good idea.

102. He never thought he'd attend an actual tea party, but then he meets someone interesting there.

103. They're in or around a pool, a lake, or an ocean.

104. They meet at a coffee shop when they've both been stood up by their online dates.

105. One of them doesn't show up for a date...but it turns out it wasn't really their fault.

106. They're both heartbroken as they say goodbye.

107. At the costume party, he thinks he knows who she is, but he's not positive.

108. They kiss, but one of them backs off and runs away for some reason.

109. She learns that he's secretly made a huge effort or sacrifice for her sake.

110. One of them sets up a big romantic gesture that goes terribly wrong.

111. One of them learns that the other is secretly planning a big romantic gesture or surprise.

112. They are grown adults, but they're acting like children – in a good way, or a bad way.

113. They are stuck alone together in the same place for days.

114. They meet in secret because nobody can know they're getting romantically involved.

115. The truth about their secret relationship comes out.

116. He's developing a crush on the lawyer he hired to help him through a nasty divorce.

117. During the wedding ceremony between the woman he loves and another man, he objects.

118. They're first drawn together because they're both appalled by the same person or situation.

119. They first make a connection because one of them defends the other one in a social situation.

120. One of them has to borrow clothes from the other.

121. They share a meaningful moment in the midst of chaos.

122. He's escorting her on a journey to meet or reunite with the man she's supposed to marry.

123. One of them discovers a terrible secret about the other's spouse or partner.

124. One of them has foreknowledge of the other's future.

125. They've been together forever, but now she has amnesia.

126. One of them gives the other a homemade gift.

127. He comes home from a trip and brings her a unique souvenir.

128. She believes he's acting this way because he's under the influence of a love potion or spell. This isn't the case.

129. He's a different race or different religion than she is, and her family or friends disapprove.

130. He wants to be with her, but her ex is trying hard to get her back.

131. They used to be a couple, and their paths cross again when one of them is assigned to interview the other for a news story.

132. She discovers his secret interest or hobby.

133. They make fun of each other, but others can tell they really like each other.

134. Neither of them can muster up the courage to confess their feelings to the other. They both talk about it to the same mutual friend.

135. She gets him to try, for the first time, something she loves.

136. One of them teaches the other how to do something.

137. They narrowly escape getting in trouble after participating in shenanigans.

138. Which one of them inherited the estate? The lawyer's trying to figure it out.

139. The police suspect her, but he's sure she didn't do it.

140. He forgoes his chance to escape a horrible situation so he can stay close to the man he loves.

141. She has mixed feelings about hiring her ex, but no one will do a better job.

142. He's kidnapped her because he desperately needs her help to save someone else.

143. She's recruiting him for a job that he can hardly believe exists.

144. Her residency, new job, or start-up business means she doesn't have a spare minute for romance…but she's tempted by him, anyway.

145. He improves himself or his life in order to win back the one who left him…and then he falls for someone else.

146. She never wanted to be involved in her family's shady business. He wants to bring them to justice…but he's attracted to her.

147. They're on a spaceship.

148. She learns that he's dating her to spite his family or get back at someone.

149. They are either watching a parade or participating in one.

150. She gets to go back in time and try again with the one she loves.

150 YOUNG ADULT PROMPTS

The majority of prompts in this book can be used in writing a young adult story, and most of the prompts on this list could be used for novels with adult protagonists.

1. A boy pursues his list of wildly ambitious New Year's resolutions, with hilarious and touching results.

2. A girl on the swim team transforms into a part-time mermaid.

3. A group of "outsiders" becomes a clique that eventually excludes others.

4. A girl's favorite author plagiarizes her fanfiction.

5. A girl who believed her friend died finds out she's very much alive.

6. Siblings hide the fact of their mother's death to avoid being put into foster care.

7. A teenager becomes a murder witness.

8. A teenager's best friend goes missing—and is widely believed to be the murderer of a family member.

9. A rule-following, straight-A student is believed guilty of a crime.

10. Two teens begin to write a fantasy novel together and then cross over into the world they've created.

11. In a dystopian future, college admissions boards have access to video footage of students' entire lives.

12. A girl always hangs out at a particular little nook at the library. Then the same boy starts taking the space every day.

13. A boy learns something terrible about his parents.

14. In a modern-day *Ferris Bueller's Day Off*, three girls ditch class for a day filled with adventures.

15. A girl who loves cosplay begins taking on the personality of whatever character she's dressed up as.

16. A girl in her teens is recruited to be a spy.

17. In a retelling of *Cyrano de Bergerac*, a boy helps his friend win a girl over through romantic and flirty texts and DMs.

18. A teen begins spending time in an abandoned house...and learns it has secrets.

19. A college student has a series of interviews for internships.

20. A college student desperate for tuition money secretly works at two different full-time summer internships at once, two city blocks away from one another.

21. A teenager survives a cruise ship sinking.

22. Anonymous notes in her locker lead her into a mystery.

23. Two teens from different social groups strike up a clandestine romance.

24. An adopted girl finds out she's one of four quadruplets and finds her other sisters.

25. A depressed girl shares tips about happiness and positivity on an anonymous social media account.

26. A teen's private diary is shared without his consent on social media, and it goes viral.

27. A college student struggles with a shopping addiction, maxing out one credit card.

28. A teen's life changes over the course of one summer as she works at a beachside café.

29. A high school student spreads a false rumor about herself to increase her social standing.

30. A boy pretends he can foretell the future…and discovers he actually can.

31. A student council election takes several unforeseen turns.

32. A teen forms a unique connection with an animal.

33. A boy's mother becomes involved with a cult.

34. A girl escapes a fundamentalist cult that's living off the grid.

35. In a world where all creative work is illegal unless commissioned by the government, teens meet to write and share poetry in secret.

36. A high school coach or teacher convinces his favorite students to cheat.

37. When a nerdy girl transfers to a new school, she completely changes her image.

38. The captain of the high school debate team does his best arguing outside of tournaments—and it gets him in trouble.

39. A teen makes a friend with someone who may or may not be an actual angel.

40. A girl tries to keep up with her schoolwork while adjusting to her newly discovered responsibilities as Queen of the Fairies.

41. A boy growing up in rough circumstances falls in love with cooking and dreams of becoming a chef.

42. A teen gives excellent advice in an anonymous advice column in the school newspaper, but is completely unable to follow the advice herself.

43. Two boys on rival basketball teams develop romantic feelings for one another.

44. A girl takes boxing lessons and gets the confidence to stand up for herself verbally as well.

45. Four high school girls form a music group and strive for success.

46. A quiet, studious boy has a secret rebellious life at night.

47. Two girls carry out an elaborate act of revenge against two other girls.

48. In order to avoid his abusive father, a boy finds ways to avoid spending time at his own house.

49. A teenager is pressured to shoot a buck on his first deer hunt with an older relative, but he can't bring himself to do it.

50. A girl struggles with the decision to tell authorities about what the star quarterback did.

51. A teen gains the ability to take the form of any other person she chooses.

52. Teens form friendships and romantic connections during rehearsals for a theater production directed by a tyrannical teacher.

53. A band of bohemian, artistic vampires recruits a newcomer.

54. With a phony resume, a teen passes as an adult and lands a corporate job.

55. A teen competes to become a national rodeo champion.

56. After planet Earth is destroyed, teen girls on a space colony feel pressured to marry and have children to propagate the human race.

57. A teen's suspicions about a teacher lead him to conduct a private investigation.

58. A boy's mother marries a very rich man, and the boy adjusts to a wealthy neighborhood and a private high school.

59. A girl tries to fit in when she transfers from a tony private school to a public one.

60. A girl's decision to post one Instagram photo a day for a

year leads her on new adventures and misadventures as she tries to find interesting pictures.

61. A boy with a history of bad behavior dates a minister's daughter.

62. Two girls on a quest to find boys to take them to prom gradually realize they have feelings for one another.

63. A teen gets a chance to live a school year all over again.

64. A boy struggles with his belief that any bad thing he imagines will come to pass.

65. A lifeguard saves the life of a celebrity's child.

66. A girl's science fair project yields results that attract the government's attention.

67. A girl finds her dead mother's teenage diary and sets out to do some of the things her mother wanted to do as a teen, but never did.

68. A boy lacking in natural athletic ability is nonetheless determined to make the team.

69. A girl on a school trip realizes she looks exactly like a girl in a Renaissance painting, and soon after, she discovers why.

70. A girl who wants to be a virgin until she gets married faces social pressure about her decision.

71. Soon after a boy was born, his father went missing. Now, a skeleton has been discovered in the basement of their former home.

72. A teen attempts to make his whole fractious extended family get along and have a nice Christmas for once in their lives.

73. A girl discovers a secret passageway in one of the office buildings she cleans at night, but nobody else seems to be able to access it.

74. A teen copes with both a hopeless crush on his best friend's older sister and a younger girl's crush on him.

75. A teen goes to extraordinary lengths to attempt to cheer up her grieving friend.

76. Much to both of their families' dismay, two teens with different faiths fall in love.

77. A teen attempts to throw a truly memorable graduation party.

78. A city kid deals with a move to a tiny farming community.

79. A teen's older sister's wedding rekindles old family feuds.

80. A boy's random acts of kindness prove contagious and lead to surprising results.

81. A girl whose mother is a hoarder attempts to have a normal life.

82. Two boys discover treasure in a local cave.

83. A girl makes a wish at 11:11 every day, but what she wishes for changes dramatically over time.

84. A boy chafes against his overachieving parents' plans for him: Ivy League school, then medical school or law school.

85. A plan to put a bully in his place goes too far.

86. A girl who's a high school bully tries to reform and make amends.

87. A boy becomes part of a test group for an experimental drug.

88. A girl supports her boyfriend as he deals with a serious illness. Unfortunately, he's not a good guy and treats her badly.

89. Two families hiding from a repressive government live in a submarine.

90. A girl dreads spending the summer with her grandparents…but it turns out to be the best summer of her life so far.

91. An intense online friendship changes when both teens wind up attending the same high school.

92. A boy makes a friend in a foreign country.

93. Two teens fall in love at a church summer camp…and months later, they can't get over it.

94. On a hunting trip, a boy mistakes a person for a deer.

95. A girl believes her mother's death was no accident.

96. A boy enters an alternate universe in search of his father.

97. A teenaged prince's advisors attempt to use him for their own political and financial gain.

98. In a matriarchal realm, a girl becomes queen at the age of

seventeen and is courted by two princes from neighboring realms.

99. An Amish girl considers whether to leave the Amish community behind.

100. A girl runs away from home, intending to live with her bohemian aunt.

101. A teen has difficulties passing his driver's license test for a very peculiar reason.

102. A boy's image and attitude change after his uncle dies and leaves him a luxury sports car.

103. At a funeral, two teens become infatuated with one another—and they arrange to meet at other funerals where neither of them knows the deceased.

104. Three very different brothers, growing up poor, learn to overcome their differences and rely on one another.

105. A girl has too many responsibilities at home, including caring for her younger siblings, because her parents are drunk and/or frequently absent.

106. An unpopular girl becomes famous for an act of bravery.

107. A boy becomes part of one of the least dangerous gangs ever.

108. A boy tries to escape the shadow of his more accomplished and more handsome older brother.

109. A group of teens become acquainted at writer meetups when they all participate in National Novel Writing

Month (NaNoWriMo), in which people attempt to complete 50,000 words of a novel in November.

110. In the 1980s, a girl creates a mixtape that expresses her feelings and what's happening in her life.

111. She says yes to being a boy's girlfriend, even though she's not interested in him, because she's never had a boyfriend before. She soon has regrets.

112. An eccentric new teacher brings inspiration to students at a high school.

113. A girl returns to school after a lengthy stay in a psychiatric ward.

114. A boy struggles with the decision to go away to a college on a full ride scholarship or to stay close to his family and his girlfriend by attending the far less prestigious university in his hometown.

115. Two friends decide to participate in a talent show. It goes horribly.

116. A girl risks helping a family escape an increasingly dangerous country.

117. Teens construct a subversive float for the homecoming parade.

118. A teenager makes friends with an aristocratic boy his own age—who happens to be a ghost.

119. A girl learns more about herself as she visits several different prospective colleges.

120. A boy buys a very expensive gift for his crush, who has no romantic interest in him whatsoever.

121. A girl's parents are nonconformists who are suspicious of authority. She rebels by joining a conservative political group.

122. A boy's social media addiction leads to insomnia and problems at school.

123. A boy plays a cruel joke on an awkward girl by pretending to want to go to a dance with her.

124. A girl discovers an unorthodox way to overcome her social anxiety.

125. At a concert, a boy freezes up after a girl asks for his name and number. Later, he tries to find her again.

126. A driven, ambitious teen is embarrassed and occasionally undermined by his laid-back, unconventional parents.

127. A girl falls in love with her best friend, and when she confesses her feelings the friend doesn't feel the same way and ends the friendship.

128. Two high school enemies wake up to find they've switched bodies.

129. A girl is hired for a babysitting job that's way beyond what she can handle.

130. Two teens who can't stand one another pretend to date in order to reach their individual goals.

131. After his mom dies, a boy goes to live with his great-aunt on a reservation.

132. A teen starts a side business out of her bedroom.

133. A boy posts hateful comments on an Internet message board daily under a fake name. Then someone reveals his true identity.

134. Two boys learn they're the descendants and heirs of King Arthur and Merlin, respectively.

135. A girl winds up with a pet llama, but she's keeping it a secret from her parents.

136. A teen takes on more responsibilities when his parent goes off to war.

137. A high school sports rivalry leads to a tragedy—and a mystery.

138. A summer camp has a sinister secret.

139. A former prison has been converted into a high school, but echoes of its past remain.

140. Two best friends set out to see the northern lights.

141. A girl tries to live a normal life despite dealing with a rare disease or condition.

142. A teen's new friend is a charismatic daredevil who leads him into adventures and trouble.

143. A teen strikes up an unlikely friendship with an elderly new neighbor.

144. A boy takes swim lessons for the first time as a teenager and falls in love with his instructor.

145. A teen is part of a group taken hostage at a church.

146. The son of the President comes of age in a world of Secret Service agents and vicious media headlines.

147. A teenager and his family become homeless after his father loses his job.

148. A teenage boy lives at the motel or hotel owned by his parents.

149. An orphan isn't sure if she can trust her new foster parents.

150. A teen learns that his father or mother is a superhero.

150 HISTORICAL FICTION PROMPTS

History is a bottomless well of inspiration for storytellers. Novelists and screenwriters create fictionalized accounts of real people and events, or they use historical settings for original storylines. Fantasy writers frequently draw on historical eras and events as well.

Historical fiction requires a lot of intensive research, but some of the ideas here might inspire someone to learn and write about a particular topic or period. And of course, a writer wouldn't need to have any special knowledge of history to use one of these prompts purely as a creative writing exercise.

I am always getting interested in random subjects on the Internet, and I started taking notes on some of them. These notes provided most of the items on this list. Some are true plot ideas, and some of them are historical facts that can provide either a creative jumping-off point or the setting for a story.

Want even more inspiration? Check out the plots for historical plays in the section on Shakespeare and other Elizabethan literature, and take a look at the historical setting prompts.

1. In 1492, two Jewish families in the kingdoms of Castile and Aragon in Spain must decide whether to convert to Catholicism or emigrate to another country following Isabella and Ferdinand's Alhambra Decree.

2. A man designing the gardens for a large estate falls in love with his client's daughter in Edwardian England.

3. In 874, Ingólfr Arnarson leaves Norway with his wife and stepbrother to escape a blood feud. He builds a house in Iceland—one of the first people to ever do so—and names the area Reykjavík.

4. In ancient Rome, a father intends to execute his son—which is completely legal for him to do at that time.

5. In ancient Rome, a father intends to sell his children into slavery to pay off some debts—also completely legal.

6. A woman establishes a hotel in the richest city in the world in 1880—Melbourne, Australia, which is in the middle of a gold rush.

7. During the Italian Renaissance, an actress in a *commedia dell'arte* troupe writes a play that becomes a sensation.

8. An English knight going off to fight in a Crusade soon concludes the whole endeavor is stupid.

9. In medieval Japan, the wife of a samurai—a trained warrior herself—leads her servants in defending her home from a Mongol raid.

10. In Victorian England, an aristocratic married woman is suspected of being the model for a controversial painting.

11. An ancient Greek athlete from a poor farming family will be granted a huge pension from the city of Athens if he triumphs in early Olympic games.

12. In 1766, Šćepan Mali becomes the ruler of Montenegro by pretending to be the Russian tsar Peter III.

13. In 1810, Archduchess Marie Louise of Austria travels to France to become Napoleon Bonaparte's second wife. At the French border, she's forced to remove all her Austrian clothes, take a bath, and get dressed in new French clothes, all according to tradition. Then she takes part in a truly lavish wedding.

14. In the sixteenth century, a European boy becomes an apprentice on a ship bound for the New World.

15. A free man who chose to become a Roman gladiator wants out, and he needs to raise the money (the *lanista*) to pay the head of the gladiators in order to regain his freedom.

16. A textile factory worker and occasional skydiver is recruited by the Soviet government to become the first woman in space in June 1963.

17. In the 1850s, white settlers build homesteads on the land originally promised by the U.S. government to the Osage nation.

18. A perfectly sane Victorian woman is locked away in an asylum by a husband who wants to divorce her and marry someone else.

19. Impoverished after the death of her parents, a young woman in the early 20th century travels from New York to Oklahoma to be a teacher in a sod schoolhouse.

20. A woman from the highest ranks of society falls in love with a coachman in Regency-era England.

21. A gentleman is about to face a challenger in a duel, but doesn't want to kill him now that he's learned more about the guy's tragic history.

22. Wu Zhao, an emperor's concubine in early eighth-century China, becomes the ruling empress.

23. A man pretending to spy for the Nazis during World War II leads them further and further astray while getting

more and more money from them and feeding valuable intelligence to the Allies.

24. In ancient Egypt, beautiful fragrances are prized, used for funeral rites, other religious rituals, and for aphrodisiacs. A woman becomes privy to secrets and scandals when she becomes the official perfume-maker to a royal court.

25. Large numbers of emus are ravaging wheat crops in 1930s Australia. The Minister of Defence deploys troops to shoot them in "The Emu War," but the birds prove wily and the effort is pretty much a failure.

26. Between December 27, 1813 and January 3, 1814, a dense fog covers London, disrupting travel and commerce.

27. A prince is kidnapped by pirates, makes friends with them, and convinces them to demand a higher ransom from his father, whom he dislikes.

28. A medieval teenage girl, pressured by her parents to marry a middle-aged man, runs away.

29. A Victorian female crime syndicate blackmails the gentry and steals from department stores and from wealthy homes, where they get employment as maids.

30. Because few women of childbearing age live in Seattle, Washington in 1864, a man named Asa Mercer recruits almost a hundred young women from the East Coast to move to Seattle. They become known as the Mercer Girls.

31. An entertainer weathers the danger and the drudgery of a USO tour during World War II.

32. Gui Zizi, a general in China's Tang Dynasty, is a Nestorian Christian who quashes the An Lushan Rebellion.

33. In 16th century Germany, a man helps a woman suspected of witchcraft escape.

34. A priestess in ancient Mesopotamia secretly gets lessons in reading and writing, although people at the time generally believe women aren't smart enough to do either.

35. After Marie Antoinette is executed, her eight-year-old son is taken to prison. A sympathetic guard helps him escape to the country. (Note: in reality, young Louis XVII died of tuberculosis after terrible abuse and neglect, and he was secretly buried in a mass grave.)

36. Jesse Stahl, an African-American cowboy, becomes famous for his daring rodeo riding.

37. A few poor families live in caves near Wick, Scotland in the early 20th century.

38. A crew member on the *HMS Beagle* survives the stress and strain involved with Charles Darwin's research trips.

39. A merchant's shared journey with another traveler on the Silk Road convinces him to convert to a different religion.

40. At the 1937 World's Fair in Paris, the German Pavilion and the Soviet Pavilion stand directly across from one another, and Pablo Picasso unveils his painting Guernica, depicting the Nazi bombing of the Basque town during the Spanish Civil War. Tensions are high.

41. In the 1650s, Peter Stuyvesant, the authoritarian director-

general of the New Netherland colony, butts heads with Adriaen van der Donck, a curious and idealistic lawyer.

42. A worker helping to construct the Brooklyn Bridge reconciles with an estranged family member.

43. In the Regency era, a tailor who makes garments with secret pockets for a spy falls in love with him.

44. Septimius Severus, an African-born governor, becomes a Roman emperor and defeats a rival's forces in battle.

45. In 1744, the world views the Great Comet with six tails.

46. A man looks into buying a suitable house on behalf of his brother, who is returning home from the war.

47. Murasaki Shikibu navigates court life in early 11th-century Japan as a lady-in-waiting while writing the world's first novel, a colossal work called *The Tale of Genji*.

48. A nurse from the Caribbean tends to wounded British troops in the Crimean War.

49. A Pony Express rider is captured by Pauite warriors.

50. When Alexander the Great invades India, the Macedonian army defeats the Agalassoi. Twenty thousand Agalassoi, despairing, set their own town on fire and cast themselves into the flames. One Agalassoi man or woman runs away instead.

51. In Regency England, a marquis whose late father gambled away most of the family fortune courts an American heiress.

52. A slave in a household of a Confederate general conveys military information to Union troops.

53. An aeronaut is hired by Union troops to spy on Confederate troops from his hot-air balloon.

54. In the early 800s, monks in an Irish monastery arm themselves and prepare for an imminent Viking raid.

55. A rich German-American family faces discrimination and hostility following the sinking of *The Lusitania* in 1915.

56. When Visigoths sack Rome, a family flees to their villa in the country.

57. In the 1880s, a Chinese man who had been working on a sugar plantation in Cuba opens a shop in the Barrio Chino, the Chinatown of Havana.

58. In a Texas town in the late nineteenth century, a judge's courthouse doubles as the local saloon.

59. The Trưng sisters, Trưng Trắc and Trưng Nhị, rule Vietnam for three years after leading a successful rebellion against the Chinese in 40 AD.

60. A dozen tornadoes rip through the Midwest in March 1925, including the Tri-State Tornado that moves through Missouri, Illinois, and Indiana, killing 695 people.

61. In 1893, suffragists in New Zealand see victory as the country becomes the first in the world to allow women to vote.

62. A sea captain named Edward Arthur Wilson begins having

visions, starts referring to himself as Brother XII, and starts a cult in Canada in the 1920s.

63. To avoid being sentenced to be a galley slave, a young man disguises himself as a lady-in-waiting in the court of Louis the Sun King in Versailles.

64. The daughter of a wealthy cacao plantation owner of Spanish descent is pressured by her family to end her childhood friendship with a *mestiza*—a girl of mixed Spanish and Native American heritage.

65. In the early 1960s, four American writers live in a run-down hotel in a foreign country.

66. A Victorian widow falls in love with her late husband's nephew.

67. The actress Dolores del Río stars in both Mexican and American films while becoming romantically involved with several actors and filmmakers in the 1930s, 1940s, and 1950s.

68. In medieval times, a man is shipwrecked in another country and given shelter by a lord there. He adapts to his new circumstances and becomes a knight in this new realm.

69. In the midst of the 1916 Uprising, gunfire around St. Stephen's Green in Dublin ceases every day so the park keeper can feed the ducks.

70. At the height of Victorian England's fern-collecting craze, a young woman changes her destiny by becoming one of the most successful gatherers of rare ferns in the wild.

71. An Englishman turns his back on England, joining King Robert the Bruce's forces in Scotland and volunteering for a dangerous mission to prove his loyalty.

72. Beginning in 1807, Ching Shih (Madame Cheng) takes over her deceased husband's pirate network, at one point controlling over three hundred junks and terrorizing both villagers and the crews of other ships.

73. A doctor in the Renaissance period, well ahead of his peers in research and knowledge, solves a murder case.

74. A Victorian gentleman learns that his wife has a scandalous past that may be publicly revealed.

75. In Kansas City during the Great Depression, 19-year-old Mary Lou Williams is the pianist, composer, and arranger for the jazz band Clouds of Joy.

76. In 1934 in Kansas City, the Democratic party machine commits widespread voter fraud and violence to win a municipal election.

77. A pirate who's done many, many people favors over the years has to call them in when he gets arrested and faces trial.

78. A couple escapes a disastrous volcanic eruption in Santa Maria, Guatemala, in 1902.

79. A nurse in the 1950s grows attached to a mysterious patient.

80. In Germany in the 1500s, the Fugger family owns a huge financial company and exerts influence over many political leaders, including King Henry VIII in England.

81. A woman of British and Afro-Caribbean descent inherits her late father's fortune and finds her way in Edwardian English society.

82. A casino owner avenges his brother in 1920s Miami.

83. Two men and one woman bring together the five Native American nations in the southern Great Lakes region to form the Iroquois Confederacy.

84. In England in the Middle Ages, a young nun in a convent is courted by a knight who wants to marry her in order to form an alliance with her noble family.

85. A Japanese soldier marries a Korean woman in 1940s Korea to help protect her from imprisonment after she becomes suspected as a dissident.

86. On July 17, 1955, Disneyland is dedicated in an "International Press Review" event plagued by a scorching temperature, non-operating water fountains, still-soft asphalt, and various other logistical issues.

87. A man enslaved by French colonists in Haiti takes part in the Revolution.

88. A woman who escaped the Great Famine in 1845 Ireland and found work as a housemaid in the United States tries to find out what happened to her sister.

89. In 18th-century India, a man from a lower caste raises his family's social status by political means.

90. A retired sea captain becomes a lighthouse keeper, but his wife and daughters object to living in such a remote place.

91. Witold Pilecki, a Polish cavalry officer, founds a Nazi resistance group in WWII and gets himself sent to Auschwitz on purpose in order to gather information about it, escaping two and a half years later.

92. In 1681, King Charles II persuades Puritan leaders in the colony of Massachusetts to lift the ban on Christmas, although many of them still consider it corrupt and refer to it as "Foolstide."

93. Buffalo Calf Road Woman, a Northern Cheyenne warrior, rescues her wounded brother from the field during the Battle of the Rosebud. Later that year, she fights alongside her husband at the Battle of the Little Bighorn, knocking Custer off his horse.

94. In the 1200s, local residents volunteer to help build Notre Dame Cathedral, though it won't be finished in their lifetime or their children's lifetimes.

95. A tattoo artist operates an underground parlor in the 1960s in New York City, where tattooing has just been made illegal.

96. A woman in the Victorian era pretends to be the lady a soldier has corresponded with through letters for the past two years.

97. In medieval times, two brothers both claim the right to inherit their late father's manor.

98. Ancient Egyptians make a successful sea voyage to the Americas. (Note: most historians do not believe this happened, but a few people point to evidence that suggests it.)

99. An entrepreneur in New York makes a fortune during the Great Depression.

100. The Stelmuze oak in Lithuania is the oldest tree in Europe: it's at least 1500 and perhaps 2000 years old. According to lore, pagans worshipped the Baltic god of thunder (Perkūnas) there.

101. After a battle, a commander winds up with an inconvenient prisoner.

102. Jewish women working in New York's shirtwaist factories go on a massive strike in 1909 and, a few months later, are granted many of their demands.

103. In the 1960s, a beloved rock star associated with peace and love is verbally and physically abusive to his wife and children.

104. In World War I, an African-American infantry unit—the "Harlem Hellfighters"—fights side by side with French troops and sees more active combat than any other American unit.

105. A pregnant widow marries a man who needs to name an heir before going off to war.

106. The man in charge of taking care of the lions, bears, and leopards who fight gladiators at the Roman Coliseum turns the animals against a cruel emperor.

107. A Frenchwoman marries a British colonel in order to get information for Napoleon's army.

108. A teenager on the streets in Victorian London pickpockets a dead man and makes an invaluable discovery.

109. A Victorian girl in London has packed to go on a grand tour of continental Europe with her family, but through a series of miscommunications, they accidentally leave her behind.

110. A group of misfits recruited for a cattle drive tangles with a band of horse thieves in the American West.

111. A governess subverts her employer's heartless plans for his children.

112. In 1754 India, the regent ruler of the Maratha Malwa kingdom dies. His mother, Ahilyabai—with the support of the Holkar army, which she leads herself, riding an elephant—becomes queen of the region.

113. A Roman noblewoman gets motion sickness from being carried around on a litter.

114. In 1736, a woman named Mrs. Ganderoon, along with a force of one hundred and twenty other needlewomen, embroiders the bridal gown and other court dresses for Augusta of Saxe-Gotha for her wedding to Frederick, Prince of Wales.

115. As a publicity stunt in 1866, a Texas train company crashes two trains into each other. Unfortunately, flying debris kills two spectators and seriously injures six others.

116. Two men who were once bitter rivals at an exclusive boarding school fight together in World War I.

117. During the U.S. Civil War, Harriet Tubman and Union Colonel James Montgomery attack plantations in South Carolina and manage to free seven hundred and twenty slaves.

118. A switchboard operator in the 1920s overhears a shocking conversation.

119. A woman born into poverty becomes a self-taught Impressionist painter and lives a surprisingly independent life in early 20th-century Paris.

120. In 1876, a yellow fever epidemic sweeps through Savannah, Georgia, and the dead are buried in the town in mass graves.

121. A British heiress serves as an ambulance driver in World War I.

122. A Havana cigar factory in the 1800s hires a local schoolteacher to read aloud to the workers in order to stave off their boredom.

123. In the 1940s in Singapore's Chinatown, Sago Lane becomes the "Street of Death." Because it's bad luck to die in your own home, immigrants with no nearby relatives who believe the end is near stay at the "death houses" to await the end. The parlors at the homes are ready for memorial services, and nearby shops sell coffins, incense, and other necessary items for funerals.

124. A Chinese alchemist, trying to make a potion to bestow immortality, accidentally creates gunpowder.

125. Annie Horniman, a British actress in the Victorian era, genuinely believes that she can astrally project herself to faraway places. She's even convinced that she's traveled to Saturn and has conversed with the people who live there.

126. In the early 1800s in New York City, virtually all leases

expire on May 1, making that the day that thousands of people move from one dwelling to another.

127. A Frenchwoman in the early 20th century is obsessed with trying to create a truly blue hybrid rose.

128. In the 1930s, African-American intellectuals wrongly assume that a novel is based on a well-known woman in Harlem.

129. Two sisters in Regency England develop a *tendre* for the same gentleman.

130. In 1652 in Zutphen, the Netherlands, the brothers François and Pierre Hémony create the first perfectly tuned carillon.

131. Adelaide Hermann starts out as an assistant to her magician husband, but when he dies in 1896, she begins performing on her own. Eventually, she becomes known as the Queen of Magic.

132. An arrogant Italian race car driver in the 1950s crashes his Ferrari, becomes seriously injured, and then attempts a comeback.

133. A woman in the early twentieth century begins receiving mysterious messages by carrier pigeon.

134. In 1887, Queen Lili'ukolani of Hawaii attends the Golden Jubilee of Queen Victoria and composes the famous song "Aloha Oe."

135. Two strangers have an unforgettable encounter when they are both wearing masks at a carnival in Venice.

136. The king is dead, but the queen has reasons to hide this fact and enlists a few of her most trusted servants to help her maintain the story that he's still ill in bed or away on a pilgrimage.

137. After an archeologist's dig, funded by several private investors, turns up nothing, he forges several antiquities.

138. A Victorian man saves a woman from a fire. She is wearing only her nightgown at the time, so her reputation is permanently ruined.

139. In the 10th century, in the extravagantly wealthy Ghana Empire, a goatherd becomes the assistant to a merchant dealing in salt and gold, and he travels in camel caravans along Trans-Sahara trade routes.

140. In 1920s Boston, Charles Ponzi carries out a large-scale, famous swindle.

141. Hans Christian Andersen, a poor Danish boy in the 1820s, lives with an abusive schoolmaster as he attends school. He writes fairy tales even though the faculty members do their best to discourage him.

142. Catherine the Great, empress of Russia, finally meets Voltaire, with whom she's been corresponding for over a decade. (Note: this is truly fictional. Although they exchanged letters for fifteen years and admired one another deeply, they never actually met in person.)

143. In the 1970s, idealistic nonconformists form a commune.

144. During the French Revolution, churches are pillaged and desecrated, and many members of the clergy are deported or sentenced to death.

145. Wolfgang Engels, a soldier in East Germany, steals an armored personal carrier and tries to drive it straight through the Berlin Wall. When it doesn't quite penetrate the wall, he evacuates the vehicle, gets tangled up in barbed wire and shot twice, and gets pulled to safety by West Berliners, who take him to a bar.

146. In Greece in 4th century BC, a man named Herostratus burns down the Temple of Artemis, one of the Seven Wonders of the Ancient World.

147. In 1907, a railroad brakeman in Mexico named Jesús Garcia Corona sees that a train car carrying dynamite has caught fire. He drives the car train backwards, downhill at full steam, saving the town of Nacozari before the dynamite blows and kills him.

148. For the 1936 Summer Olympics in Berlin, the Nazis invent the torch relay as a way to link their regime to ancient Greece, and they popularize the Olympic emblem of the five interlocking rings.

149. Jim Beckwourth, born into slavery in Virginia, becomes a blacksmith and then a fur trapper before being captured by the Crow nation. He lives with them for many years, rising to the rank of chief, and goes on to become a trader, store keeper, rancher, hotel owner, and an agent and scout for the U.S. government.

150. After a couple of decades of selling cookies they baked themselves, the Girl Scouts begin selling commercially produced and branded Girl Scout cookies in 1936.

150 GENERAL FICTION PROMPTS

I put this list together with contemporary mainstream and literary fiction in mind and sprinkled in some ideas for thrillers as well. Many of them could also be used in other ways. Some of these are more likely to be overarching plots, and some of them are better suited for smaller plot points in novels (or as inspiration for short stories).

1. Two sisters travel together to explore the city of their birth, which they remember only vaguely.

2. A group of friends who were roommates in their early 20s become roommates again decades later.

3. A therapist begins to suspect her grieving patient of murder.

4. A scholar discovers the location of the "Golden Library"— the priceless library that Ivan the Terrible had hidden or buried in the sixteenth century.

5. A woman learns for the first time that a boy she went to high school with had a huge crush on her.

6. A family's home is destroyed by raging wildfires in California.

7. A wedding venue is changed at the last minute, with guests notified in secret, to avoid being the target of organized crime.

8. A woman tells all her secrets to an Uber driver on a long drive. The driver later begins dating the woman's sister.

9. A guy recovers from a breakup by having a spa day with his best female friends.

10. Two siblings, both married with children, solve financial difficulties by all moving into one house together.

11. A pilot makes an emergency landing on the farm.

12. A college student is mistakenly identified as a terrorist.

13. Someone wins an award that embarrasses him.

14. A wife discovers that her husband has been repeatedly looking at the Facebook pages of his ex-girlfriends.

15. An eco-conscious man convinces his wife and family to live "off the grid."

16. A woman tries to save a building with historic or sentimental value from being torn down.

17. A man gets a call informing him that his wife is dead in a foreign country. He didn't know she'd gone on a trip.

18. A group of dissidents set out to bring a giant corporation to its knees.

19. A married couple confronts the fact that their autistic son is showing signs of regression, losing verbal and social skills he once had.

20. A woman suspects someone she knows is a criminal and sets a trap to catch him.

21. An older woman who lost her high-paying job pretends everything's fine even though she's barely scraping by.

22. Two actors can't stand each other and don't want to shoot scenes together.

23. DNA evidence proves a man's innocence after he's been in prison for thirty years.

24. A woman gets surgery to look more like the Photoshopped pictures of herself she shares on social media.

25. A bachelorette party isn't what anybody expected.

26. A man's daughter goes missing, and through investigation, he discovers she's been abducted by someone he trusted.

27. After the death of his grandfather, a man teaches his grandmother to drive for the first time.

28. A woman deals with several different kinds of parents after she sets up a new business driving children to and from their after-school activities and play dates.

29. A family of four celebrates all of their birthdays, Mother's Day, and the mother and father's anniversary, all during the month of May (known to them as "Mayhem.")

30. Roommates take in a stray dog and hide its existence from the apartment manager in a building that doesn't allow pets.

31. A couple sells their house to a woman who sues them a year later claiming they didn't disclose structural issues.

32. A young man gradually realizes his best friend has become completely absorbed in something ridiculous, cruel, or both, and he tries to bring his friend back to his senses again.

33. A professor uncovers a massive plagiarism syndicate that eludes all anti-plagiarism detection software—and wants a cut of the profits.

34. A woman goes on a photography safari in Tanzania and forges a strong connection with a fellow tourist.

35. A man picks a fight with a younger, bigger guy in order to prove to others—or himself—how tough he still is.

36. A man who prefers to keep his work life and his private life separate is pressured by his boss to attend the holiday office party—and to bring his wife.

37. A woman fakes a serious illness for social media attention and money.

38. A family forgoes their Christmas gift-giving to help another family in need.

39. A new public sculpture sparks a bitter community fight.

40. A meteorite crashes into a family's house, and one family member takes it as a divine sign.

41. An out-of-shape mother trains for a marathon. At first, nobody believes she can do it.

42. A family deals with an unexpected and not particularly welcome guest for Thanksgiving dinner.

43. A retiree purchases used newspaper printing equipment for a song and begins publishing an outlandish newspaper.

44. A mother tries to make up for the fact that she walked out on her children, and hopes to be a part of her grandchildren's lives.

45. A bride-to-be wants to mend fences with her father so he'll walk her down the aisle.

46. A divorcing woman whose husband is moving out of the house needs a roommate, fast—and finds one who's very different from her.

47. A professional hair and makeup artist, in trouble with the law or with an organized crime syndicate, changes her appearance several times as she hides in plain sight.

48. A man adjusts to life after losing a leg in a car accident.

49. A woman who's frustrated with her lack of options takes a job in a big city ninety miles away from home, which puts a strain on her relationship with her husband and daughter.

50. A campaign manager learns that his candidate, who has a stellar record of public service, has a terrible secret in her past.

51. A woman buys a ticket to the world's oddest and most exclusive flea market.

52. A man walks in on his fiancée as she's saying something terribly unflattering about him to her best friend.

53. Family members' lives are turned upside down when they allow a famous director to shoot a movie on their farm.

54. A woman grows jealous of her best friend's new romantic relationship and attempts to break it up.

55. A family tries to increase the profits of their small maple

syrup business by involving groups of tourists in the sugaring process.

56. A young woman follows the advice of an antiquated guide to charm, with hilarious and touching results.

57. A woman sets out to write a rulebook for a successful life; the events in her own life lead her to constantly revise it.

58. An undercover FBI agent dates a man who works for a crime boss in order to get information.

59. When a woman loses one of her employees at her struggling small-town beauty salon, her elderly mother volunteers to help her out by working for free. She just needs some training.

60. A couple who seems to have an ideal marriage announces they're getting divorced. Their best friends, another married couple, re-evaluate their relationship and make big changes.

61. Two people keep the date or appointment they made ten years ago.

62. The new pastor at a church deals with vindictive parishioners who are angry that the last minister was ousted.

63. After a woman survives both a freak accident and a poison gas attack on a subway, she suspects some entity is trying to kill her.

64. A woman loans nonprofit money to a friend who claims to be in dire straits and promises to pay it back within a couple of days. He later refuses to pay.

65. A bestselling author pretends to live a very different life in order to research a character in his upcoming novel.

66. An Uber driver becomes a drug smuggler.

67. After a young woman breaks off a serious relationship with a man who seemed like he would've been a perfect son-in-law, her parents scheme to bring the two back together.

68. A woman kills an attacker in self-defense and faces trial for murder.

69. Weeks before the wedding, a groom regrets his choice of best man.

70. A man becomes known for the songs he writes about the details of his mundane life.

71. A man in the afterlife, who believed he was unimportant on earth, witnesses the profound and wide-ranging effects his death has on others. He then tries to find his way back in time to prevent his own death.

72. Two people planning their own 25th anniversary party realize they each have very different recollections of key events in their shared history.

73. Twin sisters convince their friends that they're able to communicate telepathically, although in fact, they're terrible at guessing one another's thoughts.

74. A teacher's life becomes complicated after an aspect of her private life becomes public.

75. A couple, friends, or siblings agree to give one another's hobbies a try.

76. A couple desperate to adopt make a terrible first impression with the adoption agency.

77. A parent looks for a job after staying home with the children for twelve years.

78. When a couple buys a fixer-upper home and it turns out to be a money pit, they burn it down and try to make it look like an accident.

79. Three generations of a family go on a cross-country road trip to attend a relative's wedding.

80. A man's secretive attempts to arrange a spectacular surprise 50th birthday party for his wife lead her to fear he's having an affair.

81. A woman's beauty procedure goes horribly wrong.

82. Parents, teachers, and teens clash over whether a subject should be taught in a high school classroom.

83. A man infuriates his parents and/or children by writing about or telling people about their very personal or painful experiences.

84. A woman wants to see Jerusalem before she dies.

85. A man has more trouble than he expected getting over the loss of a pet.

86. A newly successful woman gives all her family members generous gifts. It causes unexpected problems.

87. A man quits his job, buys a trailer, and spends a year traveling across the country.

88. A woman resorts to shady measures in order to make her startup business a success.

89. A man finds a newborn baby in a tote bag on the subway.

90. An art restorer discovers a work of art is a fake—but revealing this would be disastrous to the struggling museum.

91. A middle-aged actor is told that if he were going to make it, he would've done it by now. He sets out to prove that person wrong.

92. A celebrity's career is destroyed after she is quoted out of context.

93. Long after a picture of her unconscious in a public place is shared far and wide, a woman conquers her addiction and struggles to build a new life.

94. Five very different people who all go to the same fast-food restaurant or diner every day get to know one another.

95. A woman gets a job at the most exclusive restaurant in the country, where reservations are made years in advance.

96. Someone tries to figure out what to do with the huge salt and pepper shaker collection their dead relative bequeathed to them.

97. A man believes he can communicate telepathically with a loved one who's been in a coma for a long time.

98. A community deals with a tiger on the loose.

99. A beloved sports figure's use of performance-enhancing drugs is revealed.

100. A woman attempts to change the bad reputation of fruitcake, her favorite Christmas treat.

101. After two years of fertility treatments, a couple is expecting quintuplets.

102. A mother is plagued with suspicions that her young child has been replaced by an imposter.

103. A man struggles with guilt and anger after a loved one's suicide.

104. A marketing team rebrands a very old-fashioned product for younger consumers.

105. A man quits his job, comes home, and learns that his wife is pregnant with their first child.

106. After a man's girlfriend breaks up with him, he becomes more and more involved with tracking her movements and her interactions on social media, all the while perceiving himself as a romantic and a victim.

107. A massive earthquake in the U.S. Pacific Northwest triggers a tsunami that washes over much of Portland, Salem, Eugene, Olympia, and parts of Seattle.

108. A man is asked to identify the dead body of his husband. He recognizes the body in the morgue, but it's not his husband.

109. A literary critic becomes disgusted with the viciousness of her own work.

110. A man who's never tried skiing before pretends to others that it's not his first time.

111. She's by far the best sales associate in the store, but she has a bad habit of occasionally giving a customer an item for free.

112. A man is in love with a woman who claims her husband is abusive. The man murders him and then learns he may have been misled.

113. The thing she admired about her husband—his ambition—makes her marriage a nightmare, because nothing is ever good enough for him.

114. A man designs a world-record-breaking amusement park ride.

115. A woman's two best friends have each privately confessed to her they're in love with one another, but are terrified to act on their feelings. They've both sworn her to secrecy.

116. A man writes an advice column under a female pseudonym. It becomes wildly popular.

117. A woman pressures her husband to hide something significant about himself or his life from her parents.

118. A man becomes increasingly alarmed at how differently his wife talks and acts when she's with her family.

119. A woman accidentally captures a murder in the background of her selfie for Instagram.

120. A woman's friends abandon her because they feel that five years after the loss of a loved one, she shouldn't still be clinging to grief.

121. A man's business relocates him to a place he never expected to live and expects to loathe. He winds up loving it.

122. People usually hire the harpist to play at wedding receptions and the occasional fancy birthday party, but this time, she's going to perform at a very different kind of event.

123. A woman is obsessed with how badly her ex-boyfriends hurt her…and is half-convinced she must not be lovable.

124. A man fires the man who stole his girlfriend several years ago—a matter that the other guy assumed was water under the bridge.

125. An ambitious executive is consumed with jealousy when a new hire seems to be the CEO's favorite.

126. Close friends, lovers, or family must say goodbye, knowing they won't see each other again for a long time.

127. A timid new guy at work finds a mentor in a clever, brash man who teaches him how to succeed and how to get away with just about anything.

128. A woman alarms her family by taking a dangerous journey while pregnant.

129. A man murders his neo-Nazi father.

130. A wealthy elderly woman is arrested for the first time in her life.

131. An airman in the U.S. Air Force kills people with drones without ever leaving his computer. His superiors accuse him of defying orders and purposely missing a target.

132. A family in an upper-middle-class neighborhood begins to live with extreme frugality in order to knock out their towering credit card debt.

133. A woman's best friend moves into her apartment building, and the woman starts to get irritated with her habits now that she's around all the time.

134. A detective can't reveal that he's an eyewitness to a murder—if people knew he was there, it would end his career. So he plants evidence to convict the killer.

135. A family disowns a son who wins the lottery soon after.

136. A grandfather gets remarried at the age of eighty, and nobody in the family approves.

137. Two sisters with a history of competitiveness plan weddings for the same summer.

138. A man and his ex-girlfriend become the best of friends and advise one another on future relationships.

139. A sister is called as a character witness in her brother's trial and offers damning testimony against him.

140. A man learns his parents are allowing his ex-wife to stay at their house for a while.

141. An office worker cannot be persuaded to stop writing emails in all caps.

142. A daughter sells the gifts her parents give to her children.

143. A mother becomes increasingly jealous of her friend's carefree childless lifestyle.

144. A husband pressures his wife to go back to work and then becomes jealous of her business success.

145. A woman tries to save her boyfriend from his out-of-control addiction to playing videogames.

146. A journalist goes undercover as a psychiatric patient to investigate a mental hospital.

147. A retired woman on a tight budget becomes an art thief. No one ever pays attention to her or suspects her.

148. A mother considers firing a nanny because she's worried her children love the woman better than her.

149. After a severe head injury, a man discovers a new gift for picking up foreign languages.

150. A poor, fun-loving woman in New York City hosts a series of cocktail parties in public spaces.

CLASSIC PLOT PROMPTS

This section of the book takes inspiration from classic and time-honored stories. Contemporary writers often find pleasure in either changing traditional stories to reflect their own world views or giving traditional stories new relevancy and power by giving them a new setting or context.

Umberto Eco famously wrote in his novel *The Name of the Rose,* "Books always speak of other books, and every story tells a story that has already been told." Many great works of literature were inspired by other great works of literature. Even Shakespeare stole ideas from ancient Greek and Roman writers and other playwrights and authors. If he did it, you can do it, too.

Some of these are plot points that I found interesting, rather than full-blown plots. I've sometimes described a story in broader terms in order to open up more creative possibilities, but you may wish to stay closer to the original material.

Because these are older stories, I haven't worried about sharing spoilers, so read at your own risk.

50 PLOTS FROM THE BIBLE

The Bible is one of the most influential books in the world. A lot of these stories are from Genesis because that book of the Bible contains so much colorful storytelling.

1. A man's arrogance annoys his brothers, so they sell him into slavery. (Joseph and his brothers, Genesis.)

2. A female leader with the gift of prophecy tells a commander of the army to go attack their enemy forces. He says okay, but only if she goes with him. She says fine, but that means a woman is going to get all the credit. They wage a successful battle. (Deborah and Jael, Judges.)

3. A nobody agrees to fight a supposedly unbeatable enemy warrior—and slays him. (David and Goliath, 1 Samuel.)

4. A prince and a warrior love each other, but the prince's father the king is jealous of the warrior and tries to kill him. (David and Jonathan, 1 Samuel.)

5. A couple gets banished from a paradise after breaking the rules. (Adam and Eve, Genesis.)

6. A nation suffers a series of terrible plagues. (Moses and the Plagues, Exodus.)

7. A man who squandered his inheritance while living a worthless life returns home humbled—and his father rejoices to see him again. (The Parable of the Prodigal Son, Luke.)

8. A respected teacher chooses to dine with a dishonest man nobody can stand. (Jesus and Zacchaeus, Luke.)

9. The inhabitants of a growing city suddenly find themselves all speaking different languages, so they can't understand one another. (The Tower of Babel, Genesis.)

10. A man is asked to kill his only son as a proof of his loyalty, and is stopped at the last moment. (Abraham and Isaac, Genesis.)

11. A man receives a list of holy laws. (Moses and the Ten Commandments, Genesis.)

12. A woman takes away a man's strength by cutting his hair. (Samson and Delilah, Judges.)

13. A boss makes some of his employees angry by paying those who worked a short time the same amount as those who worked a long time. (The Parable of the Workers in the Vineyard, Matthew.)

14. A king falls in love with the wife of one of his soldiers. He sends the soldier to the front lines and orders the commander to have the rest of the troops retreat so the soldier is killed in battle. (David and Bathsheba, 2 Samuel.)

15. A chariot of fire drawn by horses of fire takes a man to heaven. (Elijah's Departure, 2 Kings.)

16. A powerful woman whose false testimony led to an innocent man's execution is thrown out of a high window. The fall kills her, and stray dogs eat her dead body. (Jezebel, 1 Kings.)

17. A man is swallowed by a huge beast and survives in its stomach for three days before getting spit out again. (Jonah and the Whale, Jonah.)

18. Dry bones and skeletons become flesh-and-blood humans and get up and walk. (Ezekiel's Vision, Ezekiel.)

19. A man receives a cash payment in order to betray his leader. (Judas and Thirty Pieces of Silver, Matthew.)

20. A man and his friends are sentenced to be burned to death, but they don't burn. (Daniel and the Fiery Furnace, Daniel.)

21. Learned men notice a new portent in the sky and believe it to be a sign of the birth of a great person. (The Three Wise Men, Matthew.)

22. A man becomes enraged by dishonest moneychangers in a temple, overturns their tables, and chases them out with a whip. (The Cleansing of the Temple, Matthew, Mark, Luke, and John.)

23. A man and his pregnant wife are traveling and they're desperate to find a place to stay, but all the hotel rooms are booked. They take shelter in a stable. (Mary Gives Birth to Jesus, Luke.)

24. A ruler promises his daughter he'll give her anything. She asks him to execute a prisoner. (John the Baptist is Beheaded, Matthew.)

25. A man murders his brother out of jealousy, and he's cursed as a result. (Cain and Abel, Genesis.)

26. An angel shows up at the jail in the middle of the night

and sets an innocent prisoner free. (Peter's Escape from Prison, Acts.)

27. Two travelers suddenly realize that a stranger is actually the man they've been telling the stranger about, although they believed him to be dead. (The Road to Emmaus, Luke.)

28. Before his inevitable death, a man sits down to a final meal with his followers. (The Last Supper, Mark.)

29. While one sister does all the cooking and preparations for her guests, her sister just sits around talking with them. (Mary, Martha, and Jesus, Luke.)

30. A man's skill at interpreting the king's dreams earns him great privileges at court. (Joseph Interprets Pharaoh's Dreams, Genesis.)

31. A man is ordered to take off his shoes because he's standing on holy ground. (Joshua and the Man With the Sword, Joshua.)

32. A woman chooses not to part ways with her widowed mother-in-law and makes a difficult journey with her. (Ruth and Naomi, Ruth.)

33. A man wrestles an angel all night and won't give up until the angel gives him a blessing. (Jacob Wrestles the Angel, Genesis.)

34. Supernatural messengers tell peasants about something incredibly exciting that's happened nearby. (The Shepherds and the Angels, Luke.)

35. A man pretends to be his older brother and tricks his

dying father into giving him the blessing reserved for firstborn sons. (Isaac Blesses Jacob, Genesis.)

36. Parents lose their child after a festival and finally find him at the church. (The Boy Jesus in the Temple, Luke.)

37. A woman convinces her new husband, a king, not to slaughter her people. (Esther.)

38. A man miraculously transforms water into wine. (The Wedding Feast at Cana, John.)

39. Men meet divine punishment for burning the wrong kind of incense in a temple. (The Death of Nadab and Abihu, Leviticus.)

40. A lion attacks a boy's parents, so the boy rips the lion apart with his bare hands. (Samson and the Lion, Judges.)

41. A catastrophe wipes out most life on earth, but a few people and many animals are chosen to survive. (The Great Flood, Genesis.)

42. A man intercedes with a mob of people about to kill a woman for her crime, pointing out that all of them are guilty of some wrongdoing. (The Woman Caught in Adultery, John.)

43. A man catches a fish and finds money inside. (The Coin in the Fish's Mouth, Matthew.)

44. At the age of ninety, a woman becomes pregnant. (Sarah Becomes Pregnant, Genesis.)

45. A man forgives his contrite brothers for the terrible thing they did to him. (Joseph Forgives His Brothers, Genesis.)

46. A woman welcomes an enemy commander into her tent, and once he's asleep, she kills him by driving a tent peg into his head. (Deborah and Jael, Judges.)

47. A man orders a storm to cease, and it does. (Jesus Calms a Storm, Mark, Luke.)

48. When soldiers receive orders to slaughter the royal family, one woman escapes with her infant nephew. (Athaliah and Jehosheba, 2 Chronicles.)

49. A man invites a lot of people to a dinner party, but at the last minute, all his guests make excuses for why they can't come. So he has his servants go out and invite poor strangers to his feast. (The Parable of the Great Banquet, Luke.)

50. There's only a little food, but miraculously, it feeds thousands of people. (Feeding the Multitude, Matthew, Mark, Luke, John.)

50 PLOTS FROM EUROPEAN FAIRY TALES AND MYTHOLOGY

A lot of the stories I came across in researching were too confusing, inappropriate, or downright disturbing to include. Some of the ones that made it in are still pretty bizarre. Many of them involve winning the hand of a princess, so there are several variations of that here, but in your story, the hero might have a completely different goal. In some cases, I'm only including part of the story, but they're all pretty easy to look up if you're curious.

1. A warrior's magical weapon is stolen by an enemy, who says he'll only give it back if he can marry the warrior's sister. The warrior agrees and later dresses up like his sister to go get it back. (Thor and Thrym the giant, Norse mythology.)

2. Two sisters befriend a bear who turns out to be a prince who's under an evil enchantment. ("Snow White and Rose Red," German fairy tale.)

3. A man ventures into the realm of the dead, hoping to find his wife and bring her back to the world of the living. (Orpheus and Eurydice, Greek mythology.)

4. A father, imprisoned with his son, creates a spectacular invention that will allow his son to escape. However, the son gets carried away and ignores a warning about the invention, which causes his death. (Daedalus and Icarus, Greek mythology.)

5. A knight's best friend is fighting and doing very well at a tournament. Near the end of the day, the knight's liege

lord orders him to go and fight his best friend, who is now exhausted from battle. The knight doesn't want to do it, but he's sworn to obey his liege. (Tristan and Lamorack, Arthurian legend.)

6. All the princesses are locked in their bedrooms at night, but in the morning, their dancing shoes are always worn out. An old soldier accepts the king's challenge to figure out what's going on. ("The Twelve Dancing Princesses," German fairy tale; versions from other countries also exist.)

7. Men escape a giant by strapping themselves to the bellies of sheep and getting away when the giant lets out his flocks to graze. (*The Odyssey*, Greek mythology.)

8. A strange knight in full armor attacks an unarmed king in the forest. He makes the king agree to meet him there in one year with the answer to a difficult question. If the king doesn't get the answer right, the knight will cut off his head. (The Wedding of Sir Gawain and Dame Ragnelle, Arthurian legend.)

9. A woman whose stepmother and stepsisters are mean to her gets dressed up, attends a ball, and wins the heart of a prince. ("Cinderella," French fairy tale; many earlier variations existed around the globe.)

10. A king receives a beautiful mechanical bird, made of gold and encrusted with jewels, that has a voice almost as beautiful as a real nightingale's. Unfortunately, the king isn't able to wind it up. ("The Nightingale," fairy tale written by Hans Christian Anderson.)

11. A man steals life-saving technology to help humankind

and is punished severely for doing so. (Prometheus, Greek mythology.)

12. A foolish prince frees a villain from his chains. The prince's wife is the one who had the guy locked up. ("The Death of Koschei the Deathless," Russian fairy tale.)

13. A woman becomes jealous of her husband's love for the children he had with his first wife, so she turns them into swans. (The Children of Lir, Irish mythology.)

14. To defend the Jewish people from a Roman emperor, a rabbi creates a man out of clay and uses a special ritual to bring it to life. ("The Golem of Prague," Czechian folk tale.)

15. Two villains murder the wisest person on earth and brew mead with his blood. Anyone who drinks the mead turns into a poet or a scholar. (Odin and the Mead of Poetry, Norse mythology.)

16. Whoever can ride their horse up a steep glass hill can marry the king's daughter. ("The Princess on the Glass Hill," Norwegian fairy tale.)

17. A king feeds a flea his own blood until the insect grows to be the size of a sheep. Then he kills it and skins it. He says any man who can guess what animal the skin came from can marry his daughter. (Gross. And poor flea.) An ogre guesses correctly and takes the princess off to his lair of horror. She escapes. ("The Flea," fairy tale written by Giambattista Basile.)

18. A girl's evil stepmother sends her to the hut of a terrifying witch, hoping the witch will kill her. Instead, the girl returns home with a lantern made out of a skull. It catches

fire and burns her stepmother and mean stepsisters to death. ("Vasilia the Beautiful," Russian fairy tale.)

19. An escaped slave helps someone who's dangerous, but injured. Later, this individual refuses to fight the slave. ("Androcles and the Lion," Aesop's fable, ancient Greece.)

20. A woman is ordered to spin straw into gold. A weird guy shows up and does it for her, but when he eventually demands her firstborn as payment, she finds a way to get rid of him. ("Rumpelstiltzkin," German fairy tale.)

21. A young man is kind to all the animals who cross his path—ducks, bees, and even ants. They help him with the feats he must accomplish to win the king's daughter. ("The Queen Bee," German fairy tale.)

22. A hunter shoots a bird, and the bird begs him to take her home instead of killing her. She tells the hunter that when she falls asleep, he should hit her in the head. The hunter does all this, and the bird turns into a beautiful woman. ("Go I Know Not Whither and Fetch I Know Not What," Russian fairy tale.)

23. A woman gives birth to a bizarre-looking baby with goat's legs and horns. She screams in horror, but the father thinks his new baby is hilarious. (The Birth of Pan, Son of Hermes, Greek mythology.)

24. A queen plans to appease a vengeful god by sacrificing her daughter to a sea monster. (Perseus and Andromeda, Greek mythology.)

25. A shoemaker and his wife are poor, but when elves start making shoes for them in the middle of the night, business starts booming. The elves only have rags to wear, so the

shoemaker's wife sews little elf outfits for them. They're so proud of how they look that they run away and don't make any more shoes, but the shoemaker and his wife have already been lifted out of poverty, and they continue to prosper. ("The Elves and the Shoemaker," German fairy tale.)

26. During a royal wedding, a white stag runs through the church, pursued by sixty black hounds and one white one. The king's advisor says the stag must be hunted, so the king sends two of his best knights after it. (Sir Gawain and Lady Ablamar, Arthurian legend.)

27. An old man grows a turnip so huge he can't pull it out of the ground. He asks his wife to help pull it, but they have no luck. They recruit the dog to join in the effort, and then the cat, and finally, when a mouse also helps, they get the vegetable out of the ground. ("The Gigantic Turnip," Russian fairy tale.)

28. A woman brags about how many children she has, enraging a god and goddess, who kills them all. (Niobe in *The Iliad*, Greek mythology.)

29. The son of a nobleman comes to court disguised as a serving boy who works in the kitchens. Some of the nobles look down on him, including the girl whose sister he soon sets out to rescue. (The Story of Gareth, Arthurian legend.)

30. A woman loved by both a mortal prince and a handsome god chooses the prince. (Idas and Marpessa, Greek mythology.)

31. The youngest son of a miller inherits only a cat. However, he's no ordinary cat, and after demanding a pair of boots,

he uses cleverness and trickery to make his new master a prince. ("Puss in Boots," Italian fairy tale, but many other versions exist.)

32. The Devil marries two sisters in succession, only to throw them both into hell. The third and youngest sister marries him, rescues her sisters from hell, and helps them all escape—but only after robbing him. ("How the Devil Married Three Sisters," Italian fairy tale)

33. A sculptor creates a statue so beautiful, he falls in love with it. Then it comes to life. (Pygmalion and Galatea, Greek mythology.)

34. A dragon in a local lake keeps eating the village's cows and the occasional maiden. A man brings the dragon an enormous suet pudding in a cart, which the dragon eats (along with the horse and cart.) Then the dragon starts to feel sick to his stomach. The man pretends to lean in to give the dragon medicine and kills him with an axe to the head. (British folk tale.)

35. A god brings his baby son to the cave of a centaur and asks him to foster the child. (The story of Asclepius, Greek mythology.)

36. When a chieftain plays his magical harp, he can make anyone who hears it begin weeping, laughing, or even sleeping, as he chooses. (The Dagda's Harp, Irish mythology.)

37. A girl gives a drink of water to an old woman who's a fairy in disguise. The fairy rewards her with an enchantment: whenever the girl speaks, jewels, gold, or flowers fall from her lips. ("Diamonds and Toads," French fairy tale.)

38. A baby girl is born, and her father gives orders to leave her outside to die. She's raised by a bear and grows up to

be a great huntress and a fast runner. (Atalanta, Greek mythology.)

39. A mouse, a bird, and a sausage (who is sentient) all live together happily for a while, but when they decide to switch who does what household task, it's a disaster. ("The Mouse, the Bird, and the Sausage," German fairy tale.)

40. A horse-tamer wishes he could ride a giant winged horse. One night, he dreams that a goddess gives him a golden bridle that will allow him to do so. He wakes with the golden bridle in his hand. (Bellerophon and Pegasus, Greek mythology.)

41. Everything a man touches turns to gold, and it's awful. (King Midas and His Golden Touch, Greek mythology.)

42. The Queen of the Fairies dies and the fairies need to elect a new one, but they have trouble deciding between two candidates. They decide whoever does the most amazing feat will win the crown. ("Rosanella," French fairy tale.)

43. An individual who is unable to attain something he wants consoles himself with the idea that the thing probably wasn't any good, anyway. ("The Fox and the Grapes," Aesop's fable, ancient Greece.)

44. A king sends out his barber to find him a wife. The barber only asks that women who would like to be considered should look into his magic mirror, which makes flaws in a person's character show up like blemishes on his or her face. Strangely enough, almost no women are interested in getting married to the king. ("The Magic Mirror," Spanish folk tale.)

45. An evil fairy curses a baby princess so that one day she'll prick her finger on the spindle of a spinning wheel and die. To keep the princess safe, another fairy puts the

princess into a deep sleep for a hundred years, one that can only be broken by a kiss from a prince. ("Sleeping Beauty," French fairy tale.)

46. A fire-breathing demon lulls warriors to sleep, then burns the castle of Tara to the ground...every Samhain, for twenty-three years, until a hero bests him. (The story of Fionn Mac Cumhaill, Irish mythology.)

47. A goddess employs a big, strong man with a hundred eyes all over his body. A god disguises himself as a shepherd and tells the man such a long, dull story that, one by one, the eyes close, and finally, he dies of sheer boredom. (Hera, Argus, and Hermes, Greek mythology.)

48. A mermaid sits on a rock every evening and gives medical advice to villagers. One local woman accuses the mermaid of being evil and pushes her seat into the river. The next day, this woman's baby has died in his cradle, and no one ever sees the mermaid again. (Scottish folk tale.)

49. A trickster god decides it would be hilarious to shave the head of his brother's wife while she's sleeping. When she and her husband are furious, he promises to give her new hair made from pure gold. (Loki, Thor, and Sif, Norse mythology.)

50. A knight in the habit of inviting rich and poor alike to Christmas feasts and giving all of them generous gifts, eventually runs out of money and lives with his family in poverty. He realizes he's been forgotten by the king, who doesn't invite him to court. But on Christmas morning, in the middle of winter, a cherry tree in his garden bears delicious fruit. He takes some of the fruit to the king, who showers riches on him and his family. (Sir Cleges and the Christmas Cherry Tree, Arthurian legend.)

50 PLOTS FROM SHAKESPEARE AND OTHER ELIZABETHAN LITERATURE

1. A man makes a deal with the Devil, trading his soul for twenty-four years of service from a demon. (*Doctor Faustus*, Christopher Marlowe.)

2. Two people who are in love and about to wed conspire to get two of their friends, who are always bickering with one another, to marry each other. (*Much Ado About Nothing*, Shakespeare.)

3. A prince returns home to mourn his father's death and finds his mother already re-married to his uncle. A ghost reveals to the prince that his uncle murdered his father, and the prince ponders revenge. (*Hamlet*, Shakespeare.)

4. After conquering France, an English king courts the daughter of a French king, who has reservations about marrying an enemy. (*Henry V*, a historical play, Shakespeare.)

5. A young woman goes through a portal at the North Pole, finds herself in an alternate universe and becomes the empress of a kingdom filled with talking animals. (*The Blazing World*, Margaret Cavendish.)

6. An army commander returns home from war in triumph, but then quarrels with other leaders and gets banished. (*Coriolanus*, Shakespeare.)

7. A nobleman forces another man at gunpoint to pray to

Satan. Then he shoots him dead, sending him to Hell. (*The Unfortunate Traveler*, Thomas Nashe.)

8. When the king becomes gravely ill, a woman comes to court with a prescription developed by her late father, a doctor. The king recovers, and as a reward, he tells the young woman she can marry any of the single men at court she chooses. She picks the guy she's had a crush on for years, and because he's not happy about it, he goes off to war. (*All's Well That Ends Well,* Shakespeare.)

9. A duke usurps his older brother's throne and banishes his niece to the wilderness. The niece disguises herself as a boy for the new adventure, and the duke's own daughter goes with her. (*As You Like It*, Shakespeare.)

10. A widowed duchess proposes to her steward and marries him—in secret, because her brothers didn't want her to marry again. *(The Duchess of Malfi*, a historical play by John Webster.)

11. A man is in love with the duke's daughter, and she returns his feelings, even though she's engaged to someone else. The man asks his friend to help him and the woman he loves elope. Unfortunately, this friend becomes attracted to the woman himself and betrays the whole plan to the duke, who locks up his daughter in jail. (*The Two Gentlemen of Verona*, Shakespeare.)

12. A woman leaves home in search of a man who was exiled but still holds her affections. She gets captured by a band of outlaws—but it's okay, because the man she loves has been elected their leader. (Also *The Two Gentlemen of Verona*, Shakespeare.)

13. A man and a woman are in love. Another man's also in

love with this woman, and he's no longer interested in the woman he used to date. (A *Midsummer Night's Dream*, Shakespeare.)

14. The King and the Queen of the Fairies are arguing because the King wants to adopt the half-mortal boy the Queen took under her wing, and she doesn't want to give him up. (Also *A Midsummer Night's Dream*, Shakespeare.)

15. Someone slips a woman a love potion, and she falls in love with the wrong person—and a really inappropriate one. (Also *A Midsummer Night's Dream*, Shakespeare.)

16. A generous man with a spending problem realizes he's in debt and asks his friends to loan him money. None of them do. He invites them all to dinner, serves only warm water, and berates them for being bad friends. (*Timon of Athens*, Shakespeare.)

17. A neighboring enemy has beaten one of the king's armies and taken its commander prisoner. Meanwhile, the king's son spends all his time drinking and carousing with lowlifes. (*King Henry IV*, Shakespeare.)

18. A man who wants to marry a noblewoman disguises himself as a slave, starts a slave revolt, and then protects her from the violence he incited in order to get her to love him. (*The Bondman,* Philip Massinger.)

19. A shipwrecked merchant lands on enemy shores and is arrested immediately because everyone there hates his country. (*The Comedy of Errors*, Shakespeare.)

20. A man shows up for another man's knighthood ceremony. Then he goes on adventures, pursued by the angry man

whose knighthood he "stole." (*Sir Clyomon and Sir Clamydes*, attributed to various authors.)

21. A man intends to get revenge on another man, but he changes his mind after learning the guy is the brother of the woman he loves. (Also *Sir Clyomon and Sir Clamydes.*)

22. A rich lord and his friends play a trick on a drunken man: they put him in the lord's grand bedroom, and when the man wakes up, they claim he's a nobleman and he's been insane for the past fifteen years. (*The Taming of the Shrew*, Shakespeare.)

23. A down-on-his-luck knight sets out to woo two married women and get their money. The women discover the scheme and set out to make a fool of him. (*The Merry Wives of Windsor*, Shakespeare.)

24. Although the duke has no idea, two of his new servants are actually the brother and the boyfriend of a woman he murdered, and they're plotting to kill him in revenge. (*The White Devil*, a historical play, John Webster.)

25. Inspired by a prophecy of witches, a woman urges her husband, a war captain, to murder the king so he can take the throne. (*Macbeth,* Shakespeare.)

26. A Huguenot king marries the sister of a Catholic king. A duke schemes to take the throne. He murders the new queen and incites Catholics across Paris to kill Huguenots. (*The Massacre of Paris*, a historical play by Christopher Marlowe.)

27. The goddess Venus arranges for her son to fall in love with the Queen of Carthage. When he leaves her, feeling he has a destiny to fulfill in Italy, she burns herself to death

on a funeral pyre. Her former suitor and her sister, upset by this, kill themselves as well. (*Dido, Queen of Carthage,* a play by Christopher Marlowe based on Virgil's *The Aeneid.*)

28. A grieving general asks his servant to kill him. The servant doesn't want to obey him or refuse an order, so he kills himself by falling on his sword. (*Antony and Cleopatra,* Shakespeare.)

29. A married man lives with his girlfriend in a foreign country, but when his wife dies, he goes home and agrees to marry the emperor's sister. (Also *Antony and Cleopatra,* Shakespeare.)

30. A man gets passed over for a promotion. Seeking revenge, he convinces his boss that his boss's wife is having an affair with the guy who got the promotion. (*Othello,* Shakespeare.)

31. A king's friend prepares to depart after a long visit. The king tries to persuade him to stay longer. The king's pregnant wife succeeds in talking their guest into this, and then the king becomes obsessed with the idea that maybe his wife and his friend are secretly in love. (*A Winter's Tale,* Shakespeare.)

32. When the plague strikes London, a rich man retreats to his country estate—only to learn his butler has been using the place for illicit purposes. (*The Alchemist,* Ben Johnson.)

33. A shepherd and bandit woos the daughter of a king and helps lead the king's soldiers to war. After the king is killed in battle, he takes the throne himself. (*Tamburlaine the Great,* Christopher Marlowe.)

34. A young man refuses to fight a challenger because he's in love with the challenger's cousin. The young man's best friend can't stand this, and starts dueling the challenger himself. When the young man tries to intervene, grabbing his best friend to stop the fight, it gives the challenger an opening and he stabs the best friend to death. (*Romeo and Juliet*, Shakespeare.)

35. An emperor's wife asks him to stay home from the Senate because she dreamed of something terrible happening to him. He ignores her and goes anyway, and his friends come up and stab him to death. (*Julius Caesar*, Shakespeare.)

36. A man gives a public eulogy that leads people to riot. (Also *Julius Caesar*, Shakespeare.)

37. A prince is taken captive during a war, and two commanders bicker over who actually kidnapped him. (*The Spanish Tragedy*, Thomas Kyd.)

38. An explorer flies to the moon in a spaceship carried by a flock of geese and meets the people who live there. (*The Man in the Moone,* Francis Godwin.)

39. A witch traps a sprite in a tree trunk. A scholar of magic frees him, demanding his loyalty and service in return. (*The Tempest*, Shakespeare.)

40. A girl grows up on an island with her father, a duke turned scholar and magician. When a ship wrecks on the island, she sees one of the stranded passengers—the first man besides her father she's ever seen in her life. The two fall in love. (Also *The Tempest*, Shakespeare.)

41. A guy makes a bet with a newly married man that he

can seduce the man's bride, and then makes the husband believe he was successful. (*Cymbeline*, Shakespeare.)

42. When a king dies, a man he'd exiled returns to court. The new king likes him a lot and gives him all kinds of gifts and privileges. No one else at court likes this. (*Edward II*, a historical play by Christopher Marlowe.)

43. A woman is about to take her vows as a nun when she hears her brother's been sentenced to death. She hurries to beg the man in charge for mercy, and he finds her very attractive. (*Measure for Measure*, Shakespeare.)

44. A man abandons his bride-to-be after her dowry gets lost at sea. (Also *Measure for Measure*, Shakespeare.)

45. Two rich old men want their children to marry. Each knows his own child is a fool; neither knows that the other young person is also a fool. *(Mother Bombie*, by John Lyly.)

46. A prince complains to his best friend that he can't go to battle because he's pining over a woman. The best friend complains that he's been trying to get these two together, and his efforts are never appreciated. (*Troilus and Cressida*, Shakespeare.)

47. A duchess summons a demon and gets arrested for it, humiliating her husband. (*Henry VI Part II*, a historical play, Shakespeare.)

48. A young woman newly married to the king and the popular wife of a duke vie for power at court. (Also *Henry VI Part II*, a historical play, Shakespeare.)

49. After conquering a city, a general falls in love with one of the captives and frees her. He hires a man to paint her portrait, but the artist falls in love with her as well and

prolongs the project in order to spend more time with her. (*Campaspe*, a historical play by John Lyly.)

50. The daughter of a jailor falls in love with a prisoner and helps him escape. (*The Two Noble Kinsmen*, maybe by Shakespeare and John Fletcher.)

50 PLOT PROMPTS FROM REGENCY AND VICTORIAN NOVELS

I've taken liberties with some of these plots in order to make them easier to use as prompts. In some cases, they're the bare bones of the plot, and in many cases, they are only a part of the novel. You can transform these elements by setting them in a different country and/or putting them in a present-day, fantasy, or futuristic context.

1. A man who was framed for a crime he didn't commit escapes prison, makes a fortune in another country, and returns in disguise to get vengeance on his enemies. (*The Count of Monte Cristo*, Alexander Dumas.)

2. An orphan boy falls in love with his foster sister. As an adult, he's still obsessed with her even though she's married to somebody else. (*Wuthering Heights*, Emily Brontë.)

3. Members of a club decide to each travel to a different place and then report what they learn back to the group. (*The Pickwick Papers*, Charles Dickens.)

4. A rich man proposes to a young employee of his only to learn that she's already secretly married to his son. (*Vanity Fair*, William Thackeray.)

5. A man searching for a sea monster meets a guy with a fantastic submarine and they explore the ocean depths together. (*Twenty Thousand Leagues Under the Sea*, Jules Verne.)

6. A guy falls in love with a woman who spurns him. Later,

he gets a job and then realizes she owns the business. (*Far from the Madding Crowd*, Thomas Hardy.)

7. In the future, humankind has evolved into two separate species. (*The Time Machine,* H.G. Wells.)

8. A woman who's new in town believes the owner of a local business is unfair to his employees, but later she falls in love with him. (*North and South*, Elizabeth Gaskell.)

9. A young woman steals money from her father in order to leave the country and elope with her boyfriend against her father's wishes, but then her fiancé gambles the money away. (*The Way We Live Now*, Anthony Trollope.)

10. A man is found dead in a room with a word written in blood on the wall, but there are no wounds on the corpse. (*A Study in Scarlet*, Sir Arthur Conan Doyle.)

11. A man believes a woman he loves is having an affair, but she's actually meeting with her brother. (*The Tenant of Wildfell Hall*, Anne Brontë.)

12. A man arranges for the abduction of his recently orphaned teenage nephew because the kid is the rightful heir to a family estate. (*Kidnapped*, Robert Louis Stevenson.)

13. A poor child falls asleep and becomes a magical creature. (*The Water Babies*, Charles Kingsley.)

14. A woman refuses two marriage proposals from good guys and marries a foreigner who winds up being mean to her. Much later, one of her former suitors takes an interest in her daughter, while the other one tells her he's still interested in her. (*Portrait of a Lady*, Henry James.)

15. A man falls in love with a woman, but she's pretty mad at him because she found out he talked another guy into breaking up with her sister. (*Pride and Prejudice*, Jane Austen.)

16. A mistreated animal comes into a better situation. (*Black Beauty*, Anna Sewell.)

17. A few visits from ghosts convince a greedy man to be more generous and loving. (*A Christmas Carol*, Charles Dickens.)

18. Facing the facts of his mortality, his unpopularity, and his worthless existence, a man makes a drastic change for the better. (Also *A Christmas Carol*, Charles Dickens.)

19. A cynical slacker redeems himself by trading places with a great guy who's been imprisoned and dying in his place. (*A Tale of Two Cities*, Charles Dickens.)

20. A rich man runs over and kills a poor child in the street, but he shows no remorse. Later, he is murdered in his bed. (Also *A Tale of Two Cities*, Charles Dickens.)

21. A woman is caught in a love triangle with her fiancé and her fiancé's father. (*The Brothers Karamazov*, Fyodor Dostoyevsky.)

22. A man desperately seeks money to pay what he owes to his fiancée so that he can leave her and run off with the woman he really loves. He then finds out that the woman he really loves has taken up with a former boyfriend again. (Also *The Brothers Karamazov*, Fyodor Dostoyevsky.)

23. A person never ages due to a sinister spell. (*The Picture of Dorian Gray*, Oscar Wilde.)

24. A girl follows an animal guide to a strange new world. (*Alice in Wonderland*, Lewis Carroll.)

25. A young man falls in love with the girl next door, but she rejects him because she sees him as a brother. Later, when he's on vacation, he crosses paths with the girl's sister, and those two fall in love. (*Little Women*, Louisa May Alcott.)

26. A man forgives his wife and his wife's lover for having an affair. His wife's lover is so embarrassed he attempts suicide, but fails. The adulterers then run away together. (*Anna Karenina*, Leo Tolstoy.)

27. A young woman teaching at a school abroad develops relationships with both the schoolmaster and a rich doctor. (*Villette*, Charlotte Brontë.)

28. A respectable man has a secret and horrible past: he sold his wife and baby daughter. (*The Mayor of Casterbridge*, Thomas Hardy.)

29. A bitter old man gets robbed and becomes the foster father for a little girl. (*Silas Marner*, George Eliot.)

30. A woman marries an old man who has no interest in her, but becomes friends with an interesting guy her own age. When the woman's elderly husband dies, he leaves a note in his will that she can't inherit anything if she marries the younger guy she's friends with. (*Middlemarch*, George Eliot.)

31. A woman only realizes she's in love with her good friend after another woman falls in love with him. (*Emma*, Jane Austen.)

32. Nobody knows that this beautiful young bride faked her

own death, abandoned her child, and assumed a new identity in order to find a wealthy husband. (*Lady Audley's Secret*, Mary Elizabeth Braddon.)

33. A boy fakes his own death, runs away from home, and teams up with another runaway for adventure. (*Huckleberry Finn*, Mark Twain.)

34. An orphan becomes a criminal's apprentice. (*Oliver Twist*, Charles Dickens.)

35. A woman gets news that the man she was once in love with has gotten married to his girlfriend. Later, she learns she was mistaken—the man's girlfriend dumped him to marry his brother instead. (*Sense and Sensibility*, Jane Austen.)

36. A young woman is heartbroken when the dashing and charming man she loves ignores her and then breaks up with her. After she recovers from a dangerous illness, she receives attentions from a man who's loved her all along. (Also *Sense and Sensibility*, Jane Austen.)

37. After discovering that his grandmother was a fairy, a young man's room turns into an enchanted wood in Fairy Land. (*Phantastes, a Faerie Romance for Men and Women*, by George McDonald.)

38. The statue of a woman comes alive. She runs away, and a man searches for her. (Also *Phantastes, a Faerie Romance for Men and Women*, by George McDonald.)

39. A woman is punished and ostracized for adultery while her husband, in disguise, seeks revenge on her lover. (*The Scarlet Letter*, Nathaniel Hawthorne.)

40. In a remote location, a scientist creates grotesque human hybrids. (*The Island of Dr. Moreau*, H.G. Wells.)

41. A young man manages to pick fights with three different guys in one afternoon, but they all wind up being friends. (*The Three Musketeers*, Alexander Dumas.)

42. A young man sleeps with a rich woman in exchange for money. In doing so, he learns a secret about her that leads her to try to get him killed. (Also *The Three Musketeers*, Alexander Dumas.)

43. A man makes a large bet with his friends that he can travel around the world in a short frame of time. (*Around the World in Eighty Days*, Jules Verne.)

44. A teacher at a school snaps and beats up an abusive headmaster. (*The Life and Adventures of Nicholas Nickleby*, Charles Dickens.)

45. A man is in love with a woman who's marrying some rich and selfish old man who's offered to pay off her father's debt in return. (Also *The Life and Adventures of Nicholas Nickleby*, Charles Dickens.)

46. A young woman falls in love with her employer only to learn that he's married to a woman he keeps locked up. (*Jane Eyre*, Charlotte Brontë.)

47. Aliens attack a country on planet Earth and crush its human army, but then they all die of some alien disease. (*The War of the Worlds*, H.G. Wells.)

48. A mischievous boy develops a huge crush on a girl at school, but he keeps messing things up with her. (*The Adventures of Tom Sawyer*, Mark Twain.)

49. A boy secretly witnesses a murder and is scared to tell anyone, even when the wrong man is blamed for it. (Also *The Adventures of Tom Sawyer*, Mark Twain.)

50. A relentlessly cheerful man's good nature is tested when he moves to a dangerous and difficult new place. (*Martin Chuzzlewit,* Charles Dickens.)

50 PLOTS FROM CLASSIC CINEMA

Most of these are plots or plot points from Hollywood movies of the 1930s, 1940s, and 1950s, though there are a few movies in here from countries other than the United States. Many of these, of course, were novels first, and a few of them were plays before they were movies.

Some of these are fairly specific, and most or all of them are not in the public domain. You can take inspiration from the stories, but you won't want to follow them too closely.

1. A man is wrongfully arrested for the kidnapping of a child and he almost gets killed by an angry mob. He fakes his death and frames the mob for the murder. (*Fury.*)

2. The young wife of an old pastor falls in love with his son from his first marriage. (*Day of Wrath.*)

3. A man pushes his wife into a singing career even though she's not that talented, leading to her public humiliation. (*Citizen Kane.*)

4. One man struggles to keep another one, who lacks good judgment and is unintentionally destructive, out of trouble. (*Of Mice and Men.*)

5. An aging movie star who wants to make a comeback hires a struggling screenwriter to doctor the script she wrote to hopefully star in herself. He moves in to her mansion, but is taken aback when he realizes she's fallen in love with him. (*Sunset Boulevard.*)

6. A woman unexpectedly inherits an estate from a man who dabbled in the supernatural. Before long, the dead man's

animated corpse makes an appearance at the house. (*The Ghoul.*)

7. The chauffeur's daughter is in love with the younger son of the family her father works for. The older son fears the growing attraction between the two will end the younger son's engagement—and spoil a lucrative business deal in the process. The older son makes romantic advances toward the chauffeur's daughter, only to fall in love with her himself. (*Sabrina.*)

8. A beautiful circus acrobat agrees to marry one of the performers in the side show because she's after his inheritance. (*Freaks.*)

9. A man is arrested for armed robberies he didn't commit. As his lawyer tries to prove his innocence, the stress is devastating to his family. (*The Wrong Man.*)

10. A pickpocket accidentally steals sensitive government information. (*Pickup on South Street.*)

11. A scientist trying to secure funding for his museum gets tangled up with an eccentric heiress and a spotted leopard. (*Bringing Up Baby.*)

12. A father and his young son search for a stolen item and the person who stole it. (*The Bicycle Thief.*)

13. A socialite marries a wealthy rancher after a whirlwind romance. After she moves to the ranch, she's appalled at the way the workers are treated. (*Giant.*)

14. The hunt for a serial killer who preys on children disrupts the operations of a city's crime lords, who pitch in to find the killer. (*M.*)

15. An expatriate painter, a singer, and a concert pianist all try to make it in Paris. The painter falls in love with the singer's girlfriend. (*An American in Paris.*)

16. A rich woman seems to take an interest in the work of a struggling artist and invites him to a dinner party. He is the only guest at the "party," and he suspects she's more interested in paying him to be her boyfriend than in his artwork. (Also *An American In Paris.*)

17. After shots are fired in a theater, a woman talks a man into taking her back to his apartment. She tells him that she's a spy who has vital information, and that assassins are tracking her down. Later that night, she bursts into his room, dying of a stab wound. She's clutching a map. (*The 39 Steps.*)

18. A retired couple travels to a big city to visit their grown children, who are too busy to spend much time with them. (*Tokyo Story.*)

19. After a treacherous prince usurps the throne, a nobleman loyal to the rightful king goes into hiding in the wilderness. Others join him, and they wage guerilla warfare against the pretender. (*The Adventures of Robin Hood.*)

20. A motorcycle club comes to a small town for a race and wreaks havoc on the community, but the police chief's daughter strikes up a romance with the gang leader. (*The Wild One.*)

21. A cruel principal runs a boarding school in Paris. The man's wife, who owns the school, and his mistress—a teacher—conspire to murder him. After they do it, his body goes missing. (*Les Diaboliques.*)

22. A rogue and the self-centered daughter of a slave owner strike up a fraught romance. (*Gone With the Wind.*)

23. Two brothers—one conservative and proper, the other a womanizer—enlist as pilots during World War I. When the conservative brother's girlfriend hits on the other brother, he gives in, and then regrets it. (*Hell's Angels.*)

24. Two brothers are taken prisoner during wartime and given the choice of sharing information or getting executed. One brother is ready to talk. The other brother kills him before he can do it, and is then executed. (Also *Hell's Angels.*)

25. A reporter who lost his more prestigious jobs in big cities due to bad behavior is writing for an insignificant newspaper. When a man gets trapped in a cave, he tries to prolong the rescue so that he can get more attention as a journalist. (*Ace in the Hole.*)

26. A man abandons his fiancée for an alcoholic, down-on-her-luck actress…who hides the fact that she's married. (*Dangerous.*)

27. A self-appointed, woman-hating travelling preacher, arrested for stealing a car, meets a bank robber in jail. The bank robber won't tell him where he hid the money he stole, and is executed for murder. When the preacher gets out of prison, he courts and marries the bank robber's widow and attempts to learn where the money's hidden. (*Night of the Hunter.*)

28. A man dates a woman who's only after his money. His daughter hates her so much she attacks the woman and disfigures her. In retaliation, the father has her boyfriend killed. (*The Furies.*)

29.	The spoiled daughter of a slave owner, engaged to a wealthy banker, shocks him and society by showing up to a ball in a red dress instead of the traditional white dress. He breaks up with her. (*Jezebel.*)

30.	Someone who routinely spies on his neighbors witnesses a murder while looking in a neighbor's window. (*Rear Window.*)

31.	Two prisoners of war dig an escape tunnel, but just before it's completed, they are transferred to a more impenetrable fortress. They manage to escape. (*La Grande Illusion.*)

32.	A rich woman tries to get a fellow traveller to prove her theory that two perfect strangers can commit murder and get away with it. (*Strangers on a Train.*)

33.	A priest is assigned to a new parish where everyone is critical of him and gives him a hard time. One person even spreads lies about him, saying his cruel words helped lead to her mother's death. (*Diary of a Country Priest.*)

34.	A new town marshal, disregarding the objections of his new bride and the concerns of the townspeople, faces a gang of killers alone. (*High Noon.*)

35.	Men are pressed into naval service on a ship commanded by a ruthless tyrant of a captain. The ship's lieutenant finally approves of a mutiny. (*Mutiny on the Bounty.*)

36.	A man with a violent past tries to start a new peaceful life as a hired hand on a homestead. He winds up fighting the ranchers who are harassing the settlers. *(Shane.)*

37.	A failed British writer turned drifter shows up at a diner in Arizona. The diner owner's daughter shows him her paintings and confides that she dreams of moving to France. When the people at the diner get taken hostage by robbers, the writer changes his life insurance policy to make the young woman the recipient and asks a robber to shoot him. (*The Petrified Forest.*)

38. An alien lands his spacecraft in Washington, DC. A frightened soldier shoots and wounds him, destroying the gift the alien was bringing to the president: a device that would've allowed him to study life on other planets. (*The Day the Earth Stood Still.*)

39. A girl finds herself in an alternate universe. Her arrival killed a witch, and the witch's sister pursues her. (*The Wizard of Oz.*)

40. An American couple vacationing in a foreign country witness a murder in a marketplace. The dying man tells them of an assassination plot that must be foiled. Then their young son is kidnapped, and they get a message that he won't be harmed as long as they don't tell authorities about the plot. (*The Man Who Knew Too Much.*)

41. A botanist in Tibet is bitten by a werewolf. Luckily, the botanist has obtained a temporary cure for werewolf symptoms: the juice of the rare mariphasa plant he collected there. (*Werewolf of London.*)

42. An aging professor is forced to retire due to ill health. He comes to grips with his unpopularity as a teacher and his failures as a husband. (*The Browning Version.*)

43. An idealistic young man is appointed to fill a senator seat after a senator's death. An older senator, well-respected but secretly corrupt, mentors him. (*Mr. Smith Goes to Washington.*)

44. A sheriff arrests the brother of a criminal, who threatens to break him out of jail. The sheriff gets his alcoholic deputy, a disabled man, and a young gunfighter to stand with him against the criminal and his gang. (*Rio Bravo.*)

45. A depressed man has the opportunity to see what the world would've been like if he had never been born. (*It's a Wonderful Life.*)

46. A woman returns to her hometown after the death of her lover, a married politician. She marries a fisherman but soon starts an affair with her husband's friend. (*Clash by Night.*)

47. A retired American boxer moves to Ireland to reclaim his family's farm. He falls in love with a local woman, but her brother refuses to consent to the wedding or let her have her dowry. She wants her American beau to confront her brother, but he never wants to fight again. (*The Quiet Man.*)

48. An army deserter and a teenaged girl who's run away from home meet up in a port city, spend time together, and deal with her creepy godfather and a gangster who's after her ex-boyfriend. (*Port of Shadows.*)

49. A rich Jewish prince is betrayed by his friend and sold into Roman slavery. After he saves a Roman commander's life, the Roman frees him and adopts him as a son. (*Ben-Hur.*)

50. A nightclub owner protects his ex-girlfriend, who he still loves, and her husband from their enemies. (*Casablanca.*)

Bryn Donovan

CHARACTER PROMPTS

The most foolproof way for writers to win the loyalty of readers is to create characters they fall in love with. When characters feel like real, interesting people, readers will follow them just about anywhere to find out what they do next. Readers will even overlook weaknesses in plotting or writing if the characters have them hooked. In a series, characters become old friends.

Even for authors, part of the joy of writing is creating characters...and getting to know them better and better. The prompts in this section are designed to help you do both of those things.

37 PROMPTS BASED ON PERSONALITY TYPING

Some people love classification systems for personalities, such as astrological signs, the enneagram, and the Myers-Briggs Type Indicator. Whether or not you believe personality typing systems have any truth to them, they're useful for fiction, revealing patterns in personality that have resonated with many.

Don't get mad at me if a prompt for your zodiac sign or personality type doesn't accurately describe you. It's all just for fictional inspiration, anyway. Write about one of these characters, and see who you come up with!

1. **Aries:** independent, arrogant, and full of energy. May have a short attention span.

2. **Taurus:** a self-indulgent person who indulges his or her favorite people as well.

3. **Gemini:** entertaining, but shallow, and probably hiding something.

4. **Cancer:** caring, emotional, and moody.

5. **Leo:** vain, but a lot of fun, with a strong sense of honor.

6. **Virgo:** intelligent, analytical, and critical.

7. **Libra:** concerned with fairness, and a bit naïve.

8. **Scorpio:** smoldering with passion and suspicious of almost everyone.

9. **Sagittarius:** a cocky adventurer.

10. **Capricorn:** a serious, disciplined, shy person.

11. **Aquarius:** a humanitarian weirdo.

12. **Pisces:** an intuitive person who can't make up his or her mind.

13. **Enneagram Type 1,** The Reformer. Trying to make himself or herself, and everything else, perfect.

14. **Enneagram Type 2,** The Giver. Always trying to please others. Doesn't feel like he or she gets enough credit for it.

15. **Enneagram Type 3,** The Achiever. Climbing the ladder of success, and looking sharp while he or she does it.

16. **Enneagram Type 4,** The Individualist. A romantic who likes to think of himself or herself as different, and who is probably having trouble paying the rent.

17. **Enneagram Type 5,** The Investigator. Super smart, innovative, and not the life of the party. Probably not even invited to the party. Wouldn't have gone, anyway.

18. **Enneagram Type 6,** The Loyalist. Responsible, but given to conspiracy theories.

19. **Enneagram Type 7,** The Enthusiast. Spontaneous and optimistic, with a complete lack of common sense.

20. **Enneagram Type 8,** The Challenger. Sometimes, a brave protector. Sometimes, just a bully.

21. **Enneagram Type 9,** The Peacemaker. Thinks everyone

should chill out and maybe binge-watch TV with him or her.

22. **Myers-Briggs Type ISTJ:** The teacher or boss everybody's terrified of who turns out to be decent at heart.

23. **Myers-Briggs Type INFJ:** The guy who doesn't say a lot, and when he does, it's something way out of left field (but kind of brilliant.)

24. **Myers-Briggs Type INTJ:** The woman who took it upon herself to update the system everyone's been using so it's more logical.

25. **Myers-Briggs Type ENFJ:** Believes the world is a beautiful, loving place, and blocks out evidence to the contrary.

26. **Myers-Briggs Type ISTP:** Has many hobbies he excels at and keeps them all secret for no obvious reason.

27. **Myers-Briggs Type ESFJ:** Organized the biggest social event of the season, and also the second-biggest social event of the season. Both times, everyone went home with adorable gift bags.

28. **Myers-Briggs Type INFP:** So quiet, almost nobody paid attention to him, until he went to prison for a noble cause.

29. **Myers-Briggs Type ESFP:** Always the first performer at open mics. Turns ordinary, boring events into performances. Alternatively delightful and exhausting.

30. **Myers-Briggs Type ENFP:** Rails against conformity, often with good reason, but is occasionally a bit of a jerk about it.

31. **Myers-Briggs Type ESTP:** He's great at taking action. Not so great at thinking through the consequences first.

32. **Myers-Briggs Type ESTJ:** An upholder of tradition. Yes, she can be boring, but in hard times, she's a pillar of strength.

33. **Myers-Briggs Type ENTJ:** Wants to boss everybody all the time. To be fair, he's really good at it.

34. **Myers-Briggs Type INTJ:** Can remember everything she ever read and everything anyone ever said or did. Horrible at reading social cues, but impossible to lie to.

35. **Myers-Briggs Type ISFJ:** Always has what you need in his backpack. Knows first aid. Bakes the best oatmeal cookies on the planet.

36. **Myers-Briggs Type ENTP:** Likes to strike up conversations about philosophy and politics with strangers. Enjoys debating, and never takes intellectual disagreements personally.

37. **Myers-Briggs Type ISFP:** Feels awkward and shy when she meets new people, yet seeks out opportunities to do so.

13 PROMPTS BASED ON
PSYCHOLOGICAL DISORDERS

I put this list in the book because I think fiction could use more heroes and heroines who struggle with mental health issues. These issues are too often stigmatized and kept secret, leading the people who suffer from them to believe they are suffering alone.

If you are like many people, you will read through this list and feel that you have at least half of these disorders. This may not be the case. Personalities are messy, and we may deal with all kinds of issues while leading reasonably productive lives. However, if mental health issues are keeping you from enjoying life, please take advantage of any opportunity you have to get the help you deserve and get better.

I'm not a medical professional, so for more complete and accurate descriptions of these conditions, please do your own research with trusted sources.

1.   **Bipolar Disorder:** his periods of exhilaration, high energy, and high-risk activities alternate with periods of sadness, fatigue, and despair.

2.   **Agoraphobia:** she struggles with a fear of public places, and activities such as going shopping or attending a party can trigger a panic attack.

3.   **Post-Traumatic Stress Disorder:** he survived a trauma such as warfare, rape, or abuse. He may suffer from nightmares or flashbacks, and he may have difficulty remembering details of the event. Reminders of the trauma may trigger a response of panic and/or depression.

4.   **Binge Eating Disorder:** she responds to some strong emotions with short periods of overeating, and during these times, she feels as though she doesn't have control over her eating.

5. **Insomnia Disorder:** for long periods of time, he is unable to get a good night's sleep and feel well-rested.

6. **Borderline Personality Disorder:** she doesn't have a clear sense of herself, leading to unpredictable behavior and unstable relationships.

7. **Narcissistic Personality Disorder:** he has an exaggerated sense of his own self-importance and believes himself to be adored by others. He lacks empathy.

8. **Schizophrenia:** she hallucinates, seeing entities or hearing voices, which are often frightening. This inhibits her ability to process information and engage in real-life interactions.

9. **Munchausen Syndrome:** he fakes or exaggerates an illness to attract attention and love.

10. **Conversion Disorder:** she suffers from pain or motor issues that defy a medical or neurological diagnosis.

11. **Obsessive-Compulsive Disorder:** she fixates on threats such as fear of contamination or fear of violence or doom regarding herself or others. She attempts to circumvent these threats through compulsive behaviors such as excessive hand washing and cleaning, counting to a certain number, or other irrational behaviors.

12. **Dissociative Identity Disorder:** he develops two or more distinct personalities or identities.

13. **Kleptomania:** she has a strong impulse to steal that's not related to her physical needs or a desire for wealth. She feels rising anxiety until she steals, and she feels a sense of relief directly afterward.

ANIMAL INSTINCTS: 50 PROMPTS

For this creative exercise, you'll write a scene or a paragraph about a character who shares qualities with one of these animals...without actually naming the animal. For instance, if you were to choose an armadillo, you might write about a knight in full armor hustling across a road.

1. rat
2. scorpion
3. wolf
4. bee
5. puppy
6. cat
7. snake
8. chicken
9. owl
10. eagle
11. dolphin
12. shark
13. hummingbird
14. sloth
15. bear
16. tiger
17. horse
18. mouse
19. flamingo
20. bat
21. doe
22. chameleon
23. weasel
24. fox
25. alligator
26. seal

27. tortoise

28. buffalo

29. gazelle

30. opossum

31. bull

32. rabbit

33. giraffe

34. elephant

35. kangaroo

36. spider

37. moth

38. swan

39. otter

40. dragon

41. prairie dog

42. moose

43. duck

44. camel

45. squirrel

46. frog

47. lamb

48. butterfly

49. vulture

50. penguin

ACTION IS CHARACTER: 50 ACTION PROMPTS

Fiction can get boring if the characters aren't active enough. And in screenwriting, action is vital.

If characters are having a long conversation, it's a lot more interesting if they're doing something else as well. In fiction, it also gives you more options for tagging the dialogue. Instead of this, for instance:

"I'm not going," Darryl said.

You can write this:

Darryl slammed the drawer shut. "I'm not going."

In the second example, you can picture Darryl and infer his tone of voice. You also avoided having to write "said," which is good, because when you're writing dialogue, those "saids" can become repetitious.

Action isn't always easy to write, though. If you struggle to get your characters to do, well…anything, you aren't alone!

For this set of prompts, write a paragraph or a scene in which a character is doing the given action. Your character might be alone or with others, and he or she might be talking or silent. You might go into the thoughts or internal monologue of the character.

1. Breaking into a building.

2. Washing blood out of a garment.

3. Playing a drum.

4. Playing roulette or a slot machine.

5. Playing with a dog or a cat—fetch, a laser pointer, etc.

6. Killing a rat.

7. Butchering a deer.

8. Chopping wood.

9. Planting seeds or a tree.

10. Digging a hasty grave.

11. Searching for a lost or hidden item.

12. Putting out a fire.

13. Vacuuming.

14. Dancing.

15. Sharpening a sword or a knife.

16. Stomping grapes.

17. Parachuting out of a plane.

18. Brushing or braiding hair—someone else's or the character's own.

19. Parking in a tight spot.

20. Getting away from pursuers by car.

21. Chasing someone on foot.

22. Sparring with swords…or fists, in a boxing ring.

23. Shooting at a firing range.

24. Playing pool.

25. Singing in the shower.

26. Blowing glass.

27. Riding a bicycle.

28. Smashing a window.

29. Packing a suitcase or bag.

30. Unpacking boxes in a new home.

31. Trying on a gown or a tuxedo.

32. Shopping at a market.

33. Deep-sea diving.

34. Washing or waxing a car.

35. Tending to a wound—the character's own or someone else's.

36. Woodworking.

37. Taking an exercise class.

38. Polishing the silver.

39. Fishing.

40. Pitching a tent.

41. Building a fire.

42. Crossing on a narrow or precarious bridge.

43. Cooking, baking, or grilling.

44. Modeling in a fashion show.

45. Creating a store window display.

46. Giving someone a shoulder or foot massage.

47. Sealing a letter or charter with wax.

48. Climbing over a fence or scaling a wall.

49. Tearing down a wall.

50. Walking into the surf.

TRUE COLORS: 50 MORE ACTION PROMPTS

The old adage "actions speak louder than words" is true in fiction as well as in real life. What characters think or say doesn't tell the readers as much about them as what they actually do. This is why F. Scott Fitzgerald famously hung a sign over his writing desk that read, "Action is character."

This is a difficult exercise that could result in fantastic characterization in your story. Even if it doesn't, it can help you improve as a writer.

Here's how it works: take one of the personal qualities listed below, and write a scene in which a character does something—maybe without saying anything at all—that proves they possess that quality. In other words, write a passage in which the character shows his or her true colors.

1. patience
2. courage
3. selfishness
4. optimism
5. charisma
6. wit
7. self-control
8. jealousy
9. irreverence
10. punctuality
11. devotion
12. cruelty
13. craftiness
14. greed
15. candor
16. cowardice
17. audacity
18. compassion

19. coldness

20. incompetence

21. disenchantment

22. conformity

23. decisiveness

24. endurance

25. independence

26. faith

27. irritability

28. composure

29. flexibility

30. enthusiasm

31. dominance

32. honor

33. intuition

34. modesty

35. peacefulness

36. warmth

37. self-loathing

38. sincerity

39. originality

40. popularity

41. intelligence

42. curiosity

43. fierceness

44. professionalism

45. cowardice

46. perceptiveness

47. anxiety

48. focus

49. prejudice

50. workaholism

THIS, AND ALSO THAT: 50 PROMPTS FOR COMPLEX CHARACTERS

Many of the characters who fascinate us in stories—and in real life—have an interesting mix of qualities. They aren't contradictions, exactly, but just characteristics that we wouldn't necessarily expect to go together. Similarly, some of the most interesting times in our lives bring on mixed reactions.

Choose one of these combinations and write a passage about a character it describes.

1. brilliant, but impractical

2. loyal, but resentful

3. joking around, but brokenhearted

4. expensively dressed, but slovenly

5. burly, but squeamish

6. polite, but aloof

7. cheery, but unhelpful

8. relaxed, but observant

9. ambitious, but awkward

10. depressed, but determined

11. pompous, but kind

12. lazy, but organized

13. conceited, but charming

14. busy, but unproductive

15. calm, but despairing

16. rude, but funny

17. neat, but a pack rat

18. timid, but vindictive

19. altruistic, but impersonal

20. over-dramatic, but persuasive

21. haggard, but attractive

22. quirky, but predictable

23. angry, but civil

24. creative, but money-minded

25. obsessed, but dignified

26. sarcastic, but loving

27. homely, but stylish

28. fun-loving, but goal-driven

29. heroic, but bored

30. immature, but a natural leader

31. old, but youthful

32. young, but crotchety

33. finicky, but sweet

34. well-bred, but brutish

35. narcissistic, but honest about it

36. triumphant, but uneasy

37. frugal, but generous

38. social, but always making faux pas

39. stoic, but tenderhearted

40. giggly, but wise

41. evil, but sentimental

42. grouchy, but encouraging

43. chatty, but secretive

44. soft-spoken, but vulgar

45. idealistic, but petty

46. frumpy, but dangerous

47. disgusted, but amused

48. exhausted, but excited

49. innocent, but manipulative

50. suspicious, but impressed

CLOTHES MAKETH THE MAN (AND WOMAN): 50 SARTORIAL PROMPTS

I've seen a few online debates about whether describing characters' clothing is important. Any type of description can be overdone, but a thoughtful detail about a character's clothes can give the reader a clue about the character. Of course, it can also lead to false first impressions, with the truth being revealed later. If a character is wearing something that's unexpected, given the surroundings, that can create a striking image or introduction.

Use one of these prompts to write about a character and what he or she is doing!

1. a wedding gown that's seen better days

2. sneakers splattered in some kind of goo

3. an oversized tee shirt with a corporate logo

4. a tee shirt from a tourist destination

5. a bespoke three-piece suit

6. gym socks with sandals

7. a hat with a black veil

8. a beekeeper's suit

9. a full hazmat suit

10. a fur coat

11. a flannel shirt

12. several necklaces worn at the same time

13. sweat pants

14. surgical scrubs

15. a red bikini

16. a tweed jacket

17. a bright yellow polka dot dress

18. a bunny costume

19. a caftan

20. a belt with a gigantic belt buckle

21. bicycle shorts

22. a chain mail shirt

23. a schoolgirl's uniform

24. a Hawaiian shirt

25. red stiletto shoes

26. a ballerina tutu

27. faded jeans

28. an all-white suit

29. a very expensive watch

30. a fanny pack

31. a fresh flower in the hair

32. combat fatigues

33. lacy lingerie

34. a festive Christmas sweater

35. dark sunglasses

36. reading glasses on a chain

37. Doc Martens

38. flip flops

39. an outfit of head-to-toe black leather

40. plaid pants

41. a trench coat

42. a hard hat

43. a beret

44. an argyle sweater

45. a jean jacket covered in pins and buttons

46. a beaded evening gown

47. a coat that's two sizes too big for the wearer

48. a mechanic's coveralls

49. tap shoes

50. a hand-knitted scarf

100 PROMPTS BASED ON REAL PEOPLE

Writers gather inspiration from people they know, people they read about, and fictional characters. Writers can get themselves in legal trouble if they write about people directly, but it's fine to use elements of someone's personality and combine them with other traits. Once you've fictionalized some of the aspects of a person and you've dropped them in a completely new storyline, the character you've created will diverge from your inspiration and become someone new.

Here's how to use these prompts. Change one or more significant things about the given person, such as appearance, age, gender, occupation, or time period. For the real people who are famous, imagine if they weren't.

Once you've got this in your head, write a scene in the character's voice or a scene starring the character.

Don't be afraid to choose a person you only know a little bit about. That will only give your imagination more free rein.

Not all of the personal ones will apply to you. Naturally, you could do this same exercise with any real person you wanted—or even with a fictional character, if you change it so much that you make it your own.

1. your grandmother

2. your grandfather

3. someone you have a crush or celebrity crush on

4. Diana, Princess of Wales

5. your sister or brother

6. Joan of Arc

7. a coworker or classmate you like

8. a coworker or classmate you wish would quit or change schools

9. your newest friend

10. Mark Zuckerberg

11. your hairstylist

12. Frida Kahlo

13. your former boyfriend, girlfriend, or spouse

14. your current boyfriend, girlfriend, or spouse

15. Serena Williams

16. one of your favorite teachers of all time

17. one of your least favorite teachers of all time

18. Elvis Presley

19. the unluckiest person you know

20. a person you admire in your personal life

21. your friend's mom

22. your friend's child

23. Julie Andrews

24. your cousin

25. Leonardo Di Caprio

26. a boss you liked

27. your worst boss ever

28. your dog or cat (imagine he or she is a person)

29. your doctor

30. Jennifer Lawrence

31. Dwayne Johnson

32. someone you know who worries a lot

33. someone who you worry about

34. Martin Luther King, Jr.

35. Donald Trump

36. an aunt of yours

37. an uncle of yours

38. Oprah Winfrey

39. a friend you'd like to get to know better

40. a friend of one of your parents

41. Albert Einstein

42. someone you love who died

43. Cristiano Ronaldo

44. Angelina Jolie

45. Will Smith

46. your niece

47. your nephew

48. a creative person you know

49. the richest person you know

50. the poorest person you know

51. Jane Austen

52. Prince

53. Audrey Hepburn

54. someone you're no longer on speaking terms with

55. someone you know who's dealing with a health problem

56. Christopher Columbus

57. King Arthur

58. Michelle Obama

59. your brother-in-law or sister-in-law

60. Buddha

61. an extremely intelligent person you know

62. Tom Hanks

63. someone you avoid discussing politics with

64. a religious person you know

65. Queen Elizabeth II

66. Muhammad Ali

67. your best friend

68. someone you're friends with even though you're very different from one another

69. the most immature adult you know

70. Amelia Earhart

71. your father

72. your mother

73. Mahatma Gandhi

74. an annoying person you know

75. an actor from one of your all-time favorite movies

76. Abraham Lincoln

77. Queen Victoria

78. a neighbor, past or present

79. Beyoncé

80. someone you know who makes terrible life decisions

81. someone you know who's very quiet

82. someone you know who's loud

83. Mary Magdalene

84. someone you know who's eighty or more years old

85. someone you know who's exceptionally healthy or fitness-minded

86. Marie Antoinette

87. J.K. Rowling

88. someone you know who's quick to get in arguments

89. someone you know who's extremely talented

90. Margaret Thatcher

91. Vincent Van Gogh

92. Marilyn Monroe

93. a famous person you'd like to invite to dinner

94. a famous person you would never hear about again if you had your way

95. Michael Jordan

96. someone you know who's very attractive

97. Winston Churchill

98. a very traditional person you know

99. a very unconventional person you know

100. someone you know a little, and about whom you're curious

---

100 PROMPTS BASED ON OCCUPATIONS

Many writers, especially newer ones, tend to write main characters very much like themselves. Sometimes that's fine, and in other cases, it makes it difficult to think objectively about a strong plot.

One of the best ways to write a character who isn't just a stand-in for yourself is to give them a job that's different from your own. Many stories don't deal with workplace experiences at all, even though they can be fascinating, so including them in your story might make it distinctive and fresh.

For these prompts, write a paragraph or a scene about a character with one of the following occupations. If you imagine what a fantastic, horrible, surprising, or hilarious day on the job might be, you're likely to come up with an interesting storyline.

If you're just using the prompt to inspire some new writing, don't worry about how much you actually know about the particular occupation (although, I'll also let you in on a secret: most of us have stored away vast amounts of information on all kinds of subjects, and we're not even aware of it). If you find yourself interested in the writing the prompt inspires, you can always research the job later.

1. florist

2. customer service representative at a call center

3. personal shopper

4. piano teacher

5. welder

6. referee

7. pharmacist

8. veterinarian

9. camera operator on a movie or TV set

10. animator for film or television

11. architect

12. bank teller

13. mail carrier

14. DJ at a nightclub

15. scuba diving instructor

16. antique appraiser

17. information security expert (or "ethical hacker")

18. concierge at a hotel

19. housekeeper in a hotel

20. doula

21. entertainment journalist

22. food critic

23. sommelier

24. event planner

25. helicopter tour pilot

26. truck driver

27. radio personality

28. nurse

29. firefighter

30. political campaign manager

31. microbrewery owner

32. bartender

33. psychiatrist

34. physical therapist

35. usher at a movie theater

36. social media manager for a nonprofit organization

37. landscape designer

38. house painter

39. camp counselor

40. FBI agent

41. private tutor

42. university professor

43. marine biologist

44. real estate agent

45. plumber

46. U.S. ambassador

47. small-town mayor

48. librarian

49. meteorologist

50. travel writer

51. interior designer

52. surgeon

53. judge

54. mixed martial arts fighter

55. Secret Service agent

56. nanny

57. organic farmer

58. forensic investigator

59. lawyer

60. perfume designer

61. overnight stocker for a retail store

62. dishwasher at a country club

63. stand-up comedian

64. theme park princess

65. Hollywood stunt performer

66. aviation rescue swimmer in the Coast Guard

67. Explosive Ordnance Disposal technician

68. flight attendant

69. park ranger

70. food truck owner

71. fortune teller

72. hedge fund trader

73. dealer at a casino

74. corporate recruiter

75. fast food worker

76. personal trainer

77. mortician

78. translator

79. nutritionist

80. speech-language pathologist

81. animal shelter worker

82. zookeeper

83. manager of a racehorse sanctuary

84. belly dancer

85. robotics engineer

86. NASCAR mechanic

87. tennis instructor

88. rabbi

89. logger

90. web developer

91. videogame developer

92. orchestra conductor

93. volcanologist

94. sales associate at a shoe store

95. police officer

96. massage therapist

97. goat farmer

98. butler

99. sniper

100. paleontologist

SHAME: 50 REASONS WHY YOUR CHARACTER FEELS GUILTY

First off, a warning. I don't believe that all of the things on this list are reasons one should feel guilty. You might have a character who's been made to feel ashamed about something that's really okay. Maybe over the course of the story, they grow into self-acceptance. You might also show a character's momentary guilt over something small to demonstrate that he or she is a caring, conscientious person.

Other things on this list are, in my opinion, mistakes. Even good people can make them. Sometimes good people make really bad mistakes. You may have a character who needs to forgive himself or herself in order to move on, or you may have a character who needs to change his or her behavior and work hard to make amends.

If you're creating a less sympathetic character, your character may have done something on this list without feeling guilty about it at all.

1. When she leaves for work in the morning, her dog looks sad.

2. He took the collar off the family cat and abandoned her in a park because they couldn't afford to feed her.

3. As a child or as an adult, he didn't notice or figure out that someone he knew was in a terrible situation.

4. She keeps imagining what it would be like to kiss her female best friend.

5. He didn't make it to his father's deathbed on time.

6. She didn't go to her grandmother's funeral.

7. Because of an illness, he can't work and has to accept the support of others or the government.

8. Despite a happy childhood and a fortunate adulthood, he struggles with depression and anxiety.

9. She frequently indulges in unhealthy food.

10. He called in sick to work when really, he just didn't feel like going in.

11. She called in sick to work and is genuinely sick.

12. He forgot someone's birthday.

13. She cheated on her boyfriend or spouse.

14. His girlfriend killed herself after he broke up with her.

15. He had sex before marriage.

16. She had an abortion.

17. He decided not to have kids, even though his parents really want grandchildren.

18. She wasn't able to breastfeed her baby.

19. His houseplant died.

20. The fruits and vegetables in her fridge went bad because she didn't eat them in time.

21. She was in a car crash that injured the other driver.

22. He accidentally hit someone's dog that ran out in front of his car.

23. Someone asked her to volunteer, and she said no.

24. He's depressed, and he knows that unlike many people, he doesn't face big problems.

25. She just splurged and bought herself an expensive item.

26. He moved to another town and his parents or relatives miss him.

27. She's ignoring somebody's texts or phone calls.

28. As a lawyer, he got his client off scot free, even though the guy really was guilty.

29. As a teenager, she bullied others.

30. He and his friends spread a fake rumor about someone just for fun.

31. She has a huge crush on her stepbrother.

32. His parents spent a ton of money on his college education, and he dropped out.

33. She thinks she loves one of her children more than the other.

34. He is in his 40s and dating someone half his age.

35. She put the clean clothes away without folding them – just threw them in the drawers.

36. As a child or as an adult, he successfully blamed his wrongdoing on someone else who was punished for it.

37. She backed into another car in a parking lot and drove away without leaving a note.

38. He's in a relationship with a kind person who loves him, but he doesn't love the person back.

39. She stole from a friend.

40. He killed a mouse in a mousetrap.

41. She had her dog put down because he was very old and miserable.

42. He got someone else addicted to drugs.

43. She was too tired to go on a date with her boyfriend or husband.

44. He gave someone a cheap or thoughtless birthday or wedding gift.

45. She doesn't visit her father, who abused her when she was growing up.

46. As a child, his horsing around or dangerous behavior led to the death of a sibling or friend.

47. She slept in on Saturday even though she had a ton of things to do.

48. He gave his kids fast food for dinner for the third time that week.

49. An old friend she lost touch with contacts her to say he misses her.

50. Although she pretends to love books, it's been two years since she read one.

CRINGE: 25 WRITING PROMPTS TO EMBARRASS YOUR CHARACTER

You learn a lot about someone from how they behave in their most embarrassing moments, and this is a great way to create a sympathetic character. You can also use these for writing about yourself in an essay or memoir.

1. Her bra comes undone or the bra strap breaks.

2. He says something inappropriate, not realizing his microphone is still on.

3. She breaks a chair or a fence she's sitting on.

4. He's gone to the wrong classroom, business meeting, or funeral.

5. She says something very personal to her best friend or partner and then realizes someone else is in earshot.

6. He breaks a glass or spills a drink.

7. Her period starts early and she bleeds through her clothes.

8. He congratulates a woman on her pregnancy. She's not pregnant.

9. She accidentally hugs a stranger, mistaking him for her father or significant other.

10. He was only pretending to know about something, and then somebody asks him detailed questions about it.

11. She takes a spectacular fall on stage.

12. He says the wrong thing during his wedding vows.

13. She walks into a pole or a wall.

14. He realizes he's been calling someone the wrong name for weeks.

15. She shows up for dinner on the wrong night.

16. Someone reads his private letter or diary entry out loud in a group.

17. He realizes his shirt is on backwards or inside out (or both).

18. She's underdressed, overdressed, or wearing something completely inappropriate for the occasion.

19. He farts while taking part in a group conversation.

20. She faints or gets sick at the worst possible time.

21. An unflattering or compromising photo of her is widely distributed.

22. A family member brings up something private in front of friends.

23. He's caught talking to himself when he thought he was alone.

24. He takes a bite of something that was only meant for decoration.

25. She sends an important email to important people with a truly unfortunate typo.

GRRR: 25 WRITING PROMPTS TO ANNOY OR ANGER YOUR CHARACTER

1. His coworker or neighbor keeps listening to awful music.

2. At the casino, she played the slot machine for an hour before giving up. The next person sat down and got a huge jackpot on the first try.

3. Someone who was caught breaking a rule, or the law, wasn't properly punished.

4. Someone stole or copied his creative work, research, or invention.

5. Someone's taking up two seats on public transit, so she has to stand.

6. There are no parking spaces, and someone double-parked.

7. Someone criticizes her cat, dog, or child.

8. His pet, child, partner, or roommate wakes him up at night for the third time in a row.

9. Her snack just got stuck in the vending machine.

10. Someone he knows keeps talking about himself or herself, dominating the conversation.

11. She's wrongly accused of a misdeed, or even punished for it.

12. The zipper of his coat gets stuck.

13. She sees someone mistreating or threatening a vulnerable individual.

14. He gets home from the store with several bags of groceries, but not the one item he went there to get.

15. Someone cheats on her.

16. Someone steals his wallet, computer, or car.

17. There's water on the bathroom floor and his socks get soaked.

18. She's asked her partner or child a hundred times to stop doing a particular thing. They've promised to stop. They're still doing it.

19. Someone eats food off his plate without asking.

20. Someone makes a cruel joke or insensitive remark.

21. Someone cuts ahead of her in line.

22. Someone defaces his property or damages his vehicle.

23. Someone interrupts her repeatedly.

24. Someone asks him too many personal questions.

25. A sick person coughs or sneezes on her.

SIGH: 25 WRITING PROMPTS TO MAKE YOUR CHARACTER FEEL LONELY

Some of these things wouldn't necessarily *make a person feel lonely, but all of them* could *make someone feel that way.*

1. He invites people to his birthday party, but all of them either cancel at the last minute or simply fail to show up.

2. People keep posting pictures from a party that she wasn't invited to.

3. He doesn't have anyone to celebrate Christmas or Valentine's Day with.

4. She eats alone at a restaurant.

5. He sits alone at the movies or a baseball game.

6. He's getting divorced, and their mutual friends are spending time with his wife and her new boyfriend.

7. She gets Christmas cards from married couples with pictures of them and their smiling children.

8. He's in a group of people who have a lot of in-jokes he doesn't understand.

9. She realizes that the woman she considers a best friend doesn't feel the same way about her.

10. A group of his coworkers never invites him along to lunch.

11. She misses the dog who used to sleep at her feet.

12. He looks out of the window of his new apartment and wishes he'd never moved away from his hometown.

13. She comes across photos or cards from a family member who has since cut her off.

14. He's in a foreign country where he doesn't speak the language well— or at all.

15. She's working a night shift all on her own.

16. He hears his partner or wife compliment someone else profusely, but s/he never compliments him.

17. He texted three people, and none of them texted him back.

18. She was excited to be invited to a party, only to realize it's a "party" where you're supposed to buy stuff.

19. He wakes up from a dream where he's with his ex, his long-distance partner, his family, or a new group of friends, and he realizes it wasn't real.

20. After buying a nice new outfit, she realizes she has no one to go out and do things with, so she has nowhere special to wear it.

21. He joined an online dating service and no one is showing any interest.

22. There's a snack item in the vending machine that nobody ever wants, and she relates to it.

23. He plays board games with himself as a child...or as an adult.

24. She always asks other people about their health, their families, and their work. Nobody asks her how *she's* doing.

25. He talks to a virtual assistant or computer program as though it's a real person.

IF ONLY: 50 WRITING PROMPTS BASED ON CHARACTER REGRETS

Stories would be boring if characters always did the smart thing. Readers can relate to characters who mess up. When characters make terrible decisions, it can even make readers feel better about their own lives in comparison.

A bad decision can hook readers, because they want to see how the person will work their way out of a mess or get over it and have a good life, anyway. And of course, in life and in fiction and the movies, a "bad" decision can turn out to have been a good one in the end.

Try writing about someone who's experienced one of the following. Some of them are bigger mistakes than others.

1. Getting a tattoo that's a huge mistake.

2. Quitting a comfortable, well-paying job.

3. Passing on a once-in-a-lifetime job offer.

4. Taking the wrong job.

5. Majoring in something they didn't really like in college because they thought it was the sensible thing to do.

6. Giving up after a short time at college, despite having a generous scholarship.

7. Buying the wrong house.

8. Breaking up with their soulmate.

Bryn Donovan

9. Getting married to someone they weren't truly in love with.

10. Staying in a miserable marriage for a long time.

11. Not asking someone out when they have the chance.

12. Not reconciling with an estranged family member or friend before they died.

13. Attacking the wrong person.

14. Stealing something valuable on impulse.

15. Misplacing or leaving behind something valuable.

16. Selling a family heirloom.

17. Taking up smoking.

18. Rejecting a manuscript that turns out to be the best-selling book of the decade.

19. Sinking one's savings into a business that turns out to be a terrible idea or a scam.

20. Driving while drunk or sleep-deprived and causing an accident.

21. Accepting help or a ride from a sketchy person.

22. Going to war.

23. Not going to war.

24. Leading a disastrous army attack.

25. Not having children.

26. Having children.

27. Not spending enough time with their spouse or their family.

28. Not fighting for joint custody during the divorce proceedings.

29. Taking on a job personally instead of hiring a professional.

30. Trespassing on someone else's property.

31. Taking a shortcut.

32. Going on a risky outdoor adventure.

33. Not asking a grandmother about her life experiences before she died.

34. Not standing up for or coming to the aid of someone else who was being attacked.

35. Making a joke at someone else's expense.

36. Voting for the wrong candidate.

37. Running for office.

38. Sparing an evil person.

39. Trusting the wrong person with a task.

40. Hiring a family member or friend as an employee.

41. Saving over an important document or deleting an important file.

42. Burning letters, poems, old photographs, or a journal.

43. Breaking a promise.

44. Keeping a promise they never should have made.

45. Placing a big bet.

46. Not moving to Paris when they had the chance.

47. Moving away from their hometown.

48. Telling someone one's deepest secret.

49. Turning one's back on one's religion.

50. Never learning to play the piano.

25 NATURAL ENEMIES PROMPTS

Conflict is at the heart of a good story, and some characters seem destined to butt heads. Of course, in some cases, the same characters may also have a lot in common. Some of the pairings on this list could be friends who bicker about a particular issue. Most of them could be true adversaries. They could even be enemies who wind up becoming friends or falling in love. Try writing about one of these pairs.

1. a vegan and a steakhouse owner

2. a warrior and a pacifist

3. soldiers of opposing armies

4. two people on opposing political campaigns

5. an evangelical minister and an atheist

6. a celebrity and a tabloid photographer

7. a moderator on a website and an Internet troll

8. a neat person and a slob

9. two people in love with the same person

10. a conservationist and a real estate developer

11. a cat lover and someone who's scared of cats

12. a jock and a nerd

13. a doctor and a faith healer

14. a prince and an anti-monarchist

15. a modest person and a person with no inhibitions

16. owners of two competing shops or restaurants in a small town

17. a small business owner and the CEO of a big retail chain

18. a city lover and an outdoorsy type

19. a fugitive and a U.S. Marshal

20. an eternal optimist and a pessimist

21. two people vying for the same promotion at work

22. a district attorney and a public defender on the same case

23. a spendthrift and a miser

24. a school principal or headmaster and a juvenile delinquent

25. a human and an alien invader

50 BIG REALIZATIONS FOR
YOUR CHARACTERS

Keep in mind that a character might have a realization that turns out to be false.

1. If she met someone like the person she used to be, she'd feel nothing but envy.

2. If he met someone like the person he used to be, he'd feel nothing but scorn.

3. The person she believed was honorable was anything but.

4. His marriage or other relationship isn't worth saving.

5. Ending his relationship was the biggest mistake of his life.

6. She made the exact same mistake her mother made.

7. He's lived up to his father's legacy.

8. Just because the rest of his family lived a certain way doesn't mean he can't expect better.

9. Although he makes a lot of excuses, his real problem is that he's lazy.

10. She's no longer faking it.

11. The end of the relationship wasn't his fault at all.

12. The end of the relationship was all her fault.

13. What he thought was a bad break turned out to be a blessing.

14. What she thought was a dream come true turned out to be a nightmare.

15. She's the friend that people call only when everyone else is busy.

16. There's no way for him to help someone who's ruining her life, because she isn't inclined to change.

17. It doesn't matter how competent he is at work; to succeed, he has to learn better social skills.

18. It's okay to ask for help.

19. Living up to other people's expectations isn't working out at all, and it's time for her to do what makes *her* happy.

20. His son, daughter, or parent is a bad person.

21. She no longer believes in the religion in which she was raised.

22. He's embraced a new faith or has found his faith again.

23. The adults in her life are making it up as they go along, just like she is.

24. Being an adult doesn't mean she has to abandon the things she loved as a kid.

25. To a large degree, he can choose to be happy.

26. She's an addict.

27. He's not as smart or talented as everyone told him he was when he was a kid.

28. Although people put her down all the time when she was a kid, she's actually quite smart or very talented.

29. Although she thinks of herself as a sarcastic person with a heart of gold, she's actually a real jerk.

30. He's way too hard on his spouse or child.

31. She no longer has friends.

32. He's actually made a real friend.

33. She's fallen in love.

34. Although he has some athletic talent, he'll never be a professional sports player.

35. Her wild daydream isn't so wild... it's possible that she could actually attain it.

36. He's become obsessed with a topic or activity.

37. There's nothing in her life that she's really passionate about. She's just drifting along.

38. Her child is now an adult.

39. What happened to him wasn't his fault.

40. He loathes his chosen career.

41. He is never going to love her.

42. She is never going to get over him.

43. She's missed out on a lot of things by giving up on herself too easily.

44. He's missed out on a lot of things by being afraid to take action in the first place.

45. It's time for him to quit and cut his losses.

46. She needs to make her family a priority.

47. He's forgiven him.

48. She's forgiven herself.

49. He needs to stop taking life so seriously.

50. Despite the heartbreak or loss she suffered, the best part of her life might still be ahead of her.

SETTING PROMPTS

A strong sense of place can be an author's secret weapon. It can transport readers to another time and place, making them forget about the real world around them. The setting can underscore the mood of a scene, or even provide the conflict. A romantic scene or a fight scene is all the more memorable if it's set in a surprising location.

You can use all of the prompts in this section in one of two ways. (Okay, chances are, you'll think of other ways to use them that I haven't even considered.)

If you struggle with description, you can use any of these prompts as practice. Write a paragraph describing the scene. A description of the setting doesn't need to go on and on; you can focus on a few key details. Many writers focus mostly on visual descriptions, but remember that including sounds, smells, and tactile details will create an even more immersive virtual reality for your reader.

You can also use these prompts as a way into a storyline. Imagine the scene, then start to write something that happens there. Don't judge yourself—just go with your imagination.

50 INDOOR SETTING PROMPTS

1. The penthouse suite.

2. An elevator.

3. An indoor trampoline park.

4. A shopping mall.

5. A nail salon.

6. A cubicle in an office building.

7. An outdated kitchen.

8. The inside of a storage unit.

9. The inside of a cedar chest.

10. A hunting lodge decorated with pelts and antlers.

11. A bicycle repair shop.

12. A chocolate shop.

13. A pizza delivery place.

14. A day care for children.

15. A day care for dogs.

16. A school cafeteria.

17. A janitor's closet.

18. A coat closet.

19. A factory floor.

20. A motel lobby.

21. A tuxedo rental store.

22. A great-grandmother's living room.

23. The abandoned salt mine beneath Detroit...which is the size of a city.

24. A basement apartment.

25. A sports bar during a big game.

26. A truck stop.

27. A furniture gallery.

28. City Hall.

29. A living room in a tiny house—five hundred square feet or less.

30. An adobe house.

31. A yurt.

32. A mosque.

33. A synagogue.

34. A nursing home.

35. A bank vault.

36. An attorney's office.

37. An insurance office.

38. A filthy motel room.

39. An underwater hotel.

40. The Oval Office in the White House.

41. A window seat.

42. A hayloft in a barn.

43. Balcony seats at an opera house.

44. A steam room.

45. A laboratory.

46. A hall lined with portraits in gilded frames.

47. An auto repair shop.

48. A liquor store.

49. A school principal's office.

50. An agricultural dome on a space colony.

50 OUTDOOR SETTING PROMPTS

1. A sidewalk café.

2. A skateboard park.

3. A basketball court in a city neighborhood.

4. The front porch of a farmhouse.

5. Slag heaps.

6. A tunnel covered in graffiti.

7. A wishing well.

8. A party on a rooftop.

9. A gazebo in a park.

10. An amphitheater.

11. London Bridge.

12. The Grand Canyon, Arizona.

13. Central Park, New York City.

14. New York City's Times Square, in the rain.

15. Outside the Eiffel Tower.

16. An outdoor bazaar or *souq*.

17. A courtyard in New Orleans.

18. An old New Orleans cemetery with above-ground graves.

19. A junkyard.

20. A recycling center.

21. A petting zoo.

22. A rainforest.

23. A desert plain.

24. Ice fields in Antarctica.

25. Lava fields in Iceland.

26. Mosquito Bay in Puerto Rico at night, glowing with bioluminescent plankton.

27. A meadow full of fireflies.

28. A boatyard.

29. A beach covered with pieces of sea glass.

30. An apartment balcony.

31. The balcony of an oceanfront home, with the ocean rising almost level.

32. The view from the top of a large water slide.

33. The view from the glass platform near the top of the Willis Tower in Chicago, over 1,450 feet in the air.

34. The Great Wall of China.

35. A treehouse.

36. A rock concert.

37. A Japanese tea garden.

38. The street of a *favela* or slum in Brazil.

39. A part of a city under federal quarantine.

40. A highway underpass, home to thousands of bats.

41. An abandoned amusement park.

42. A hundred stone pillars, supporting nothing.

43. A topiary garden.

44. Bison on a prairie.

45. A swimming pool behind a Bel Air mansion.

46. The flying reindeer training grounds at the North Pole.

47. A school of pink dolphins in the ocean.

48. A town square full of cats.

49. A broken and abandoned railroad track.

50. A rocket launch site.

100 HISTORICAL SETTING PROMPTS

1. A blacksmith's shop in a medieval village.

2. An alehouse in a medieval city.

3. The front seat in a covered wagon.

4. A general store on the U.S. frontier.

5. An Iroquois longhouse.

6. An Oglala Lakota tipi.

7. A Pueblo cliff dwelling.

8. The Shanghai Race Club in the 1930s.

9. A fishmonger's stall in Victorian London.

10. A home turned into a hospital during the U.S. Civil War.

11. A Mayan temple.

12. The servant's quarters in an English country house in the early 20th century.

13. Backstage at the Globe Theater in Elizabethan times.

14. On the set of a motion picture in 1940s Hollywood.

15. A five-and-dime store in the U.S. in the 1950s.

16. A women's dormitory at a university in the 1960s.

17. A grand hacienda on a vast sheep ranch in Mexico in the 1700s.

18. An olive orchard in Biblical times.

19. The cave of a family of Neanderthals.

20. A coffee house in colonial Boston prior to the Revolutionary War.

21. A dressmaker's shop in Belle Époque Paris.

22. The slums of Dublin in 1914.

23. A speakeasy in the U.S. during Prohibition.

24. The city of Mecca, filled with pilgrims, in the late 1100s.

25. A log cabin in the U.S. in the 1800s.

26. A one-room schoolhouse on the American prairie.

27. A trolley car in San Francisco in the early 1900s.

28. The watchtower of a medieval castle.

29. A surgical operating theater in the 1800s.

30. The scullery in a Victorian house.

31. A sleigh ride on a snowy day.

32. The Winter Palace in Russia in the time of Peter the Great.

33. A secret Soviet bunker during the Cold War.

34. A street filled with horses and carriages.

35. A steamboat on the Mississippi River.

36. The Apollo Theater in Harlem in the 1930s.

37. A seaside picnic in Regency England.

38. A scriptorium, where medieval monks copy and illuminate manuscripts.

39. A public execution (this could be in many different eras and places).

40. A church on Easter Sunday in the 1950s.

41. Cruising on Main Street in the U.S. on a Saturday night in the 1950s.

42. Under the boardwalk on Coney Island in the 1950s.

43. A croquet game on an English lawn in the 1860s.

44. A newspaper office in the 1940s.

45. Stonehenge, soon after it was erected.

46. The Taj Mahal, soon after it was built.

47. The Alamo Mission in the weeks before the Texas Revolution.

48. A trading post in Hudson's Bay, Canada in the late 1700s, where wool blankets are exchanged for beaver pelts.

49. A Viking ship headed to Britain for a summertime raid.

50. The *RMS Celtic*, an ocean liner built by the White Star Line, on its maiden voyage from Liverpool to New York

City in 1901 (for those of you who like *The Titanic,* except for the sinking part).

51. A fishing boat in the Mediterranean in Biblical times.

52. A glitzy discotheque in the 1970s.

53. A shop in the Haight-Ashbury district of San Francisco in the 1970s.

54. A roller-skating rink in the 1970s.

55. An underground punk show in the 1980s.

56. A VHS video rental store in the 1980s.

57. Prince Charles and Lady Diana's wedding procession route on July 29, 1981.

58. The slave quarters on an antebellum plantation in the U.S. South.

59. A Fourth of July celebration on the U.S. bicentennial, 1976.

60. The Library of Alexandria before the fire.

61. The Pentagon during the Cuban Missile Crisis of the 1960s.

62. Paris in the 1920s—when Langston Hughes, Josephine Baker, Ernest Hemingway, F. Scott Fitzgerald, Gertrude Stein, Djuna Barnes, and other creative American expatriates were there.

63. The shop of a master craftsperson in Elizabethan England.

64. The construction site of the Pyramids.

65. Ellis Island on opening day.

66. Greenwich Village in the 1950s.

67. The Stonewall Riots in Greenwich Village, New York City: June 28, 1969.

68. The Berlin Wall when it came down: November 9, 1989.

69. A nightclub in Storyville, New Orleans's red-light district, in the early 1900s.

70. Vienna in the time of Mozart.

71. Hyde Park, London, in the 1820s.

72. London on V-E Day, May 8, 1945.

73. The spa town of Mariánské Lázně in the Golden Era of the late 1800s.

74. Australia in 1900, the year before independence.

75. Sobrino de Botin in Madrid, Spain—the world's oldest continuously operating restaurant—in 1725, right after it first opened.

76. A boarding house in the Texas panhandle during the Dust Bowl.

77. A fallout shelter in the 1950s.

78. A Negro Leagues baseball game in the 1930s in Kansas City, St. Louis, Baltimore, Birmingham, Chicago,

Brooklyn, Indianapolis, Memphis, Pittsburgh, or Philadelphia.

79. A cathedral in a medieval city.

80. An imperial palace in China.

81. The construction site of Rockefeller Center during the Great Depression.

82. The Parthenon in Athens, Greece, dedicated to the goddess Athena, in 400 BC.

83. The Parthenon in the early 1460s after the Ottoman conquest, when it was being used as a mosque.

84. A village well in Israel in the time of Jesus Christ.

85. The Hanging Gardens of Babylon, created around 525 BC by King Nebuchadnezzar II for his queen, Amytis. (Note: this is only one theory about the gardens, which may or may not have actually existed.)

86. A French chateau in the 1600s.

87. Hautvillers Abbey in the 1670s and 1680s, when the cellarer Dom Pérignon was inventing Champagne.

88. A tannery in Marrakesh in the 1100s.

89. A crinoline shop in 1880.

90. A tobacconist and sweet shop in 1880.

91. A barbershop in the 1950s.

92. A public bathhouse in ancient Rome.

93. Mexico in the 1820s, when the newly independent nation is in chaos and Spanish general Augustin de Iturbide becomes a dictator.

94. A farmstead in the Cotswolds, England, in the early 1900s.

95. The servants' dining hall in the basement of an English country house in the early 1900s.

96. The offices of Enron, the Houston energy company, in 2001, when their fraudulent accounting practices were coming to light.

97. A meeting of the White Rose, a German anti-Nazi group, near the University of Munich in the autumn of 1942.

98. Moton Field in Tuskegee, Alabama, where black military pilots (Tuskegee Airmen) trained, in the summer of 1941.

99. The flight school for WASPs, Women Airforce Service Pilots, in Houston, Texas in 1942.

100. A Pan Am airplane in the 1960s.

50 PROMPTS ON CARS, PLANES, TRAINS, BOATS, AND MORE

1. A packed passenger plane sitting on a runway on a hot summer day.

2. Behind the wheel of a monster truck at a monster truck rally.

3. Behind the wheel of a truck loaded with nitroglycerin, the active ingredient in dynamite.

4. A refrigerated car on a freight train.

5. A subway car on the Paris Metro.

6. The first-class car on the bullet train travelling between Tokyo and Kyoto.

7. The backseat of an old car in a grocery store parking lot at night.

8. The back of a hearse.

9. A tiny, messy bathroom on a commercial airplane.

10. A helicopter above a metropolis.

11. A helicopter above a war zone.

12. A blimp above a stadium.

13. A school bus filled with children.

14. A school bus with passengers who aren't children, that isn't heading to or from a school.

15. The front seat of a U-Haul van on the highway.

16. A used car lot at midnight.

17. An airport terminal at two a.m.

18. An SUV off the road in the desert.

19. The deck of a yacht.

20. A canoe in a swamp.

21. The back seat of a ride-hailing vehicle (such as Lyft or Uber.).

22. The driver's seat of a stretch limousine.

23. A Greyhound bus.

24. A rowboat on a pond.

25. A private jet with every luxurious amenity.

26. An RV in Manhattan.

27. A luxury sports car on the streets of a small town.

28. The dining car in a train.

29. The lounge on a cruise ship.

30. The driver's seat of an ambulance.

31. The driver's seat of an armored car carrying cash.

32. The back of a prisoner transport vehicle.

33. The driver's seat of a garbage truck.

34. The observation car on a train.

35. The back of a police car.

36. The front seat in a fire engine.

37. A motorcycle in an alley.

38. A Vespa in a small town.

39. A snowmobile in the mountains.

40. A sports car in an ice storm.

41. The driver's seat of an Army tank.

42. A sailboat on a sunny bay.

43. A gondola on a canal in Venice.

44. A houseboat.

45. A hang glider over a canyon.

46. A Model T Ford.

47. A spacecraft circling Jupiter.

48. The driver's seat of a tractor in a cornfield.

49. A small plane, crashed and in flames.

50. A ski lift.

DIALOGUE PROMPTS

Many fiction writers enjoy writing dialogue more than any other part of the story and feel confident about their ability to write it. When you're writing a story, dialogue can be a great place to begin.

As you're writing, keep in mind that different characters should express themselves differently. One might be inclined to cursing, while another might never use coarse language. One might say everything that's on her mind, while another might speak in shorter sentences—and say less in general. Giving each character his or her distinctive voice is another way to make the characters real to the readers.

200 GENERAL DIALOGUE PROMPTS

Most of the prompts on this list are open-ended so they can lend themselves to many different kinds of stories. Start with one of them, write a conversation around it, and see where it takes you!

1. "Ma'am, is this your dog?"

2. "No, it's really not that complicated. He's a bad person."

3. "Hey...what's wrong with your face?"

4. "The king is missing."

5. "Ah yes, come in. Close the door behind you."

6. "Dude. It's three in the morning."

7. "Um, sorry. That one's not for sale."

8. "You've got thirty seconds to explain to me what you're doing here."

9. "Didn't anyone ever tell you who your real daddy is?"

10. "I know this may be hard to believe, but I'm on your side."

11. "Never heard of that being used as a murder weapon before."

12. "Just sit around and cry, then. I don't have that luxury."

13. "I'm sorry. I thought you were someone else."

14. "That's the nice thing about telling the truth. You don't have nearly as much to keep track of."

15. "Of course we're best friends. No one else would put up with our shenanigans."

16. "That's the least of your worries."

17. "You look different from your profile picture."

18. "Do you trust me?"

19. "You found it on the beach? You know, when most people take a walk on the beach, they pick up seashells."

20. "Sir. This is for children only."

21. "I haven't tried this on a human yet, but it should work."

22. "What? I meant it as a compliment."

23. "Who put this in my coat pocket?"

24. "I can't do this anymore."

25. "You think you're so good-looking, but deep down, you're the kind of ugly that Photoshop can't fix."

26. "I know you did your best, but it wasn't enough."

27. "Even if I could stop it, I wouldn't."

28. "You have got to see this."

29. "Guess who made the evening news?"

30. "I don't really think of myself as a thief..."

31. "Are you just going to keep walking by my house or are you going to come in?"

32. "We do things a little differently in this century."

33. "Please return to your assigned seat."

34. "Are you banned from all Taco Bells, or just that Taco Bell?"

35. "I can't believe I used to think he was attractive."

36. "You *are* speaking to the manager."

37. "Where are your clothes?"

38. "Well, this contest isn't going to rig itself."

39. "Hi, I'm calling about your ad?"

40. "I can't believe I'm telling you this."

41. "I should have told you this a long time ago."

42. "I am only telling the truth when I say that you have not behaved completely as a gentleman in this matter."

43. "I thought we were friends!"

44. "That's not a good look."

45. "It's a genetic trait, but it's exceptionally rare."

46. "I love you, but I don't even think I know who you really are."

47. "She's evil, but she does have a point there."

48. "I didn't know you could talk."

49. "Sweetie, what were you thinking?"

50. "What makes you think it was an accident?"

51. "Sorry. You're the first person I've spoken to in ten years."

52. "I don't suppose you've got a blowtorch around here?"

53. "I know you're here. You may as well show yourself."

54. "Get a job!"

55. "Actually…I do know of a reason why these two shouldn't get married."

56. "According to this, you owe them eighty thousand dollars."

57. "We thought at first that it was part of the performance."

58. "It's been a while since I've seen y'all in church."

59. "I would break his thumbs right now if I could."

60. "Why are you helping me?"

61. "That's the worst reason I've ever heard to have a baby."

62. "I didn't even recognize you!"

63. "Is it worth breaking your vows over?"

64. "I told you not to read that."

65. "Put the turkey down."

66. "I didn't ask to be abducted."

67. "That's the most disgusting thing I've ever heard."

68. "Where did you learn how to do that?"

69. "How could you do this to me?"

70. "I thought *you* had him!"

71. "Humility is not one of my many virtues."

72. "How can you stand living here?"

73. "She's young, fertile, and from a good family. What more do you need to know?"

74. "Sometimes being a total geek pays off."

75. "You don't have the correct paperwork."

76. "Careful not to break the—oh."

77. "I wasn't going to say anything, but yeah."

78. "I'd love to help, but I want to keep all my money in case I want to spend it on other things."

79. "Well aren't you the cutest little thing?"

80. "Why is that your password?"

81. "Please don't use sarcasm. It confuses me."

82. "After we lost you, things just weren't the same."

83. "If you were logical you would've killed me already."

84. "Well, that could've gone better."

85. "Sometimes I feel like she's still at my side."

86. "We've been waiting two hours."

87. "Your services are no longer required."

88. "I feel like we've met before..."

89. "Does he hit you?"

90. "Yes, it's a questionable line of work, but I'm good at it."

91. "She's in the building."

92. "Wow! It's an honor to meet you."

93. "You were in a crash. Can you tell me your name?"

94. "This used to be a great country, but people like you are destroying it."

95. "I'm cured. I swear."

96. "My chances of living to a ripe old age are unfortunately excellent."

97. "Let's face it: you don't exactly blend in."

98. "Forgive me if I'm misreading things, but do you want to make out?"

99. "The next time you shoot a guy, don't do it on national television."

100. "We'll need to take a blood sample to be sure."

101. "Maybe you don't believe in them, but they definitely believe in you."

102. "Just get out there and smile and act like everything's fine."

103. "Keep your head down!"

104. "I still miss being with you."

105. "She is a heretic and a danger to us all."

106. "Well change it back!"

107. "Those were his last wishes?"

108. "Yeah, we're still legally married, but it doesn't mean anything."

109. "I'm not mad at you for lying. I'm mad at you for being so bad at it."

110. "Ugh, I still have glitter all over me."

111. "I know it's going to hurt to leave—like cutting off your leg to get out of a trap—but you have to do it."

112. "If it's beluga caviar, yes, but if it's cheap caviar, no."

113. "I've been patient for five minutes!"

114. "I'm not the best, but I have the best timing."

115. "Just because you're bitter doesn't mean you're smarter than everybody else."

116. "That's a discussion for another time."

117. "Take it easy. There's plenty to go around."

118. "Are you embarrassed to be seen with me?"

119. "Yes, who's this?... My worst enemy? I'm sorry, you're going to have to be more specific."

120. "He's gone from normal crazy to off-the-rails crazy."

121. "What are you talking about? I don't have a sister."

122. "You know who always wants more money? Rich people."

123. "I don't think that's a good enough reason to bring someone back from the dead."

124. "You're the one who left. Not me."

125. "It's an acquired taste."

126. "She's not getting a dime out of me."

127. "I didn't even know you were in the country."

128. "I know he's the worst, but he's still family."

129. "Of course I'm scared. I'm not an idiot."

130. "What do you mean you've never pumped your own gas?"

131. "I couldn't sleep because of the crying in the next room."

132. "Did you make that yourself?"

133. "You were in there so long I got worried."

134. "Nobody ever suspects nurses."

135. "It seems they got the translation wrong. What it really says is…"

136. "Don't apologize. Of course you're upset."

137. "No, this isn't the point of no return. That was a few points back."

138. "Do you smell something?"

139. "It seemed like a good idea at the time."

140. "What am I supposed to do with all these extra rubber duckies?"

141. "Make that whining brat shut up."

142. "Once the spring snows melt, we shall know."

143. "It was an insurance convention. Stuff happens."

144. "I didn't feel hurt. I didn't feel anything."

145. "You must be mistaken. No one's lived there in thirty years."

146. "In four minutes they'll enter the atmosphere."

147. "95 percent of this news program is filler, and the rest is lies."

148. "I felt so dirty that I just wanted to die."

149. "The website didn't mention this part of the tour."

150. "That's going to cost you extra."

151. "Who left this in the sink?"

152. "Don't mix those two things unless you want to be throwing up all night."

153. "Obviously, I look different from my last incarnation."

154. "Apart from being grouchy all the time, I'm a really good husband."

155. "Hang on, this is going to hurt. A lot."

156. "I'm not sorry I did it, but it was a horrible experience."

157. "Calling him mentally ill is an insult to mentally ill people."

158. "You've never seen a horse quite like this one."

159. "If you're not having an affair with him, why did you call him sixty-eight times in two weeks?"

160. "I don't know why I waited so long to do this."

161. "Whatever you do, don't open your eyes."

162. "Am I free to go, officer?"

163. "I don't want to do anything this weekend but sleep and eat ice cream."

164. "In retrospect, drowning her was a mistake."

165. "You cast a spell? What kind of spell?"

166. "If you don't tell her, I will."

167. "I'm the only one who gets to overrule. Now sit down or I'll have you removed from this courtroom."

168. "Can I pet the cows?"

169. "Quit whining. The woman won."

170. "Eh, he's a good kid, but he started hanging around in the wrong crowd, got caught up in some stuff."

171. "What *do* you want?"

172. "What do *you* want?"

173. "This is definitely my worst birthday yet."

174. "That's not what your mom said."

175. "I just think it's weird that he never leaves his apartment."

176. "She could change, but most people don't."

177. "I've got a choice here. I can be angry about this all day, or I can try to enjoy myself anyway."

178. "You're the laziest revolutionary ever."

179. "She followed me into the casino screaming."

180. "You're never going to get a husband if you keep turning down proposals."

181. "Who are you talking to?"

182. "Sorry about your car."

183. "You throw this guy a lifeline and he tries to hang himself from it."

184. "Everyone is calling me The Watcher, but I don't know what I'm supposed to be watching, and at this point it seems awkward to ask."

185. "Put it in a black duffel bag and bring it to the following address at 2 a.m."

186. "I am the most humble person you are ever likely to meet."

187. "Thank you in advance for your cooperation in this matter."

188. "I've kept this baby alive for a full year now and I'm very proud of that."

189. "She doesn't have much to contribute besides enthusiasm."

190. "This is why I don't have a lot of friends."

191. "I've figured out my life's true purpose."

192. "Human? Not anymore."

193. "I would like to apologize for sending you that picture. It was meant for someone else."

194. "Take me to the body."

195. "I should have warned him, but I wanted to see how it would play out."

196. "Thank God you're here!"

197. "Give her a break. The afterlife can get really boring."

---

198. "I said good day, sir!"

199. "I'm not sad and single. I'm fabulous and available."

200. "Where am I?"

50 TOPICS FOR ARGUMENTS

All good stories have conflict, and that often includes characters arguing with one another. Antagonists fight with the heroes, allies have disagreements, and friends, family members, and couples have quarrels with one another. These can range from amusingly petty to deadly serious.

Choose any of these topics and write an argument between two or more characters.

1. directions, or the best route to take

2. household chores

3. an infidelity or a flirtation

4. whether to let a hostage go

5. where to go on vacation

6. who to spend the holidays with

7. how to spend the weekend

8. whether they should have a baby

9. what to name a baby

10. how a child should be disciplined

11. whether an employee should be fired

12. whether they should attack or retreat

13. whether someone behaved properly at a social event

14. how someone should dress

15. whether something is a justifiable purchase

16. a person's bad grades

17. whether a law or rule is reasonable

18. what TV show or movie to watch

19. a person's overeating

20. a person's overspending

21. a person's refusal to get necessary treatment

22. a person's failure to honor a commitment

23. whether someone should be working harder

24. whether someone is working too much

25. whether someone is using a mean or disrespectful tone of voice

26. a person's past history of abuse

27. a person's current pattern of lying and secrecy

28. a person's choice of romantic partner

29. a person's choice in friendship

30. whether to take out a loan

31. one person's decision not to loan or give money to the other

32. a loan that was never paid back

33. a person's decision to cut her hair…or grow out his beard

34. whether she's a bad listener

35. whether someone should go to bed at a decent hour

36. who is the rightful heir to the throne

37. whether an ancient text should be taken literally

38. whether a prophecy is legitimate

39. whether a ritual is necessary

40. whether a TV series or a series of books has gone hopelessly downhill

41. whether to end a person's artificial life support

42. who the better candidate is

43. where someone should go to college

44. whether an occupation is immoral

45. who's going to take the dangerous mission

46. whether life is too hard for seeing-eye dogs and drug-sniffing dogs

47. what temperature the house or car should be

48. whether to move to another country

49. whether a photograph or video has been manipulated

50. exactly what happened on that particular night

50 THINGS SOMEONE CAN ASK

Questions and requests create innate tension in dialogue. Will the person get what they want, whether it's a favor or a straight answer? Sometimes the asker is in a vulnerable position, and sometimes the person being questioned is.

I wrote these prompts in second person for the sake of clarity and brevity, but you'll probably write in the voice of your character, not yourself.

1. Ask someone to crash on their couch.

2. Ask someone to take over flying the plane.

3. Ask God for a sign.

4. Ask someone for a little hint.

5. Beg someone to spare your life.

6. Beg someone to spare your friend's or loved one's life.

7. Beg someone to take your life.

8. Ask someone to give you a black eye.

9. Ask for a job.

10. Ask for a day off from work.

11. Ask for a raise.

12. Ask someone for a sizable amount of money.

13. Ask for forgiveness.

14. Ask how to atone for a grave misdeed.

15. Ask how to get on someone's good side.

16. Ask someone to go on a road trip with you.

17. Ask someone to move to another country with you.

18. Ask someone why he sent the incriminating letters, messages, or texts he did.

19. Ask someone why a stolen item is in her possession.

20. Ask someone if the crime another person accused him of is true.

21. Ask a stranger a personal, inappropriate question.

22. Ask someone to look after your baby for a while.

23. Ask someone for an autograph.

24. Ask someone to consider plastic surgery.

25. Ask someone why he saved your life.

26. Ask someone to betray her leader.

27. Literally ask for the shirt off someone's back.

28. Request an entrée that's not on the menu.

29. Ask a merchant if she can procure an unusual item.

30. Ask someone to withdraw from a political race.

31. Ask someone to retreat in a battle.

32. Solicit advice on a quest.

33. Solicit advice on one's love life.

34. Ask someone to tell a lie for you.

35. Ask someone to keep a secret.

36. Ask someone if he needs help.

37. Ask someone to stop talking.

38. Beg someone to be your mentor.

39. Beg for food.

40. Beg for medical assistance.

41. Ask someone on a date.

42. Ask someone if you can kiss her.

43. Ask someone to marry you.

44. Ask for a volunteer for a dangerous mission.

45. Ask someone for access to a restricted area.

46. Ask if the deceased had any enemies.

47. Plead with the hotel manager for someplace to stay even though there are no vacancies.

48. Ask Santa for something you're highly unlikely to get.

49. Beg someone not to leave.

50. Ask someone to please go away.

50 THINGS SOMEONE CAN EXPLAIN

Write a paragraph or two in your character's voice explaining one of the following things. Keep in mind that your character may actually be giving terrible advice or an irrational explanation.

1. Why one shouldn't cremate a dead body.

2. How he got that scar.

3. Why she chose that tattoo.

4. Why he seemed to have dropped off the face of the earth for the past ten years.

5. What makes rain in the country so dangerous.

6. Why she moved to the city.

7. Why he left his job.

8. Why she applied for this job.

9. Why one should always choose the middle seat in an airplane.

10. Why she dropped out of college.

11. Why he started college at the age of seventy.

12. Why she went on a cruise alone.

13. Why he did his own investigation of the murder.

14. Why she gave a car to a stranger.

15. Why there's a huge crater in the center of the metropolis.

16. Why she defected from the army.

17. Why they always eat oysters on Fridays.

18. Why there's a second moon now.

19. Why he lives on a boat.

20. Why nobody called the police.

21. Why he refused to pay for his son's college education.

22. Why she attempted to climb Mount Everest.

23. Why humans ignored climate change.

24. Why they went deep into credit card debt again after digging out of it.

25. Why he missed his flight.

26. How the small town's festival got started.

27. How to steal a diamond necklace.

28. How to crash a wedding reception.

29. How to avoid being taken advantage of in a divorce.

30. How to get a promotion without working hard.

31. How to quit drinking.

32. How to save the horses when a wildfire is headed toward the ranch.

33. How to get a great bargain on a used car.

34. How to get rich quick.

35. How to be a good girlfriend or boyfriend.

36. How to turn a regular stick into a magic wand.

37. Why he's digging up a grave.

38. Why she let everyone think she was unable to speak.

39. Why he has a map of various warehouses.

40. Why she leaves her Christmas tree up all year.

41. Why he refuses to own a microwave.

42. Why she gained a hundred pounds.

43. Why someone else described him as a sociopath.

44. Why a certain person who everyone admires is actually a terrible person.

45. Why they need to stage an intervention.

46. Why he fired the actor from his play or movie.

47. Why he adopted ten stray cats.

48. Why the marriage was over before they even went on their honeymoon.

49. How saying a prayer changed everything.

50. How she made a fresh start.

OTHER FICTION PROMPTS

This section invites you to draw inspiration from disparate and unusual sources: made-up titles, images, sounds, Tarot cards, particular types of scenes, and more. The more frequently you write, the easier it will be to get inspired, even from the most random things you read and experience.

100 TITLE PROMPTS

These are all titles that I've invented. At the time of editing this book, we couldn't find any of them being used as actual fiction titles, but we could've missed one, and I know that this could change at any time.

I think the best way to use them as writing prompts is to do some fast writing. Pick one, maybe set a timer for five minutes, and as quickly as you can, write out a beginning or a scene from a short story or novel with that title.

I doubt you'll wind up using one of these for a title of a finished story, but I totally approve of doing so!

1. What We Did In London

2. That's Where You're Wrong

3. Run the Table

4. The Soldier On The Bridge

5. Single Serving

6. Like Heroes Often Do

7. The Odor Of Salt

8. Music Box Magic

9. She Whose Opportunity Escapeth Her Not

10. Ammo And Diesel

11. Café Afternoons

31. Barefoot June

32. The Devil And His Brother

33. Meeting On The Mezzanine

34. Well, Actually

35. When The Dead Return

36. The Lamplighter's Oath

37. Mortal Honor

38. It Happened At The Tulip Festival

39. Extra Large Supreme

40. Trainhopping

41. By A Bad Road

42. The Alien In The Archives

43. Current Address

44. Shameless Flattery

45. Sparkling Sands

46. The Winery Diaries

47. Dangerous If Provoked

48. The Umbrella Code

49. Songs For An Irish Wake

69. A Harp Played By The Wind

70. Bad Girls Make Good Spies

71. The Bibliophile

72. The City We Left Behind

73. Mornings At Birdie's

74. Step Aside

75. The Parrot In The Palace

76. Dreamers And Makers

77. Never Let Me Down

78. One Weekend In Autumn

79. Trick Or Trade

80. As Always, My Apologies

81. Champagne And Chocolates

82. Savage Force

83. Five Dogs, Two Houses

84. The Stars Above The Plains

85. The Patron Saint Of Irony

86. The Amethyst Key

87. Underground Bride

88. One Hundred Flights

89. The Vengeance Of A King

90. Sweet Like Mangoes

91. Appaloosa Canyon

92. Only On This Day

93. Ms. Worldwide

94. Lies I Believed As A Child

95. The Boy In The Powder-Blue Tux

96. Browser History

97. Waitressing For Rich People

98. Learning To Flirt

99. Starlink

100. The Lost Cello

200 IMAGE PROMPTS

Images can serve as powerful symbols in writing. In fact, a whole school of poetry, called Imagism, developed around the idea of letting images speak for themselves. An image doesn't have to be a symbol to be memorable, and even ordinary images can serve as triggers for creative thinking.

1. A grown woman sitting in a tree.

2. A plane writing a message in the sky.

3. A greeting card with part of the inside torn off—where the signature would be.

4. A woman cuddling a tiger cub.

5. Work boots or hiking boots caked with mud.

6. A keychain with a few dozen keys.

7. Camels and their riders trekking across the desert.

8. A hooded figure in the shadows.

9. A big bunch of balloons floating off into the sky.

10. Hands covered in oil.

11. Bare feet in the sand.

12. A boa constrictor coiled on the sofa.

13. Glitter in an hourglass.

14. Koi circulating in a pond.

15. A bonfire in the woods.

16. A row of test tubes.

17. Tools hanging on a pegboard.

18. An organ transplant cooler.

19. A shattered window.

20. A spun glass figurine.

21. A drink in a coconut, with a paper umbrella.

22. Snow in someone's hair.

23. A bunch of fake flowers.

24. A dog's wet nose, close up.

25. A Ouija board.

26. The blue flame of a gas stove burner.

27. A rifle hanging over a fireplace.

28. An eagle gliding over the river.

29. Illuminated windows of a tall hospital building, seen from the city street.

30. Someone jumping off the side of a cliff into the ocean.

31. A sofa covered with plastic.

32. A red–and–white striped barbershop pole.

33. A coffee can stuffed with coins and crumpled single dollar bills.

34. A hangman's noose.

35. A child's face covered with freckles.

36. A large cage.

37. A bathtub filled with milk.

38. A set of dumbbells.

39. A torn screen door.

40. A bottle of sunscreen.

41. A row of marching ants…indoors or outdoors.

42. A sponge floating in a bucket of dirty water.

43. A broken thermometer.

44. The view of the clouds from the cockpit of an airplane.

45. A pink canopy bed.

46. The rubble of a demolished building.

47. A smashed phone.

48. A poorly done tattoo.

49. The skull of a cow.

50. Palm trees swaying in a strong wind.

51. Pages of sheet music littering the floor.

52. A well-loved stuffed animal.

53. A telescope pointed out the bedroom window.

54. A daisy with half the petals pulled off.

55. Dry, cracked earth in a drought.

56. A chrysalis.

57. A bright red house amid a snowy white landscape.

58. A thermostat turned all the way up.

59. A starfish in the shallows.

60. A typewriter.

61. A wild animal's eyes glowing in the dark.

62. The pupil of a human eye contracting.

63. A palm reading chart.

64. A forest floor covered with autumn leaves.

65. A lace sleeve.

66. An antique perfume bottle.

67. A crowd of people reaching their hands into the air.

68. Two men in suits standing in a cornfield.

69. A jeweled chalice.

70. A retainer.

71. A spacecraft sitting on the surface of a misty planet.

72. A guitar case.

73. A marble sculpture of two lovers.

74. A floor covered with packing peanuts.

75. A park bench under a streetlight.

76. A huge tree stump with many, many rings.

77. A sparkler.

78. A bin full of cans and bottles to be recycled.

79. A quartz crystal reflecting rainbow hues.

80. Smooth black stones in a riverbed.

81. A golden cross pendant on a chain.

82. A vase of dried, dead roses.

83. A tie-dyed tee shirt.

84. An emergency exit sign.

85. Cut-up credit cards.

86. A gold medal.

87. A chalkboard covered with equations.

88. Racks of clothing at a thrift store.

89. Piles of dirty laundry.

90. A painted fan.

91. A long chain ending in a broken shackle.

92. Someone in a parachute descending to earth.

93. Ticket stubs.

94. An ancient Egyptian sarcophagus.

95. A big spider in the bathtub.

96. A windmill.

97. A superhero costume.

98. A dog wearing a cone.

99. A teacup turned upside down.

100. A fork in the road.

101. Toadstools growing in an indoor location.

102. Long fingernails with chipped polish.

103. A boat decorated with Christmas lights.

104. A mobile over a crib.

105. A box filled with electrical cords and cables.

106. A frozen fountain.

107. Eggs in a nest.

108. A rusted cannon.

109. An army marching in formation.

110. A wig on a wig stand.

111. A bicycle on a roof.

112. A souvenir thimble.

113. An antique Christmas ornament.

114. A figurine of a saint.

115. A charm bracelet with many charms.

116. Soldiers in uniform standing on a street corner.

117. A sand castle.

118. A propane tank.

119. A plastic dinosaur.

120. A school of swimming jellyfish.

121. A paint can overturned on the floor, with a big puddle of paint.

122. A toe ring on a middle toe.

123. A solar eclipse.

124. A shopping cart filled to the brim with only one item.

125. A two-headed snake.

126. A ballerina tutu.

127. Birds on a telephone wire.

128. Used paintbrushes in a coffee can.

129. Velvet curtains drawn across a stage.

130. Ready-to-assemble shelves that still need to be assembled; instructions and pieces strewn across the floor.

131. A crash test dummy.

132. A baby hedgehog.

133. Lemons floating in a swimming pool.

134. A lizard in the bathroom.

135. Hair dyed bright turquoise.

136. A vintage trailer.

137. A freeway with traffic at a standstill.

138. Banners of *papel picado* (colorful tissue paper cut into intricate designs; a Mexican folk art and traditional decoration).

139. A puzzle piece on the floor.

140. A bedraggled horse.

141. A toddler in a snowsuit.

142. A set of barbells.

143. A huge bruise on a leg.

144. A word traced onto a filthy car.

145. Shipping boxes with bubble wrap.

146. A machete.

147. A stone wall.

148. A hornet's nest.

149. A ballcap.

150. A Mardi Gras mask.

151. The fossilized tooth of a saber-tooth tiger.

152. A man carrying a surfboard on a New York subway.

153. A rusted bed frame; no mattress.

154. Two hummingbirds fighting.

155. Blue veins showing through white skin.

156. Beet juice on a cutting board.

157. A smashed tomato on the pavement.

158. A lighthouse.

159. A row of parked motorcycles.

160. A sparkling chandelier.

161. A pair of cowboy boots.

162. A car skidding on the ice.

163. Dandelions gone to seed.

164. A refrigerator door covered in magnets, children's art, coupons, and more.

165. A sweater with an elaborate pattern.

166. Seaweed on the beach.

167. A canned ham.

168. A pair of boxing gloves.

169. A dance floor that lights up.

170. A pinball machine.

171. A walking stick with a brass mermaid handle.

172. A makeup case filled with cosmetics and brushes.

173. A zebra skin rug.

174. A paper clip bent out of shape.

175. A dentist's chair.

176. A stack of soda cans.

177. A sunrise in the rearview mirror.

178. Frozen pizzas from a crashed semi truck spilled all over the road.

179. A pineapple.

180. A woman with a bandana obscuring most of her face.

181. A neon sign advertising foot massages.

182. Sun streaming through lace curtains.

183. An earring near the shower drain.

184. A snow globe.

185. A bag of French fries on the edge of a bathtub.

186. A woman with a shaved head.

187. Soap bubbles floating on the breeze.

188. A night landscape seen through cracked eyeglasses.

189. A cozy interior seen through fogged eyeglasses.

190. A baby wearing sunglasses.

191. A magnifying glass.

192. A car decorated with balloons, tin cans, and "Just Married" signs.

193. A jet leaving a trail in the sky.

194. Muddy footprints on the carpet.

195. A throng of marathon runners.

196. A snowflake on an eyelash.

197. A raindrop on a leaf.

198. Children's chalk drawings on a sidewalk or driveway.

199. An origami fox.

200. A half of a walnut.

50 PROMPTS BASED ON SOUNDS

1. Write a scene that features a warning siren of some kind.

2. Write a scene that features the sound of thunder.

3. Write about a character who's thrilled when she hears a certain sound.

4. Write about a character who's furious when he hears a certain sound.

5. Write about a character who's terrified when she hears a certain sound.

6. Imagine someone who has a noisy neighbor at home or at work, and write about the situation.

7. Describe a character's voice from another character's point of view.

8. Describe the sounds at an airport, and set a scene there.

9. Describe the sounds on a street in a past century, and set a scene there.

10. Write a scene that includes the sounds of modern-day city traffic.

11. Write a scene that includes the sound of a waterfall.

12. Write a scene that begins with the sound of a doorbell ringing.

13. Write a scene that ends with the sound of church bells ringing.

14. Imagine a situation in which champagne corks are popping, and write about it.

15. Imagine a situation in which guns are firing, and write about it.

16. Write a scene in which a rooster is crowing. Make it in a place where no one would expect to hear a rooster.

17. Most people consider this to be a pleasant sound—but your character hates it.

18. Most people consider this to be an irritating noise—but your character loves it.

19. Write a conversation in which people have to shout over the noise.

20. Write a conversation in which people have to whisper.

21. Write a scene that features an automated voice.

22. Write a scene that features the sound of breathing.

23. Write a scene that plays out in complete silence.

24. A character is trying to keep someone else from noticing certain sounds.

25. These sounds make it clear that your character is home. Describe them.

26. No one would ever expect these sounds to be coming from your character's apartment. What's going on?

27. Imagine a situation in which fireworks are exploding, and write about it.

28. Imagine a situation in which autumn leaves are crunching underfoot, and write about it.

29. This cheerful sound is the backdrop to a dire situation.

30. This serious sound is the backdrop to a pleasant or hilarious situation.

31. Write a scene in which someone's phone rings at a wildly inopportune time.

32. Write a scene that features booing and heckling.

33. Write a scene that features cheering and a standing ovation.

34. Include a dog, wolf, or coyote howling in a scene.

35. Include the chirping of crickets or the droning of locusts in a scene.

36. Describe the sounds at a busy diner and set a scene there.

37. Describe the sounds at a seashore and set a scene there.

38. A voicemail or recording rocks your character's world.

39. The voice over the intercom says something highly unusual.

40. Radio static or a garbled recording makes a message difficult for your character to understand.

41. One character is able to hear something that the other characters can't.

42. Describe how it sounds when creatures of another species talk to one another.

43. Write a scene that features the sounds of a gym or locker room.

44. Write a scene that features the sounds of an elevator.

45. Include the squeaking of a Styrofoam cooler in a scene.

46. Include the sound of breaking icebergs in a scene.

47. Describe the sounds at a nightclub and set a scene there.

48. Describe the sounds on a construction site and set a scene there.

49. Write a scene in which a character mistakes one noise for another.

50. Write a scene in which someone hears a sound they have never heard before in their lives. What does it turn out to be?

50 PROMPTS BASED ON SMELLS

Most writers tend to under-utilize the sense of smell in their writing. This sense is strongly linked to the part of the brain that stores memories, and smells can elicit strong emotional responses.

1. A character encounters a smell that transports him back to another time in his life.

2. Include the scent of clean laundry in a scene.

3. Include the scent of limes in a scene.

4. Write a scene that includes the smells of spring.

5. Write a scene that includes the smells of a summer vacation.

6. Write a scene that incorporates the smell of gasoline.

7. Write a scene that incorporates the smell of formaldehyde.

8. A character loves the way someone else smells.

9. A character hates the way someone else smells.

10. Write about your character's associations with the smell of vanilla.

11. Write about your character's associations with the smell of baby powder.

12. Write a scene that incorporates the smells of a beauty salon.

13. Write a scene that incorporates the smells of a sickroom.

14. A character encounters a smell that confuses her.

15. A character encounters a smell that infuriates him.

16. Write a scene that includes the smell of apples.

17. Write a scene that includes that new-car smell.

18. Include scented candles in a scene.

19. Include the scent of burning or melting plastic in a scene.

20. Write a scene that takes place in a greenhouse filled with flowers.

21. Write a scene in which barnyard smells feature prominently.

22. A character notices a smell that fills him with dread.

23. A character notices a smell that makes her expect something good.

24. Use the smell of blue cheese in a scene.

25. Use the smell of menthol in a scene.

26. Write a scene that includes the smell of dirt.

27. Write a scene that includes the smell of something from another planet.

28. A character encounters a smell that makes her stomach growl.

29. A character encounters a smell that makes his stomach turn.

30. A character encounters a smell that makes her eyes water.

31. Include the smell of movie popcorn in a scene.

32. Include the smell of money in a scene.

33. Write a scene that incorporates the smells of Christmas.

34. Write a scene that incorporates the smells of a state fair.

35. A character asks someone else about a smell.

36. A character attempts to remove or mask a smell.

37. Write a scene that incorporates the smells of a grade school building.

38. Write a scene that incorporates the smells of a frat house.

39. A character encounters the familiar smells of the place where he works.

40. A character encounters smells that are exotic to her.

41. Include the scents of a bakery in a scene.

42. Include the scents of an Italian restaurant in a scene.

43. Write about a character's negative associations with a smell.

44. Write a scene that features a rare perfume.

45. Write a scene that includes the smells of a forest.

46. Write a scene that includes the smells in a cave.

47. A character encounters musty smells.

48. Use the smell of new carpet in a scene.

49. Write about a character with a very strong sense of smell.

50. Write about a character who has no sense of smell at all.

50 PROMPTS BASED ON TOUCH
AND PHYSICAL SENSATIONS

These prompts are about tactile sensations and about the way people feel physically. Some of them are about being in physical distress, which can keep readers' attention and elicit their empathy. Some are physical reactions to emotion, which can help readers feel the emotions more themselves. Write about a character experiencing one of the following things.

1. shortness of breath and a racing heartbeat after running or other physical exertion

2. jumping into cold water

3. easing into a hot bath

4. getting a deep tissue massage

5. an aching neck from spending too much time on the computer

6. blistered feet from wearing ill-fitting shoes

7. feeling so sleepy, it's hard to keep his eyes open

8. feeling so frightened, adrenaline rushes through her body and makes her tremble

9. feeling so angry, a vein pulses in his neck

10. feeling a flutter in her stomach when she sees or talks to her crush

11. heated cheeks—from embarrassment or anger

12. a tight throat—from emotion or even incipient tears

13. the feel of velvet

14. the feel of wool

15. the feel of modeling clay

16. a burning tongue and a runny nose from eating something spicy

17. a burning tongue from drinking a beverage that's too hot

18. feeling the caffeine from her morning coffee hitting her system

19. feeling groggy after a nap

20. sweating in the hot sun

21. squishy mud underfoot

22. stones underfoot

23. dizziness

24. nausea

25. a gentle breeze

26. a cold, biting wind

27. putting weight on a sprained ankle

28. menstrual cramps

29. scratching an itch

30. getting a hug

31. the feel of a cat or dog curled up in his lap

32. a hornet sting

33. the feel of smooth satin

34. the feel of slippery soap

35. hairbrush bristles against her scalp

36. someone playing with her hair

37. a fever

38. a numb mouth after getting Novocain at the dentist

39. a needle prick

40. a pinprick

41. a high heel stepping on his bare foot

42. feeling shaky from hunger

43. feeling satisfied after a meal

44. the feel of a hot car seat

45. the feel of rough tree bark

46. an earache

47. a dislocated shoulder

48. the feel of something slimy

49. the feel of something sticky

50. the feel of something prickly

25 CHRISTMAS PROMPTS

I've done a lot of creative work in my career that centers on Christmas, so I couldn't resist including a list of Christmas prompts for stories.

1. Two people are secretly romantically interested in one another. They agree to share Christmas dinner together, just as friends, because a family holiday isn't going to happen and all of their other friends are already busy.

2. A department-store Santa who was once a Navy SEAL becomes concerned about the safety of a shopper and follows her home.

3. A person is on a difficult quest to find or make a particular gift for someone else.

4. A Christmas card arrives in the mail fifty years after it was sent.

5. The Christmas ornament is supposedly enchanted.

6. A man who has just become fabulously wealthy is picking out gifts for friends and family.

7. A woman is transported to a Christmas in a past century.

8. To impress her, he learns the words to every verse of her favorite Christmas carol. And he doesn't even like carols. Or Christmas. Or singing.

9. She embarrasses herself at a Christmas party.

10. A boat is decked out in Christmas lights.

11. One of the figures in the Nativity scene has been replaced by something completely different.

12. After the blizzard hits, they're stuck together for a while, and they have to stay warm.

13. After her neighbors complain about her outdoor Christmas decorations, she escalates the situation.

14. Two strangers wind up participating in a holiday activity together.

15. Someone has been cutting down and stealing trees from the Christmas tree farm.

16. Someone resorts to desperate measures to get home for Christmas.

17. This is the worst Christmas gift he could've imagined.

18. They're putting up a Christmas tree at the hospital.

19. It's Christmas, and he's determined to make amends.

20. Whose reindeer is this and what is it doing here?

21. She receives a gift wrapped in newspaper and duct tape.

22. At the palace, Christmas is very different from what she's used to.

23. Okay, he's not Santa, but he did have a very good reason for breaking into the house.

24. After Santa's sleigh takes off, elves realize that one bag of toys didn't get packed.

25. An actual angel shows up at the kids' Christmas pageant.

150 UNUSUAL AND BEAUTIFUL
WORDS AS PROMPTS

Like a lot of writers, I collect words that are unusual and/or that I just like the sound of, hoping to use them someday. In a few cases, I just like the word for existing. Here are some of my favorites from my journals, along with their definitions. If you have a large vocabulary, you may already know most of these!

Words are subjective, and you might dislike some that I find lovely, but that's all right—there are a lot of them here. I've stuck to English words except in cases where a foreign word has been pretty much adopted into English. Pick a favorite and use it to jump-start a journal entry, poem, or story. Perhaps you'd also enjoy starting a list of your own.

1. **amaranthine**

    An adjective meaning either a. undying, unfailing, or b. a pinkish-purply-red color, like the amaranth flower.

2. **winterbourne**

    A noun meaning a stream that flows only or mostly in the wintertime.

3. **florilegium**

    A noun, meaning an anthology or volume of writings.

4. **chaparral**

    A noun meaning a biome characterized by very dry summers, and very wet winters, and shrubs adapted to live under those conditions. It can also refer to a dense thicket of shrubs. I learned this word when living in Arizona, a state with many expanses of beautiful chaparral.

5. **palimpsest**

A noun referring to a manuscript or tablet on which the original writing or text has been erased and written over... but traces of the original text remain.

6. **sequacious**

An adjective meaning intellectually servile, or devoid of independent or original thought.

7. **tyro**

A noun meaning a beginner or a novice. I like the energetic and forceful sound of this word coupled with the meaning.

8. **meliorism**

A noun referring to the belief that the world tends to get better, and we can help it along.

9. **apophasis**

A noun. This is the act of bringing up a subject by pretending you aren't going to bring up ("We won't discuss the way you messed this up last time.")

10. **vellichor**

A noun meaning the wistful feeling one gets in used bookstores. Amazing word, I know.

11. **supertemporal**

An adjective describing something eternal or beyond time.

12. **balefire**

A noun that seems like it belongs in fantasy novels. It's an outdoor fire used as a signal.

13. **caesura**

A noun. I know this one from studying poetry: it's a break or pause in the middle of a line of verse. It can also be used for some other kind of break or interruption.

14. **nyctophilia**

A noun, meaning a preference for the darkness or the nighttime.

15. **noctivagant**

An adjective somewhat related to the above—it describes someone who wanders in the night.

16. **troika**

A noun from the Russian describing a group of three people, especially three people in charge.

17. **carmine**

A noun that means a red pigment made from cochineal (an insect), or a vivid crimson color in general.

18. **iceblink**

A noun meaning the reflected light in the sky over an ice field.

19. **trouvaille**

A noun meaning a fortunate find or an unexpected windfall.

20. **emprise**

A noun meaning an ambitious, adventurous, and/or chivalric undertaking.

21. **dysphoria**

   A noun. I love the word "euphoria," and I like knowing that "dysphoria" is its opposite: a state of feeling extremely unhappy or embittered.

22. **eudaemonism**

   A noun meaning the philosophy that personal happiness and well-being is the most important ethical goal.

23. **impavid**

   An adjective meaning undaunted or fearless.

24. **parallax**

   The noun is often used in astronomy. It refers to the way the position of an object appears to be different when viewed from different positions. It's also sometimes used specifically to describe the difference between the view of an object through a camera lens and the view through a separate viewfinder.

25. **kickshaw**

   A noun meaning a worthless trinket. I always guessed this originated in Victorian England, but it's much older: Merriam-Webster says its first known use was in 1597.

26. **lambent**

   An adjective meaning softly glowing or radiant. It can also refer to brilliance in words or expression.

27. **griffonage**

   A noun meaning terribly messy handwriting.

28. **gibbous**

An adjective meaning either humpbacked or swollen; often used to describe the moon when it's more than half full, but not completely full.

29. **macarize**

A verb meaning to declare something or someone happy or blessed.

30. **archipelago**

A noun that means a group of scattered islands.

31. **nacreous**

An adjective that sounds distasteful to me but has a pretty meaning: resembling mother-of-pearl.

32. **flummery**

A noun. It's an archaic word for nonsense or trickery, but it's also a type of dessert.

33. **oblation**

A noun meaning the act of making an offering or sacrifice in worship.

34. **oblectation**

A noun meaning pleasure or delight.

35. **sybarite**

Somewhat related to the above; a noun meaning a person who's a hedonist, devoted to pleasure and luxurious living.

36. **paladin**

A noun meaning a military leader or a champion of a cause.

37. **scintilla**

A noun related to "scintillating," this means a spark or a trace.

38. **effleurage**

A noun. It's a term from massage, meaning a light stroking movement.

39. **ephemera**

A noun that refers to paper items that are often thrown away but that someone has saved, such as tickets, flyers, old letters, and postcards.

40. **riparian**

An adjective describing something related to or located on the bank of a river.

41. **callithump**

A noun meaning an out-of-tune band or a loud parade.

42. **telos**

A noun meaning a final purpose or ultimate end.

43. **chypre**

A noun meaning a kind of perfume with earthy and mossy base notes and citrusy top notes. It's really a French word, and it's pronounced sort of like "SHEEP-ruh."

44. **sillage**

Another noun I learned from the perfume world. It refers to the degree to which the scent lingers in the air when perfume is worn. For instance, if a perfume has a strong sillage, you'll take care to apply it very lightly so you don't overpower everyone.

45. **aestival**

   Also spelled "estival," but that looks more like a typo to me. This is an adjective describing something related to summer.

46. **capricious**

   An adjective describing someone or something who's impulsive or impossible to predict.

47. **numinous**

   An adjective, describing something that has a supernatural or spiritual quality.

48. **pennyworth**

   A noun meaning a good deal or a bargain.

49. **vicissitude**

   A noun meaning the quality of being changeable or up to fate; or a good or bad thing that happens by chance.

50. **dendrophile**

   A noun meaning a person who loves trees or forests.

51. **nexus**

   A noun meaning a link or connection. It can also refer to a connected series of things.

52. **arcanum**

   A noun meaning a mystery, a secret, or secret knowledge.

53. **bellicose**

   An adjective meaning pugnacious or eager to fight.

54. **opprobrium**

   Ahh, I love this word. It's a noun meaning condemnation or harsh criticism.

55. widdershins

An adverb describing a left-hand or counter-clockwise direction.

56. astrolabe

A noun referring to an antiquated instrument to calculate the position of celestial bodies.

57. imprimatur

A noun meaning the license to print or publish, especially one granted by the Roman Catholic church or by a government.

58. elysian

An adjective used to describe a blissful or heavenly place.

59. quixotic

An adjective describing someone or something that is so idealistic or romantic as to be foolish and impractical. From Cervantes's classic novel *Don Quixote*.

60. evanescence

A noun describing the quality of disappearing or vanishing like vapor.

61. intermezzo

A noun meaning a short interlude between longer movements of a musical composition or a short independent musical composition. It can also be used to refer to a short diversion or interlude.

62. baragouin

A noun meaning unintelligible speech or jargon.

63. **élan**

An adjective borrowed from the French, meaning enthusiasm, dash, or brilliant style.

64. **maffick**

A verb meaning to celebrate loudly, publicly, and extravagantly.

65. **sophrosyne**

A noun referring to moderation or healthy self-control.

66. **pericardia**

The membranous sac around the heart.

67. **ossuary**

A noun meaning a place where bones are kept.

68. **chatoyant**

An adjective describing a gem that has a changeable luster or color.

69. **apostate**

A noun referring to someone who has rebelled against or has refused to recognize a religious faith. It can also refer to someone who's defected; a traitor.

70. **jewelweed**

A noun. This is a flower—a type of impatiens. I've read that it's a natural treatment for poison ivy, poison oak, and other rashes and skin irritants. I have no idea if this is true. The combination of something rare and valuable and something common and unwelcome makes it an interesting word to me.

71. **tessellate**

A verb meaning to decorate with mosaics, or to cover a surface with a pattern of a repeating single shape.

72. **acanthous**

An adjective meaning prickly or spiny.

73. **peripeteia**

A noun meaning a sudden and surprising change of fortune, especially in a work of literature.

74. **stentorian**

An adjective describing a booming or thundering voice.

75. **aggiornamento**

A noun meaning the act of bringing something up to date.

76. **mordacious**

An adjective meaning sarcastic or biting.

77. **petroglyph**

A noun meaning a prehistoric rock carving.

78. **novalia**

A noun meaning lands that have just been claimed or reclaimed for cultivation.

79. **rimose**

An adjective describing something with many clefts or cracks.

80. **apricity**

A noun meaning the warmth of the sun in wintertime.

81. **bitterroot**

A noun. It's a succulent herb in the purslane family, sometimes used for herbal remedies.

82. **soubrette**

A noun meaning a flirtatious young woman in a comedy, or an actress who plays that kind of part.

83. **vespertine**

An adjective describing something that's related to or occurs in the evening.

84. **esbat**

A noun meaning the meeting of a group of witches.

85. **tellurian**

An adjective describing something related to the earth, or an inhabitant of the earth.

86. **jejune**

I learned this adjective from reading Evelyn Waugh's *Brideshead Revisited* when I was an adolescent. It describes something devoid of interest or meaning.

87. **calyx**

A noun meaning the green cuplike part at the base of a flower.

88. **byzantine**

An adjective describing complicated systems with a great deal of confusing bureaucracy. It's derived from the ancient city of Byzantium and the Byzantine Empire.

89. **limn**

A verb meaning to draw, paint, describe, or delineate in detail.

90. **razzamatazz**

Also spelled "razzmatazz," and related to "razzle-dazzle." A noun meaning the quality of being showy, gaudy, or spectacular.

91. **votary**

A noun meaning someone who is devoted to a subject or way of life. It can also mean a dedicated admirer.

92. **famulus**

A noun meaning an assistant or secretary, particularly to a scholar or a magician.

93. **aegis**

A noun meaning support, protection, or patronage.

94. **lucida**

A noun meaning the brightest star in a constellation.

95. **outré**

An adjective meaning strange, unconventional, or "out there."

96. **pluvial**

An adjective meaning rainy or somehow related to rain.

97. **verdant**

An adjective meaning green and lush with vegetation. It can also mean someone who doesn't have much experience or good judgement.

98. **sangfroid**

A noun from the French, meaning the quality of composure or coolness under pressure.

99. **desideratum**

A noun for something wanted and/or believed to be necessary.

100. **hijinks**

A noun also spelled as two words, "high jinks." It means horseplay, rambunctious activities, and shenanigans.

101. **mellifluous**

An adjective describing something that is smooth and pleasant to hear.

102. **gossamer**

An adjective meaning light, translucent, or delicate, like fairy's wings.

103. **valetudinarian**

A person in poor health who's preoccupied with their ailments.

104. **lodestone**

A noun referring to the mineral magnetite. It can also refer to something that has a strong attraction.

105. **lacuna**

A noun meaning a missing space or gap. I've most often seen this refer to memory.

106. diktat

A noun meaning a harsh decree or order, particularly one imposed on a defeated party.

107. parvenu

A noun meaning someone who has recently become rich and/or important, and hasn't yet adapted the manners, dress, or home to match.

108. donnybrook

A noun, archaic I think, meaning a brawl.

109. martinet

A noun meaning a strict enforcer of rules.

110. somnambulist

A noun meaning a sleepwalker.

111. invidious

An adjective describing something that tends to cause jealousy or resentment.

112. maelstrom

A noun meaning a violent whirlpool; also used to refer to a turbulent matter.

113. sapient

An adjective meaning full of wisdom.

114. Bacchanal

A noun referring to a hedonistic and excessive party or celebration.

115. supine

An adjective meaning facing upwards.

116. moxie

An adjective meaning energy, determination, and daring.

117. titivate

A verb meaning to spruce up.

118. volvox

A noun. It's actually just a type of algae, but I think it's a great word.

119. renascent

An adjective referring to something reborn or gaining renewed energy.

120. canard

A noun meaning a widely shared but unproven belief. It can also mean a hoax or fabricated story.

121. irenic

An adjective describing someone who advocates for peace or reconciliation.

122. karst

A noun. It's a rocky landscape formed by erosion, characterized by towers, ridges, caves, sinkholes, and fissures.

123. cartophile

A noun meaning someone who loves maps.

124. **protean**

An adjective describing someone or something able to assume different forms, or describing someone or something diverse or versatile.

125. **sonoluminescence**

A noun. I like the concept as much as I like the word. It refers to the light that some liquids give off when certain intense high-frequency sounds or ultrasonic waves pass through them.

126. **obstreperous**

An adjective meaning loud, boisterous, or out of control.

127. **minatory**

An adjective meaning menacing or threatening.

128. **marmoreal**

An adjective describing something that's similar to or related to marble.

129. **gasconade**

A noun meaning excessive boasting.

130. **pervicacious**

An adjective meaning stubborn and refusing to change one's mind.

131. **klaxon**

A noun meaning a loud mechanical horn—usually an emergency or warning alarm.

132. laodicean

A noun referring to someone who doesn't care much about religion or politics.

133. verdigris

A noun meaning the green patina that forms on copper, bronze, and brass. It can also refer to that shade of green (which is a little blueish).

134. aliferous

An adjective describing someone or something with wings.

135. nocent

An adjective that's the opposite of innocent! It means guilty or harmful.

136. afterclap

A noun. This is an unexpected negative consequence of an event that was assumed to be over and done with. Isn't that a great word? I love it.

137. sussurus

A noun, meaning a murmuring, buzzing, or whispering sound.

138. bricolage

A noun meaning something put together out of whatever materials or ideas happened to be available.

139. fantod

A noun meaning a state of tension or irritability.

140. torpor

A noun meaning a state of inactivity in which one is barely conscious.

141. sacristy

A noun meaning a room in a church where sacred objects are stored.

142. prolix

An adjective meaning garrulous and tending to discuss things in too great of detail.

143. lazaretto

A noun meaning a hospital for patients with contagious diseases.

144. madid

An adjective meaning wet or moist.

145. paean

A noun meaning a song of praise or thanksgiving.

146. uxorious

An adjective meaning excessively fond of or devoted to one's wife.

147. lethe

A noun meaning oblivion or forgetfulness; derived from the river Lethe in Greek mythology.

148. margaritomancy

A noun meaning divination using pearls.

149. pronoia

This is a neologism, but I'm really fond of it. It's the opposite of paranoia: the sense that people are secretly out to help you, and the universe itself is conspiring in your favor.

150. **lexiphanic**

An adjective describing someone who uses fancy or obscure words in a pretentious way.

50 WRITING PROMPTS INSPIRED BY TAROT

Tarot cards have long been a source of inspiration for writers and artists. The divinatory messages and timeless archetypes often appeal to creative minds. You don't have to believe in the ability of Tarot cards to predict the future in order to use them to send your imagination in a new direction.

For this list, I've used all of the major arcana and some of the minor arcana. I've taken a lot of creative liberties with Tarot card meanings, and with any of my writing prompts, I think you should do the same.

1. **The Fool:** write about someone beginning a new adventure or journey, with no idea of where it might lead.

2. **The Magician:** write about someone performing real magic or the illusion of it.

3. **The High Priestess:** write about a female religious figure.

4. **The Empress:** write about a powerful pregnant woman.

5. **The Emperor:** write about a stern patriarch.

6. **The Hierophant:** write about someone who insists upon convention or conformity.

7. **The Lovers:** write about two lovers who face a difficult choice.

8. **The Chariot:** write about someone taking a victory lap, literally or figuratively.

9. **Strength:** write about someone fighting a wild animal.

10. **The Hermit:** write about someone who has isolated himself or herself in search of some truth.

11. **Wheel of Fortune:** write about a stroke of extraordinary bad luck.

12. **Justice:** write about a guilty person's punishment or an innocent person's reprieve.

13. **The Hanged Man:** write about someone who calmly makes a huge sacrifice.

14. **Death:** write about the end of a life, relationship, job, or living situation that brings relief.

15. **Temperance:** write about someone who uses patience or self-control in a difficult situation.

16. **The Devil:** write about someone giving in to temptation.

17. **The Tower:** write about a city or citadel under attack.

18. **The Star:** write about the one thing that gives a character hope when things look bleak.

19. **The Moon:** write about a disturbing dream.

20. **The Sun:** write about an event filled with sunshine and joy.

21. **Judgement:** write about a character who realizes he has a calling or a purpose to fulfill.

22. **The World:** write about someone who's on top of the world.

23. **Two of Wands:** write about someone making a decision between two jobs or two creative ventures.

24. **Four of Wands:** write about some type of homecoming.

25. **Five of Wands:** write about five people arguing about how to achieve a goal.

26. **Seven of Wands:** write about someone defending their property.

27. **Nine of Wands:** write about someone who is exhausted but still striving.

28. **Knight of Wands:** write about someone making a grand gesture.

29. **King of Wands:** write about a leader giving a speech to rally the troops.

30. **Ace of Cups:** write about a gift of love.

31. **Three of Cups:** write about a small celebration with friends.

32. **Four of Cups:** write about someone who absolutely cannot get motivated.

33. **Six of Cups:** write about someone who is nostalgic for her childhood.

34. **Eight of Cups:** write about someone who is abandoning a dream.

35. **Page of Cups:** write about someone giving a toast.

36. **Queen of Cups:** write about someone who's uncannily intuitive.

37. **Two of Swords:** write about someone making a decision when both options are bad.

38. **Five of Swords:** write about someone who's alienated his friends or family.

39. **Six of Swords:** write about someone who is forced to move to a new residence or go on a journey.

40. **Eight of Swords:** write about someone who feels trapped, but really isn't.

41. **Ten of Swords:** write about someone who's been stabbed in the back.

42. **Knight of Swords:** write about someone who makes a rash and extreme decision.

43. **Queen of Swords:** write about an intellectual who's lacking in emotion.

44. **Ace of Pentacles:** write about someone who just got a great job offer.

45. **Three of Pentacles:** write about a graduation.

46. **Five of Pentacles:** write about someone who has become destitute or homeless.

47. **Seven of Pentacles:** write about a harvest.

48. **Nine of Pentacles:** write about someone enjoying the good life.

49. **Page of Pentacles:** write about someone starting a new business.

50. **King of Pentacles:** write about a generous billionaire.

25 PROMPTS TO MELT PEOPLE'S HEARTS

Some of these might even make readers cry a little, since many of us are even more likely to tear up at kindness and goodness than we are at sad events. Readers are likely to remember a sweet moment in a story, and it can even make them feel better about life and about the world.

1. Someone gives a lonely person a gift.

2. A parent, friend, or significant other gives him a gift that reflects respect for his life choices or support of his dreams.

3. A child gives her a piece of artwork that depicts her in a flattering or affectionate light.

4. He helps or stands up for an opponent or rival.

5. A person falls asleep cuddling with an animal.

6. An animal cuddles with a stuffed animal.

7. A dog or cat is adopted from a shelter and seems overjoyed to be heading home at last.

8. Someone does an act of kindness in secret.

9. Two people who have been married for sixty or more years are still romantic and flirty with one another.

10. A person finally achieves her childhood goal...when she's in her nineties.

11. Someone brings flowers or a treat to the person he loves for no particular occasion.

12. Someone waits a long time in a car or a waiting room for the person she loves.

13. He remembers how she takes her coffee or tea.

14. She re-creates a holiday or special event because they missed it.

15. When she's taking a shower, he puts her bathrobe in the dryer and wraps her up in it as soon as she gets out.

16. He sings a goofy made-up song to his kid.

17. Someone hugs someone who doesn't expect it...and who realizes he loves it.

18. The people in a workplace, school, or community join together to do something kind.

19. He visits his grandma or great-aunt regularly.

20. She starts a standing ovation for her friend's performance or speech (which, to be honest, is only okay).

21. He gets flustered—and touched—by an unexpected compliment.

22. He repairs someone else's item after it got broken.

23. She makes a spur-of-the-moment decision to make a big sacrifice for someone else.

24. He's a tough guy, but he's brought to tears for a sentimental reason.

25. She returns to the place she was the happiest.

50 "MEET CUTE" IDEAS

"Meet cute" is a screenplay writing term in which two people, destined to fall in love, meet for the first time. Sometimes, the meeting is awkward; in fact, many, many meet cutes involve the characters actually bumping into one another.

A scene that brings two perfect strangers together can be funny and memorable. First encounters are just as important in fiction.

This list isn't limited to romance. You could also use these prompts to think about how two future best friends meet—or take things in a more sinister direction, and use them to introduce future enemies, or a future predator and his or her victim.

1. She mistakes him for an intruder.

2. He mistakes her for his online date.

3. She keeps contacting tech support because nothing's working since she installed the upgrade on her computer. He's the tech support guy.

4. Their dogs seem to be attracted to one another.

5. He leaves his hot dog unattended for a moment, and her dog eats it.

6. They both recapture or subdue a wild animal or creature on the loose.

7. She kicks off her shoes—and one hits him.

8. She's a real estate agent, and the woman shows up for her open house.

9. He works for the admissions department, and he's giving her a tour of the university.

10. They attend a meetup or political rally and no one else is there—not even the organizer.

11. They're both pulled onstage by a performer.

12. She accidentally spills a beer on him at a concert or sporting event.

13. He drowns his sorrows at a bar after discovering that his girlfriend's cheating on him. She's the bartender.

14. It's his day to move into the apartment. She's not finished moving out of it yet.

15. He sees her struggling to move a piece of furniture—or a large and unusual item—into her new apartment, and he lends a hand.

16. She's his new neighbor, and she knocks on the door asking to borrow an unusual item.

17. She responds to his online ad for an unusual item for sale.

18. They're bidding against one another at an auction.

19. When they were small children, he had a big crush on her and passed her a love note in class.

20. She comes over to get her friend's belongings from his apartment after he and her friend break up.

21. He meets her at the restaurant, believing she's asked him on a date. It's really an elaborate setup of her grandmother's, who knows him and thinks he's a nice boy.

22. At a party, she asks him to pretend to be her date so a guy who's been pestering her will leave her alone.

23. After a party, he contacts her to apologize on behalf of his best friend, who was drunk and rude.

24. After a party, she asks the host for the number of a guy she enjoyed talking to. The host, confused, gives her the number of a different guy.

25. They spar in a martial arts class.

26. They're assigned to be partners in a dancing or cooking class.

27. He finds and returns her lost item.

28. She chases after him to return something he dropped. He was leaving it behind on purpose for the other secret agent to pick up.

29. He's in the ER after his daredevil behavior led to an accident, and the other man is the doctor.

30. They both become volunteer firefighters at the same time.

31. They both decided to rob the store, house, or museum on the same night.

32. She's a police officer who mistakes him for a fleeing suspect.

33. A tyrannical judge arrests a feisty prosecutor in contempt of court, and he's the deputy who reluctantly removes her from the courtroom.

34. At the City Council meeting, one of them speaks up in favor of a proposal, and one speaks out against it.

35. He always likes to dip his fries in barbecue sauce, so he's disappointed the restaurant doesn't have any. From the next table, she hands him the small bottle of it she carries in her purse.

36. He's an awkward guy in general and at a dinner party, he makes a reference that no one else gets—except her.

37. They share a ride to or from the airport.

38. He plays a violin in the subway, and he's so good, she has to stop to listen.

39. She's a workaholic who comes into the office before dawn. He's the new security guard who lets her in.

40. They're cheering for their children at a soccer game or recital.

41. She's the face painter he hired for his child's birthday party.

42. They seem to have purchased tickets for the same seat at an event...

43. Or they've somehow made a reservation for the same hotel room, bed and breakfast suite, or rental cabin.

44. He sees her near the lake. Takes another good look. Distracted, he walks off the edge of the pier into the water.

45. He sees her by the side of the road, trying to fix her bicycle, and stops to help.

46. She's arguing with a friend or date about some obscure subject and he chimes in to support her point of view.

47. He accidentally walks in on her while she's bathing or showering.

48. She's an Ivy League student working on her advanced calculus homework at a café. He's a barista, and he looks over her shoulder and corrects her work. She's irritated. But he's right.

49. They meet at the wedding rehearsal, where she's the maid of honor and he's the minister.

50. They're the only two single people at the New Year's Eve party, and they agree to kiss at midnight for good luck.

Your characters, like you, sometimes need to get out of the house or away from work and have a little fun. If you're writing a romance and you want your couple to do something fun together, these prompts might give you some ideas. Of course, you can also make things go horribly wrong for a different kind of story! Some of these could also be used for friend or family time in your story.

I've included some ideas that are more urban, and some that would make more sense for small town or rural settings. Some are very expensive, for stories about wealthy characters, while others don't cost a thing. It can be a lot of fun if one of the characters is used to the activity, while the other is completely out of his or her element. If you get some ideas here for things to do with your significant other in real life, so much the better.

Your characters could...

1. Visit an aquarium.

2. Go four-wheeling or ATVing.

3. Go to a Renaissance festival.

4. Go to a basketball, baseball, football, or hockey game. This could be professional, minor league, college, high school, or Little League.

5. Take a hot yoga class.

6. Go to the state fair.

7. Attend a wine tasting, whiskey tasting, or chocolate tasting.

8. Attend a rock concert.

9. Go rock climbing …in real life or at an indoor gym.

10. Visit a museum.

11. Take turns performing karaoke at a bar.

12. Drive out to the country to look up at the stars.

13. Watch fireworks.

14. Go berry picking in the early summer, or apple picking in the late summer or early fall.

15. Go on a hike to see the autumn leaves.

16. Go sledding.

17. Play miniature golf.

18. Tour a vineyard, brewery, or coffee roasting facility.

19. Have a photo shoot.

20. Go ice-skating.

21. Go to church together.

22. Make dinner together.

23. Bake cookies together.

24. Go to the beach.

25. Go to the zoo or a wildlife sanctuary.

26. Test-drive an expensive sports car.

27. Go fishing on a lake.

28. Take a day cruise on her yacht.

29. Ride bikes.

30. Meet for cocktails at a jazz club.

31. Meet at the dog park.

32. Take dance lessons.

33. Go to a farmer's market.

34. Take a hot air balloon ride.

35. Go on a nighttime helicopter ride over the city.

36. Take a walk in an old graveyard.

37. Visit a commercial haunted house before Halloween.

38. Go horseback riding.

39. Go to an archery range.

40. Play ping-pong or pool.

41. Go thrift store shopping.

42. Attend a free lecture.

43. Attend a child's play or concert.

44. Go bowling.

45. Go to a racetrack...could be cars, could be horses.

46. Tour a historic home.

47. Play a board game.

48. Make s'mores, outdoors or over a fireplace at home.

49. Go to the opera.

50. Attend a party together.

50 FIGHT SCENE IDEAS

1. Two people fight without waking or disturbing a third person.

2. Someone uses an object that isn't usually considered to be dangerous as an effective weapon.

3. It's impossible to tell the real opponents from the ones who are illusions or holograms.

4. People fight in zero gravity.

5. People fight underwater.

6. People fight in a building that's on fire.

7. Two people fight, and an unlikely bystander saves our main character.

8. Two people fight, but when a third person attacks our main character, his other opponent saves him.

9. Fortunately, his blood is also a weapon.

10. One of the fighters is drugged or drunk.

11. Someone's trying to unmask the person who's attacking him.

12. Someone finds out that she's fighting the person she meant to join forces with or save.

13. Someone fights while wearing something that makes them appear the opposite of tough or intimidating.

14. They fight naked.

15. They fight in Times Square on New Year's Eve.

16. A protester and counter-protester fight.

17. Someone shoves his opponent into a body of water, and then rescues him when it's apparent he'll drown.

18. Someone gets help from an animal.

19. A friend, co-worker, or ally suddenly attacks someone.

20. One person dumps a gallon of something over the other person's head.

21. One person chokes the other with a computer cord.

22. One person chokes the other with a string of Christmas lights.

23. Someone defends herself from an attacker while driving at top speed.

24. They fight in a hospital, which makes it easy for the main character to patch himself up afterward.

25. Bullying the bartender or server was a mistake.

26. She knocks out two men with one move.

27. They fight in a locked closet.

28. He celebrates his victory too early.

29. Someone leaps from a considerable height to land on an opponent.

30. Someone breaks the rules of the duel.

31. Her opponent vaporizes before she can stab him.

32. He accidentally wounds a bystander.

33. Someone was only pretending to be knocked out.

34. Her weapon gets stuck.

35. Priceless objects get damaged in the brawl.

36. Someone uses a bed sheet in the struggle.

37. The fight is a ruse to distract people from what's really going on.

38. Someone repeatedly tries to avoid the fight to no avail.

39. Someone takes refuge in a disgusting place.

40. He finds himself battling a creature he didn't believe existed.

41. They fight on slick ice.

42. He fights three challengers in succession.

43. Her glasses get destroyed and she can barely see.

44. He steals his opponent's car, not realizing his allies rigged it with an explosive.

45. Someone's ridiculous move or antic catches an opponent off guard.

46. Someone loses an opponent in the crowd and then finds her again.

47. A garden tool becomes a deadly weapon.

48. Someone hurls a shopping cart through the air.

49. Someone gets bashed with a crown or tiara.

50. He accidentally kills his opponent.

50 DESPERATE MEASURES

For most writers, one of the main goals is to tell a story that isn't boring. One way to keep things interesting is to have a character do something they thought they'd never do in order to reach a goal or to prevent something terrible from happening. For much less angsty scenes, it's also inspiring—and touching—to see someone make do with what they've got.

Here are fifty examples of things your characters could do.

1. Sell a beloved or important possession in order to pay for something he (or someone he loves) desperately needs.

2. Make a Halloween costume with items sitting around the house.

3. Cook for a dinner party or reception with food that's already in the fridge and cupboards.

4. Live off canned food for a month...with no stove in sight.

5. Murder an innocent person in order to keep him from giving information that would lead to the deaths of many others.

6. Escape by jumping on the boxcar of a freight train headed who knows where.

7. Eat or drink something poisonous so the enemy will do the same.

8. Improvise when no tampons or sanitary pads are available.

9. Escape via the sewer.

10. Pretend not to speak English in order to avoid a conversation.

11. Get married to someone he's not interested in so he can stay in the country.

12. Get married to someone she's not interested in so her children will be provided for.

13. Hide in the bathroom for an hour to avoid another guest at the party.

14. Cut and color her hair in order to match someone else's driver's license or passport.

15. Inject himself with a substance in order to test his hypothesis about it.

16. Beg a new mother to nurse a baby who isn't her own.

17. Drive a car without your glasses or contact lenses to escape.

18. Do all your Christmas shopping at the last minute, at a convenience store or an airport gift shop.

19. Make a coffee filter out of a paper towel or some other material.

20. Stitch up a wound with non-medical materials and no prior experience or knowledge of how to do so.

21. Try out a dangerous magical spell.

22. Make an alliance with a former enemy.

23. Ask a dangerous monster for help.

24. Infect her blood with a vampire-killing virus and then offer herself to a vampire.

25. Go to the dance or the party with someone he doesn't really like, because he needs to be there for another purpose.

26. Commit a robbery to get the money for a life-saving medical treatment or procedure.

27. Break the chairs and burn them in the fireplace to stay warm.

28. Cut off his leg to get out of a trap or to stop the infection from spreading.

29. Wash her hair with bar soap because there's no shampoo and conditioner.

30. Risk drinking water from a questionable source rather than dying of thirst.

31. Take shelter somewhere disgusting in order to stay warm.

32. Stay with a sketchy stranger rather than staying on the street.

33. Participate in a crime to gain the trust of a gang or crime syndicate in order to take it down.

34. Shoot his friend dead in order to spare him a more prolonged and painful death.

35. Go two nights without sleep in order to make a deadline.

36. Bring the chickens into the house after the coop burns down.

37. Sell her hair for money.

38. Sell his plasma for money.

39. Make a grilled cheese sandwich or a fried egg on a clothes iron.

40. Build furniture out of cinder blocks, discarded doors, and oil drums.

41. Build a house out of shipping containers and recycled lumber.

42. Head out with his wagon and team of horses into a blizzard to retrieve food and supplies for the tiny town on the prairie.

43. Get out of the car and relieve herself behind a shrub when the freeway traffic is so bad that she won't get to the next exit for another hour.

44. Abandon ship even though he doesn't exactly know how to swim.

45. Use someone else's credit card after filing off part of the name, telling the sales associate it got stuck in a faulty machine.

46. Burn the house to the ground because it's haunted.

47. Raid dumpsters for food.

48. Use a dab of body lotion or some gel from an aloe vera plant in lieu of hair gel.

49. Live in the basement of the home he was evicted from until he can figure out his next move.

50. Pack up and move to another city in the middle of the night to get away from someone.

---

50 HAPPY EVER AFTER PROMPTS

Happy endings are frequently maligned. Some people will argue that they aren't like real life—but the fact that real life is painful, difficult, and unjust is exactly why so many people prefer happy endings in their books, TV shows, and movies. A happy resolution that feels realistic and "earned" can take more finesse and talent than leaving a story unresolved or ending in despair.

1. The dog and the owner find each other again.

2. The innocent man is acquitted.

3. The captive escapes.

4. The special event turns out perfectly.

5. She gets the job.

6. He gets the promotion.

7. She starts her own business.

8. The business is saved.

9. The underdog wins.

10. They discover a cure.

11. The patient recovers.

12. They have a baby.

13. She gets away with it.

14. He sees the light and changes his ways.

15. The rescue is a success.

16. It can fly.

17. He accepts the wedding proposal.

18. The house is restored to its former glory.

19. The magnificent animal is successfully returned to the wild.

20. The former enemies are now friends.

21. The student graduates.

22. The orphan is adopted.

23. The father and son reconcile.

24. The superpower is restored.

25. He makes it home safely at last.

26. She finally travels to the place of her dreams.

27. He learns how much everyone really cares about him.

28. They save the planet/town/park from destruction.

29. The curse is broken.

30. The best candidate wins the election.

31. She inherits the estate.

32. The war is over.

33. The unjust law is changed.

34. The beloved one returns.

35. The wrongdoer is exposed.

36. The two confess their love for one another at last.

37. They make it to safety.

38. Her work finally gets the respect it deserves.

39. The former lovers renew their commitment.

40. He does what everyone said he would never be able to do.

41. She reveals her secret, and her revelation is met not with condemnation, but understanding.

42. He learns that he made a big positive difference.

43. The public park, school for underprivileged children, free hospital, or other benevolent institution opens.

44. The monster is killed.

45. She dares to chase the dream she's been ignoring all along.

46. It arrives just in time.

47. She finds evidence that the deceased person always loved her, despite everything.

48. He learns the truth about what really happened – and it's much more positive than he'd imagined.

49. She is granted a second chance and makes the most of it.

50. The dead person has come back to life.

100 POETRY EXERCISES

My background is in poetry, so I couldn't help but include a list of poetry-writing exercises.

Of course, most, if not all, of the writing prompts in this book can be used for poetry. I would especially recommend the autobiographical prompts, image prompts, and sound prompts for inspiration.

This section includes not only prompts, but also other exercises and suggestions for getting inspired. Some of them can be used for fiction and journaling, too!

I think the best way for poets to get inspired—and to learn—is to read a lot of poetry. But hopefully, you'll find plenty of approaches here that get your creative juices flowing as well.

1. Pick a song on your iPod, phone, or a playlist at random and let it influence you as you quickly write a first draft of a poem.

2. Go to a café, library, or fast food restaurant. Sit where you can see the door. Write a poem about the next person who walks in.

3. You can also do this in a public place where there are a lot of people talking: write a poem based on an overheard conversation.

4. Write a poem in the form of a shopping list.

5. Write a poem in the form of a to-do list.

6. Write a poem that's a set of directions or instructions.

7. Write a poem that incorporates copy from a real set of directions or instructions—in a manual, on a product label, etc.

8. Write a poem about a wild animal. Mary Oliver has written many poems like this that might inspire you, including "The Hermit Crab," "The Shark," and "Wild Geese."

9. Write a poem from the *point of view* of a wild animal.

10. Write a poem from the point of view of an inanimate object.

11. Write a poem that's purely a dialogue between two or more people.

12. Take a long walk and take a journal along. Sit down outside and write a poem.

13. Take a long drive and bring a way to record yourself. Try dictating lines of a poem out loud. Say whatever comes into your head. You can use only the good stuff later when you put it down on paper.

14. Write a poem from the point of view of a famous person you like.

15. Write a poem from the point of view of a famous person you loathe.

16. Write a poem in which some words have been crossed out and replaced with other words.

17. Write a poem inspired by a piece of art. (By the way, the

word for a poem or literary work inspired by visual art is *ekphrasis*. Pretty cool, right?)

18. Write a poem with a refrain: a line or a few lines that repeat, like the chorus of a song.

19. Write a poem that's a prophecy: about your life, someone else's, or about the world. César Vallejo's poem "Black Stone on a White Stone," translated from the Spanish, might inspire you.

20. Write a poem that's a series of made-up epitaphs on gravestones.

21. Set your alarm for two hours earlier than you usually wake up. Put a notebook and pen next to your bed. When you wake up, free-write for about fifteen minutes. ("Free-writing" means "writing down whatever pops into your head, without thinking too hard about it.") If you woke up in the middle of a dream, use the dream as inspiration; otherwise, just write whatever comes into your head. Go back to sleep. Later, turn your free-writing into a poem.

22. Go somewhere you won't be disturbed. If you get interrupted a lot in your home, some libraries will allow you to rent a room with a door you can close to the world. You can also try going to a park.

    Set an alarm to go off in three minutes. Close your eyes and breathe deeply. Attempt to clear your mind as much as possible, just focusing on your breathing. When the alarm goes off, very calmly fill out a page with free-writing.

23. Write a poem that's an email or letter to someone, living or dead.

24. Write a poem that's an open letter to a whole group of people.

25. Do this one with a friend. Each of you writes down two nouns and two verbs. Then you switch with one another and write the best poem you can in twenty minutes using their words. (You can conjugate the verbs however you like.)

26. I got this one from one of my poetry professors, though I'm sorry to say I can't remember which one: start with a poem written in a language you don't speak a word of, and "translate" it into your native tongue.

27. Rewrite an old poem—19th century or earlier—into a modern one. Make more changes, until you've gotten completely away from the source material.

28. Write a poem in which every line begins with the same word. You can change that in revision...or maybe you won't want to.

29. For this one, you'll need to either write in a notebook or journal, or on your phone. Go to a store that would be a weird place to write a poem—like a convenience store, a department store, or a drugstore—and write a quick poem.

30. Write a poem that focuses on one color. Federico García Lorca's poem "Somnambulist Ballad," translated from the Spanish, or Diane Wakoski's poem "Blue Monday" might inspire you.

31. Write a poem designed to get yourself through the hard times. Langston Hughes's poem "The Island" might inspire you.

32. Write a poem expressing joy or gratitude. e.e. cummings's poem "i thank you God for most this amazing" might inspire you.

33. Write a poem that's a series of positive affirmations. It's okay if they're weird. In fact, it's almost certainly better if they're weird.

34. Write a poem that's a series of questions.

35. Write a poem that's in the form of an interview, with questions and answers.

36. Write a pantoum. A pantoum is a poem with four-line stanzas. Lines 2 and 4 of the first stanza become lines 1 and 3 of the following stanza. And then lines 2 and 4 of that stanza become lines 1 and 3 of the next one…you get the idea. (Do an Internet search of pantoums to see examples.) Write as many stanzas as you want, but lines 2 and 4 of the final stanza should be lines 1 and 3 of the first stanza.

37. **Write a poem in iambs.**

   An iamb is a combination of an unstressed syllable followed by a stressed syllable. If you have a line written in iambs, the rhythm is like this:

   da-DA da-DA da-DA da-DA da-DA

   Shakespeare's sonnets are great examples of poetry written in iambs. Actually, they're in iambic pentameter, which means there are five "da-DAs" in every line. And of course, they're rhymed.

   But for this exercise, you don't have to rhyme, and you don't have to make the lines all the same length. You can have a line with two iambs, like this:

I wonder why

Followed by a line with eight iambs, like this:

our parents left us in the woods that night with no granola bars

Do whatever you want! Just try to get the rhythm right.

38. **Write a haiku—or several.**

   The original Japanese form of haiku is specific to the Japanese language. If you want to know more about that, do an Internet search on haiku and "cutting words." It's fascinating!

   The English version of haiku is usually a three-line poem in which the first line has 5 syllables, the second has 7 syllables, and the third has 5 syllables. It's a fun way to write short poems.

   Because Japanese haiku frequently focus on a specific image from nature, you might want to try doing the same.

39. Write a poem that's a collection of six-word stories.

40. If there's a poet you just *love*, read about ten poems by them. Then pretend you're them and write a new poem. You'll think you're imitating their voice, but you'll really be learning more about your own...

41. Or pretend you're a particular fictional character, and write a poem while you're pretending you're them.

42. Have you ever had the experience of misunderstanding a lyric in a song? Use the phrase or line you *thought* you heard in a poem.

43. Write a poem about dawn.

44. Write a poem about midnight.

45. Write a poem that argues for something ridiculous.

46. Write an acrostic poem. The first letter of each line spells out a word vertically down the left-hand side of the page. Even for serious poets who would never try to publish an acrostic poem, this is a great exercise to get creative juices flowing.

47. Write a poem that includes homonyms—words that have the same sound but different spellings and meanings, such as "presents" and "presence," "piece" and "peace," etc.

48. Tell your subconscious (or your muse, if you prefer), *out loud,* that it/she/he has a half hour to inspire you. Take a half hour to clean or tidy up. Then write.

49. Ask a friend for a random subject for a poem. Whatever they say, write a poem about it.

50. Close your eyes, flip through a book, and put your finger on a page. Whatever word you're pointing at, use it as a poem title and write that poem.

51. If you want to force yourself to get back into the writing habit: make yourself write a poem a day for a week.

52. If you're really serious about it: make that a poem a day for a month. (If you live in the U.S. or Canada, you might do this in April. Both countries recognize April as National Poetry Month.)

53. If you're really, really serious about it: post a new poem every day for a month on social media, even if some of them are pretty bad. (You may get more readers on

Facebook than you'd ever get if you published in some literary journals.)

54. Write a poem that's a series of imaginary tweets or an imaginary Facebook post.

55. Read a science article and let it inspire a poem.

56. Read a business article and let it inspire a poem.

57. Read an article about sports and let it inspire a poem.

58. Write a poem that proves, disproves, or rewrites a familiar cliché.

59. Write a poem saying goodbye to someone or something. It could be a happy poem, a sad poem, or both.

60. Write a poem confessing to a crime you did not commit.

61. Write a poem bragging of a triumph you have not accomplished (or not yet, anyway).

62. Write a poem that uses a word or two that you just invented. Lewis Carroll's poem "Jabberwocky" might inspire you.

63. Write a poem about an imaginary or idyllic place. Samuel Taylor Coleridge's description of Xanadu in his poem "Kubla Khan" might inspire you.

64. Write a poem set in a real city or other place…but not one that you've ever visited.

65. Write a poem late at night, by hand, by candlelight.

66. Fill a page with free-writing…with your eyes closed.

67. Or fill a page with free-writing using your non-dominant hand. (This idea and the one before it can help you tap into less rational, more creative thought patterns.)

68. Write a poem that's a list of numbered reasons. Reasons for what? That's up to you.

69. Write a poem that's a list of rules...or rules to break.

70. Write a poem about a certain food. Kevin Young's odes to food, including "Ode to Okra," and "Ode to Pepper Vinegar," might inspire you.

71. Write a poem about physical pain you've experienced.

72. Write a poem about physical pleasure you've experienced.

73. Write a poem about being in a hurry. Eliminate punctuation and break the lines in odd places to mimic a fast pace.

74. If you work a day job, try writing a poem on your lunch hour. The poet Frank O'Hara did this. You can check out his book *Lunch Poems*.

75. Do you have a smartphone that allows you to set alarms? For an entire day, carry it with you. Set alarms to go off at odd times every hour. Every time the alarm goes off, write down a few lines of random poetry. At the end of the day, take a look at what you've got and see if you can put it together into a poem.

76. Alternately, get together with writing friends, set a half-hour timer, and write in silence together for the whole thirty minutes. This is a great method for writers who are easily distracted.

77. Write a poem about mist.

78. Write a poem about lightning.

79. If you're an Internet addict, take a whole weekend off from the Internet and then write a poem. See if the break changes your thinking!

80. Write a poem that is a magical spell.

81. Write a poem from the point of view of an angel.

82. Write a poem from the point of view of a ghost.

83. Write a poem about the human body (yours, someone else's, or in general), or about just a part of it.

84. Write the first draft of a poem using a Sharpie and a big piece of poster board or sheet of butcher paper.

85. Ride public transit and write a poem. If you regularly ride public transit, take a new route.

86. Be safe, but: walk in a neighborhood that's new to you, and then write a poem.

87. Attend a poetry reading. While sitting in the audience, discreetly write a poem of your own…

88. Or, write a poem while listening to a speech or lecture.

89. Write a poem with very short lines—two or three words, four at the most. Gwendolyn Brooks's poem "We Real Cool" may inspire you.

90. Write a poem with very long lines. Walt Whitman's collection *Leaves of Grass* may inspire you.

91. Write a poem inspired by a familiar story. Anne Sexton's collection *Transformations* may inspire you.

92. Write a poem that's a curse.

93. Write a poem that's a prayer.

94. Write a poem that takes place before a fight.

95. Write a poem that takes place after a party.

96. Write a poem addressing two people about to get married.

97. Write a poem addressing a newborn baby.

98. Write a series of seven short poems—one for each day of the week.

99. Write a series of twelve short poems—one for each month of the year.

100. Use a funny saying on a tee shirt or a bumper sticker as the title of your poem.

AUTOBIOGRAPHICAL AND BLOGGING PROMPTS

This section is especially for people who write personal essays, nonfiction, memoirs, or blogs. If you interview others, you may find ideas for questions in this section. And if you manage a social media account, the prompts here could also spark more content to keep your followers engaged. Share a fun fact or two about you—and ask people to do the same.

If you're an aspiring blogger, or if you've been blogging for a while and could use some new ideas, I hope this section will help!

Any writer or creative person with social media accounts knows how important it is to inspire comments and engagement. Here's one of the great secrets of conversation (and it's not actually that secret): most people love to talk about themselves. You might find questions in this section that you can pose to your followers.

This section can help with your fiction or screenplay writing as well. If you assume the point of view of a character, write in their voice, you're likely to uncover new truths about them that will make your story richer.

100 GENERAL AUTOBIOGRAPHICAL PROMPTS

1. Tell your story about a stroke of luck that turned out to be unlucky, or a time when you should have been careful of what you wished for.

2. Tell your story about how a setback or unfortunate event turned out to be a blessing in disguise.

3. Tell your story about a time you lost something important to you.

4. Write about a time you learned an important lesson.

5. Write about a lesson you never seem to learn.

6. Write a letter to your younger self (you choose the age) with advice.

7. Write about the best time you had in the past year.

8. Write about the worst time you had in the past year.

9. Write about a significant change you've made in the past five years.

10. Write about what the number 10 means to you. You can write about a child at the age of 10, a 10th anniversary of something, or about 10 as a dress size, a shoe size, a perfect score... you get the idea.

11. Write about one way in which your life is better than it was ten years ago.

12. Tell your story about an amazing place you visited.

13. Tell your story about a challenging vacation or road trip.

14. Tell your story about a car you owned or drove.

15. What part of the day or night is your favorite, and why?

16. Which meal of the day is your favorite, and why?

17. Write about one of the weirdest foods or drinks you've ever tried.

18. Write about a past experience of yours that few other people share.

19. Write about one thing that energizes you.

20. Write about one thing that exhausts you.

21. Write about what the color orange means to you. It could be a team color, a school color, the favorite color of someone you love, a color in nature, or so on.

22. Write about the time you got to meet somebody famous... or write about a famous person you would like to meet, and why.

23. Write about one of your guilty pleasures.

24. Write about a way you indulge yourself.

25. Write about a time you got an exciting delivery in the mail.

26. Write a letter to someone that you could never send...but you wish you could.

27. Write about the contents of your purse, backpack, or wallet, or about one item in there.

28. Tell your story about a time when you were so sad, you felt like you almost couldn't go on.

29. Write about the last time you cried.

30. Write about the last time you laughed really hard.

31. Write about everything that's making you happy today.

32. Write about something you love to shop for...something you hate to shop for...or about loving or hating to shop in general.

33. Describe an interaction you had with a stranger.

34. Describe an interaction you had with the police.

35. What's one thing you wish people would ask you about? What would you tell them?

36. What's one thing you wish people would never ask you about again? Why?

37. Write about a time when you dealt with someone who behaved in a disturbing way.

38. Write about a time when you were completely confused.

39. Write about one thing that confuses you right now.

40. Write about a time you truly felt like an adult...or, if you're not an adult yet, write about a time when you felt like you were really growing up.

41. Tell your story about a time you felt old.

42. Tell your story about a time you felt like a kid (assuming you are not one).

43. Tell your story about fire. It could be a house fire, a forest fire, a bonfire, candles...any fire.

44. Tell your story about water: the ocean, a swimming pool, a bathtub, a drink of water...any water.

45. Write about a time that someone gossiped or lied about you.

46. Write about a time when you were dancing and you loved it...or hated it.

47. Write about what Monday means to you.

48. Describe your trip to a state fair or amusement park, or write about why you would or wouldn't like to go to one.

49. What's an activity that a lot of people seem to enjoy that isn't fun to you at all?

50. What's something you love doing that hardly anyone you know is interested in?

51. Write about whether you curse a lot, or not at all...and why.

52. Tell your story about running. You might have been running after someone or something, from someone or something, or running on purpose.

53. Write about a memorable time you attended, participated in, or watched a sporting event.

54. Write about three things (not people) that you can't live without.

55. Tell your story about a time you threw caution to the wind... or about a time when, looking back, you wish you had.

56. Tell your story about a time you felt ignored or taken for granted.

57. Tell your story about when you had to wait for a very long time.

58. Write about what you would do with an extra million dollars.

59. If you had to live in any era other than the present one, when would you choose? Do you think you would like it better than this era? Why?

60. If you could live someone else's life for just one day, whose life would you choose? How do you think it would go?

61. If they were making a movie of your life, what actor would you want to play you? What advice would you give her on really getting the role down?

62. In a zombie apocalypse, do you think you would survive for a long time, or would you be one of the first to go? Why?

63. If you had the opportunity to go on a ten-year trip to outer space, away from friends and family (though you would still be able to talk to them), would you say yes or no?

64. If you had one superpower, what would it be? How would you use it for good—or would you?

65. If you had a full month to learn something new, what would you learn?

66. Write about something that you didn't learn or figure out for a very long time, even though it seems basic or obvious in retrospect.

67. Write about something that you were obsessed with for a while... or something you are still obsessed with.

68. Write about your secret daydream of being heroic or famous.

69. Write about a decision that was (or is!) very difficult to make.

70. Tell your story about one of the worst decisions you ever made.

71. Tell your story about one of the best, most brilliant decisions you ever made

72. Write about a situation that you've been struggling with for years.

73. Tell your story about the time you felt the fear and did it anyway.

74. Tell your story about the time you succeeded at something because you just. Didn't. Give. Up.

75. Write about what the word *peace* means to you.

76. Tell your story about how you won something, like a contest, a game, an award, or a raffle.

77. Do you feel a strong urge to win at games, arguments, and contests, or are you fairly indifferent to victory as a motivation?

78. Do you believe success is a matter of talent, luck, or hard work? Or is it a combination of two or all of them?

79. Write about something you did in the past year that made you proud.

80. Write about a small thing you accomplished this week.

81. Write about something you would do differently if you had the chance to do it all over again.

82. Tell your story about a time you were treated unfairly or cheated out of something.

83. Tell your story about a time you cheated at something.

84. Tell your story about overcoming a disadvantage you were born with.

85. Tell your story about the last time you made a fool of yourself. (We all do it!)

86. Write about a reason why you're pretty sure other people are jealous of you. (Can you blame them?)

87. What's a way in which you just can't help but show off? Or are there a few ways you do this?

88. What's something you're really looking forward to in the next six months, and why?

89. Write about a big lifetime goal of yours that the people close to you know about.

90. Write about a secret wild dream or ambition that almost nobody knows about.

91. If you could choose only one: would you rather be more attractive than you are now or more intelligent than you are now? Why?

92. Would you rather have ten percent more income, or four extra weeks off every year? How come?

93. Write about a place that you hope to never return to again…or a place you detest going every time you have to go.

94. If you could get a free two-week vacation to one other place in the world, where would you go?

95. Tell your story about backing out of something or leaving something. Why did you do it? Are you glad you did?

96. Tell your story about being rejected. How did you deal with it?

97. What's something that you lie about or hide regularly? It can be a silly thing or something important.

98. Write about a recurring dream you have or just a strange dream that stuck with you.

99. Tell your story about a time your life suddenly changed in a big way.

100. Tell your story about trying something for the first time.

50 PROMPTS ABOUT CHILDHOOD

1. Describe one of your earliest childhood memories.

2. Write about something that was a big part of your childhood that today's kids will never know about.

3. Describe your favorite toy or game when you were five.

4. Write about a game that you invented when you were little.

5. Write about a photograph that was taken of you as a child.

6. Write about something you loved doing when you were young.

7. Write about something you hated doing.

8. Tell your story about a pet you had as a child or about your encounter with an animal.

9. Tell your story about learning to do something as a child, such as tying your shoes or reading.

10. Write about a book or a series of books that you loved when you were growing up.

11. Write about the TV shows you watched as a kid.

12. Write about music you enjoyed listening to or a song you liked to sing.

13. What was your favorite kind of make-believe when you were a child? For instance, did you pretend to be a superhero, a princess, or a cat?

14. Tell your story about your first best friend as a child. How did you meet them? How did you play together?

15. Tell your story about a neighbor you had when you were growing up.

16. What was your favorite meal when you were little? Do you still like it now?

17. Tell your story about a time when a babysitter or relative looked after you.

18. What was something you misunderstood as a child? It might be the definition of a word or something about adult life.

19. Tell your story about a time you were embarrassed as a child.

20. Tell your story about a time you embarrassed a parent or another adult.

21. Tell your story about an outdoor adventure in your childhood.

22. Tell your story about a trip or a visit you enjoyed when you were little.

23. Describe growing up rich, poor, or middle class. Were you aware of it at the time? How did it affect you? Did you know children with different economic circumstances from yours?

24. When you were young, were you aware of race and ethnicity? Did you know other children of different races and/or ethnicities? How did growing up the race or ethnicity you are affect you?

25. Write about something that terrified you as a child.

26. What's something you wanted badly when you were young? Did you get it? If so, was it everything you hoped? If not, did it matter?

27. Tell your story about a lie you told that was very obvious... or a lie you got away with.

28. Tell your story of a time you behaved badly.

29. Write about an instance when you felt proud of yourself when you were a kid.

30. Describe someone who bullied you as a child. Why do you think they did it?

31. Tell your story about a trip to another town that you enjoyed when you were little.

32. Write about a place in your own town that you loved to go to as a kid.

33. Write about a time when you got lost.

34. What was your favorite season of the year when you were growing up—winter, spring, summer, or fall? Why?

35. What was your favorite time of the day when you were growing up? How come?

36. Tell your story about a time you celebrated a birthday or a holiday as a child.

37. Write about believing in Santa Claus.

38. Tell your story about a childhood crush.

39. Explain why you were a difficult child to raise.

40. Explain why you were an easy child to raise.

41. Tell your story about a fight you had with a sibling or another child.

42. Write about something you did when you were young that was actually pretty dangerous.

43. Write about what it was like when you were sick and stayed home from school as a kid...or about a time you only pretended to be sick so you could stay home.

44. Write something about a bike or scooter you had as a child.

45. Write about a time when you were swimming or playing with water.

46. Describe an art or craft project you liked doing as a kid.

47. Write about being on the playground or at a park.

48. Write about a childhood sleepover or slumber party.

49. When you were a kid, what did you want to be when you grew up? Does any part of that dream appeal to you now, and if so, is there a way you could still experience or enjoy

it? (If you grew up to be what you imagined, write about that!)

50. If you could go back and give your child self some things to make your childhood happier, what you would give her or him?

50 PROMPTS ABOUT YOUR IDENTITY AND PERSONALITY

1. Write about what you see as one of your best qualities.

2. Write about one of your most useful talents.

3. Do you fit your astrological sign? Why or why not?

4. Describe the benefits of being an introvert or an extrovert.

5. Describe the challenges of being an introvert or an extrovert.

6. In what ways do you fit the stereotypes of your gender, and in what ways do you differ from the stereotypes?

7. What's something that people don't learn about your personality unless they get to know you very well?

8. Is it easy or difficult for others to get to know you? Why?

9. Write about the ways that you're silly...and about the ways you're pretty serious. (If you're pretty much all silly or all serious, write about that.)

10. Tell your story about a time that you were either more high-strung or more laid-back than others might have been in your situation.

11. Write about a particular phobia or fear you have. If you're not scared of anything, write about that!

12. Are you someone who likes the idea of sticking to a routine? If so, why? Is it easy for you to do so, or do you struggle with it? If you don't like the idea of a routine, why not? Are you trapped in one anyway, or free of routines?

13. Write about a way in which your personality or behavior has changed quite a bit in the past several years.

14. Write about a way that you would like your personality or behavior to change.

15. How much do you think people can change themselves? Do you think personality is mostly ingrained in people, or do you think people can be pretty much anyone they want to be?

16. Write about an aspect of your identity or personality that not everyone finds acceptable.

17. Do you feel like you need a lot of approval from the people around you, or do you do pretty much whatever you want without worrying about it?

18. Do you like to make decisions carefully, weighing all the information and the pros and cons? Or do you just jump into things and follow your heart? Either way, how is that working out for you so far?

19. Do big changes in your life excite you, or freak you out? Or both?

20. Write about some things you worry about that you probably don't need to worry about.

21. What's something that makes you almost irrationally happy?

22. When you're happy, how do you usually express it? Or do you usually keep it to yourself?

23. Write about something that makes you almost irrationally angry.

24. When you're angry, how do you usually express it? Or do you usually keep it to yourself?

25. Write about something that makes you green with jealousy...or write about how and why you're not really prone to jealousy.

26. Do you tend to move fast and get things done quickly, or do you see yourself as moving at a slower pace? What are the benefits and drawbacks of your default speed?

27. Do you consider yourself an optimist, a pessimist, or a realist? If you're a pessimist, do you aspire to be more positive, or do you believe pessimism has its advantages?

28. Is it easy or difficult for you to say no? Why do you think you're like that?

29. Write about a time when someone else complimented your personality in a way that surprised or flattered you.

30. How sensitive are you to your indoor environment? Can you ignore things like annoying noises, ugly views, or poor lighting, or do things like this make it hard for you to work or to enjoy yourself?

31. Write about how the weather or the season affects your personality.

32. What are two or three roles that define you the most? Parent, spouse, Christian, Buddhist, son, daughter, nature lover, runner? Why are these the most important?

33. Are you somebody who holds a grudge or a hurt for a long time, or do you find it easy to let it go?

34. Are you good at getting work done ahead of a deadline, and if so, what helps you do that? Or do you procrastinate like most people? If so, how?

35. Is it easy for you to pick up on hints and social cues, or do you need people to tell you things directly?

36. Do you frequently suspect individuals, organizations, and authorities of hidden and sinister motives, or do you mostly trust others? Why do you think you're like this?

37. Do you think a lot about becoming rich or becoming more rich? Or is wealth not a focus for you?

38. Do you strongly identify with your work? Is it a part of who you are? Or is it just what you do to make a living for yourself or to take care of your family?

39. If you are married or if you are a parent, do you feel like your role as a spouse or as a parent is a big part of your identity?

40. What is your sexual orientation? Do most people know this about you? If so, how? If not, why not?

41. Write about something that you're a fan of—such as a

sports team or a TV show—and what that says about your personality or identity.

42. Do you think of your body as a part of your essential self? Or is it merely a vehicle that gets you around?

43. Tell your story about a time when you felt like you could truly be yourself.

44. Tell your story about a time when you didn't feel like you could be yourself at all.

45. Do you think your name fits you? Why or why not? Does your name affect how other people perceive you? Do you like it?

46. If you could secretly choose a nickname or a title for yourself, what would it be?

47. Write about a significant event or life experience that shaped your personality or identity.

48. Do you think you're generally in touch with your emotions, or does it sometimes take you a while to realize how you're feeling?

49. Are you lacking in confidence, confident...or sometimes over-confident?

50. Fill in the blank, and then write more about it: "I am more than just a _____."

50 PROMPTS ABOUT YOUR
BELIEFS AND VALUES

1. Do you have the same religious beliefs that you had as a child? If so, why? If not, how and why did they change?

2. Write about an aspect of your religious denomination or community now (or something about atheists or agnostics, if you are one) that you wouldn't mind changing.

3. Do you believe that people who hold different spiritual views from you are mistaken? If not, how can you both be right?

4. Would you be able to marry someone who had a different view on religion than you do? If you already did this, how is it working out?

5. Write about whether you believe self-denial—such as fasting, chastity, or voluntary poverty—can make someone a better person.

6. If you meditate, write about the benefits. If you don't, write about whether you believe it would benefit you.

7. Write about a time when you prayed for something or cast a spell for something, and it worked...or about a time it didn't.

8. Write about your thoughts regarding the Law of Attraction—the idea that positive thoughts attract positive

things to your life, and negative thoughts attract negative things to your life.

9. What superstitions do you believe in or follow? Do you do certain things to avoid bad luck or make wishes in certain ways?

10. Write about someone you admire for the way they live out their beliefs and values.

11. Where and when is it appropriate to discuss religious beliefs openly, and where and when should people keep it to themselves?

12. Do you feel comfortable with everyone knowing about your particular beliefs or lack of them? Or do you feel that you need to hide this in some situations? Why?

13. Do you believe you have an obligation to sway or convert others to your belief system or lack of one? Why or why not?

14. Write about a misconception many people have about the people who follow your religion (or about atheists or agnostics, if you are one).

15. If you were going to take a spiritual pilgrimage, religious or secular, what would that be like? If you already follow a tradition that includes pilgrimages, write about why you would or wouldn't like to go on one—or write about the time you did.

16. Write about when and/or where you feel the most spiritually connected to a deity or to the universe as a whole.

17. Describe a ceremony or ritual, religious or secular, that had or has deep meaning for you.

18. Tell your story about a time that you participated in a service or ceremony of a faith that wasn't your own.

19. Write about when you think it's morally acceptable to lie. If your answer is "never," write about why you think that.

20. Write about when you think it's morally acceptable to steal. If your answer is "never," write about why you think that.

21. What do you think is the most underrated virtue?

22. Write about a prejudice that you overcame...or about how you're still working on overcoming one.

23. Write about whether you believe in ghosts, and why.

24. Write about whether you believe in the Devil, demons, or evil spirits, and why.

25. Write about whether you believe in angels or fairies, and why.

26. Write about whether you believe or suspect there's intelligent life on other planets, and why.

27. Write about something you believe that isn't a particularly popular belief.

28. Write about something that you don't believe exists...but you really wish it did.

29. Discuss a religious or ethical principle that you believe is right but have trouble following.

30. Write about an object you own that has religious, spiritual, or symbolic significance to you.

31. Do you believe that things happen for a reason, or do they just happen randomly? Why do you think this?

32. Do you believe that you have a lot of control over your destiny or future? Why or why not?

33. Do you believe in life after death, and if so, what do you think happens? Do you feel certain about this, or do you have doubts?

34. Write about why your beliefs or lack of them make you morally or intellectually superior to others...or why they don't.

35. Write about why you believe it is or isn't okay to eat animals and animal products.

36. Write about whether you believe women and men should fulfill different roles or take different paths in life based on their gender.

37. Write about why you believe baby boys should be circumcised or should not be uncircumcised...or why you believe it doesn't matter much either way.

38. Write about something you did (or didn't do) that you're proud of from a moral or religious standpoint.

39. Share a quote or a verse from a sacred text that you believe in strongly, and write about why.

40. Write about whether you think it's all right for humans to develop artificial intelligence.

41. Write about whether you think people ought to be allowed to end their lives when they have terminal illnesses or are old and ready to die.

42. If you believe in reincarnation, write about who or what you think you might have been before. If you have actual memories of past lives, write about those.

43. Write about how you know whether something is a sin or morally wrong.

44. Consider the seven "deadly sins"—pride, envy, gluttony, lust, anger, greed, and sloth. Do they all seem like sins to you? Why or why not?

45. Do you believe that human beings are naturally evil, naturally good, or naturally more or less neutral?

46. Do you believe people are punished for their sins? If so, how are they punished, and by what or whom?

47. Do you believe that people are rewarded for their good deeds and kindness, and if so, how does that work?

48. Discuss why a particular religious belief that other people hold makes no sense to you...even if you respect their right to believe it.

49. Write down some questions you would like to ask a deity, whether you believe in this deity or not.

50. Write your own morning prayer or meditation.

50 PROMPTS ABOUT FAMILY

1. Write about the benefits of being an only child—or the advantages of having siblings.

2. Do you believe people should try to maintain relationships with family members, no matter what? Or can there be good reasons to cut off or disown someone in your family?

3. Write about a death in your family.

4. Write about a birth in your family.

5. Write about a trait you inherited or picked up from a parent.

6. Write about a way in which you are very different from a parent.

7. If you don't have children: do you or did you want them? Why or why not?

8. If you have children: what is one thing that surprised you about being a parent?

9. What's one mistake you think a lot of parents make when they're raising children?

10. What do you think are the most important things a parent can teach a child?

11. Do you think it's important for a family to sit down together at the dinner table? Why or why not?

12. Tell your story about what makes your family different from other families you know.

13. In your family, do you feel like you are the favorite, the outcast, or neither?

14. Discuss why you do or don't consider pets to be family members.

15. Tell a story about a pet, past or present.

16. Discuss whether you consider people who aren't related to you by blood as family.

17. If you became a billionaire, would that change your relationship with your immediate family? If so, how?

18. Tell your story about a family rift or feud.

19. Tell your story about a family reconciliation.

20. Do your parents and/or siblings live in the same town as you, or do they live far away? Do you consider that a good thing or a bad thing?

21. How often do you talk to your parent(s) and/or your sibling(s), and what do you usually talk about?

22. If you have a sibling or siblings, write about the personality traits or habits they have in common with you.

23. If you have a sibling or siblings, write about ways that they are completely different from you.

24. Do you think that some actions count as child abuse, even if they aren't physical abuse? If not, why not? If so, which ones?

25. Write a letter to a family member or relative who died. It could be someone you are close to or a distant ancestor.

26. Where were your ancestors from originally, or do you know? Do you think that's part of who you are now, or do you think it's irrelevant?

27. How does your family handle conflicts and painful issues? Do you hash it all out, or just try to forget about it? Either way, how well do you think that works for your family?

28. How does your family express affection? Are you hugging and effusive, or more reserved? Has this affected how you relate to others?

29. Tell your story about an activity your family did together for fun—one time, or on a regular basis. If your family doesn't do anything together for fun, write about that.

30. Write about something that you think would be really fun to do with your family someday.

31. Tell your story about an ordeal your family went through.

32. Write about why you're proud of one of your family members.

33. Write about why you worry about one of your family members.

34. Write about a time you envied someone else because of their marriage or family situation.

35. Write about a time you felt sorry for someone else because of their marriage or family situation.

36. Describe a family photo, new or old, and write about why you like it or dislike it.

37. Tell your story about a prank that you or someone else in your family played on another family member.

38. Write about your family's best or worst habit.

39. Write about having trouble balancing time with your family and other parts of your life...or write about how this isn't difficult for you at all.

40. Write about a time you were a good parent, a good sibling, or a good child.

41. Write about a time you felt guilty as a parent, sibling, or child.

42. Tell your story about a family member doing something for the first time.

43. If you have grown siblings or grown children, are you surprised at how they turned out? Or are they the same people they were when they were small?

44. Write about a family member's experience with a disability or a physical or mental health condition.

45. Tell your story about the last time you were *furious* with someone in your family.

46. Tell your story about living with a parent as an adult...or write about why you would never want to do that.

47. Tell your story about a secret a family member kept from you...or a secret you kept (or are still keeping) from a family member.

48. Do you think it's acceptable for a parent to snoop in their child's bedroom? Why or why not?

49. Tell your story about an overprotective parent...or a negligent parent.

50. Write down a funny story that your family likes to tell again and again.

50 PROMPTS ABOUT FRIENDSHIPS AND RELATIONSHIPS

1. Write about how a person can tell if they're really in love.

2. Do you consider yourself hopeful or cynical about romance? Why do you have that outlook?

3. Discuss one of the most important qualities you think people should look for in a friend.

4. Discuss one of the most important qualities you think people should look for in a romantic partner.

5. Discuss a quality that you think is overrated when choosing a romantic partner.

6. What do you consider to be "deal breakers" in a marriage or romantic relationship?

7. Tell your story about how you met your spouse, significant other, or one of your best friends.

8. Tell your story about when a friend (or a group of them) made your day.

9. Tell your story about when a friend (or a group of them) broke your heart.

10. Describe what you think would be a perfect cheap romantic date.

11. Describe what you think would be a perfect expensive romantic date.

12. Write about how you find it easy—or hard—to make new friends.

13. Tell your story about a time when you forgave a friend or a friend forgave you.

14. Tell your story about a time you went out of your way to be a good friend.

15. Write about one thing you wish you could change about your significant other.

16. Write about one thing your significant other wishes they could change about you.

17. Tell your story about one of the most romantic experiences of your life.

18. If you're not married but would like to be someday, describe your perfect wedding. If you're married, write how you would plan your wedding if you were doing it all over again today.

19. Do you believe in soul mates? Why or why not?

20. Tell your story about having an unrequited crush on someone.

21. Tell your story about a time when someone you weren't interested in romantically had a crush on you.

22. Write about one of the best ways a romantic partner or friend can show that they care about you.

23. Write about a couple you know who's been together and happy for a long time. Why do you think things have worked out for them?

24. Write about a couple you know who had a disastrous breakup. Why do you think they couldn't make it work?

25. Write about a former friend or someone you used to date that you still miss sometimes.

26. Write about a bad relationship or a friendship that you stayed in way too long.

27. Are you attracted to people who are a lot like you or people who are very different from you? Explain.

28. What is something you love to talk about...that you wish your friends would ask you about more often?

29. Do you think it's all right for couples to have some secrets from one another? If not, why not? If so, what secrets are acceptable?

30. Do you want friends who will be candid with you, even if it's not flattering, or do you prefer friends who flatter you no matter what?

31. Do you think expensive engagement and/or wedding rings are a good idea? Why or why not?

32. Do you think big, over-the-top public proposals are a good idea? Why or why not?

33. Write a few paragraphs or a numbered list entitled: "The Perks of Being My Friend."

34. Write about a time when a friend tried to take advantage of you.

35. Write about a time you felt left out of a group.

36. If a newly married couple asked for your advice on how to have a happy marriage, what would you tell them?

37. Is it okay to break up with someone by text? Why or why not?

38. Write about a time you were devastated by a breakup...and how you got over it.

39. Write about a time when you found out a friend or significant other lied to you.

40. Write about a time when you were embarrassed to have a friend or significant other learn something about you.

41. Do you think couples can be happy together despite big differences in politics or religion? Why or why not?

42. Tell your story about being friends with or dating someone who your family didn't approve of.

43. Write about a big argument you had with a friend or significant other.

44. Write about a place that's special to you and a friend, a group of friends, or a significant other.

45. Do you believe that it would be easy for you to be friends with an ex, or would it be close to impossible?

46. Write about your first kiss. If you've never been kissed, write about your hopes and fears about a first kiss.

47. Do you feel like you have enough friends, or do you want to make friends with more people?

48. Which is more important to you: having a whole bunch of friends or having a few very close friends?

49. Write about something sweet that your friend or significant other often does for you.

50. Write about a time with a friend or romantic partner when you could not stop laughing.

50 PROMPTS ABOUT HEALTH
AND APPEARANCE

1. Describe a physical feature of yours that you really like.

2. Tell your story about a time when someone else complimented you on one of your physical features.

3. Are you shy about your body, such as when you change clothes in a locker room? Or are you comfortable with it? Why?

4. Do you think it's morally okay for people to wear little or no clothing in public, or do you think it's wrong? Why?

5. Has your attitude about your appearance changed over the years? Do you care less or care more about the way you look?

6. How would you describe your personal style? Has it changed over the years? Do you think you would like it to change in the future?

7. Do you think people make snap judgments about you based on your appearance? Are they accurate or not?

8. Write about a tattoo you have and its significance, a tattoo you would like to get...or why you would never, ever get a tattoo.

9. Do you wear makeup? If so, do you enjoy it? If not, would

you ever want to? Do you feel pressured by society to wear makeup or not to wear it?

10. Tell your story about a time you got injured or you were in an accident.

11. Tell your story about getting surgery or a medical procedure.

12. Tell your story about a memorable visit to the office of a doctor, dentist, or optometrist.

13. Write about a time when your body was very sore.

14. Write about a time when you were really sick.

15. Write a note apologizing to a part of your body for insulting it in the past.

16. Write a note thanking a part of your body for doing such a good job.

17. Tell your story about a time that you were impressed by what your body could do.

18. Tell your story about dealing with an addiction, mental or physical health problem, or disability.

19. Do you believe in any alternative health practices, such as homeopathy, faith healing, crystals, or reiki? If not, do you think it's okay for other people to believe in them?

20. Write about a kind of exercise or physical activity you enjoy.

21. Write about three healthy foods that you really like.

22. Write about a clothing item or a style of clothing that you never feel comfortable wearing.

23. Write about a clothing item or type of clothing you would wear if it were socially acceptable...or write about things you wear even though others may find it strange.

24. Write about a time you had to really dress up for an event. Did you enjoy it?

25. Tell your story about being criticized or praised for your health or for a medical decision.

26. Write about getting a haircut, a shave at a barber shop, a manicure or pedicure, or a massage.

27. Write about a health or beauty obsession, a fashion trend, or a way of eating that you find absolutely ridiculous.

28. Write about a time when you weren't getting enough sleep.

29. Tell your story about a time when you were so stressed that it affected your physical health.

30. Tell your story about a time you went on a diet or exercise program, or a time when you trained for a team or an event.

31. On paper, invent a smoothie, healthy herbal tea blend, or other healthy drink. Write about why you think you would enjoy it and/or why it would make you feel better. (Feel free to try it out later.)

32. Do you believe that people take too many drugs to treat their moods or mental health issues? Or do you believe that psychiatric medications are mostly a good thing?

Do you believe that some people you know *should* be medicated?

33. Write about your thoughts on recreational drugs.

34. Do you think a lot about the nutritional value of your food and how natural it is? Or do you not concern yourself much about it?

35. Write about the best advice on your health or appearance that you've ever been given.

36. Write about the worst advice on your health or appearance that you've ever been given.

37. Write about something in your everyday routine or environment that's detrimental to your mental health.

38. Write about something in your everyday routine or environment that's detrimental to your physical health.

39. Write about three things that almost always improve your mood.

40. Write about three things that almost always make your body feel better right away.

41. Write about how your body has changed as you've gotten older.

42. Do you believe you'll live to a very old age? Why or why not? Do you want to?

43. Write about one of your favorite outfits or your favorite pair of shoes.

44. Write about your dream outfit or item of clothing—something you don't own, but would like to.

45. Tell a story that has to do with your hair or your lack of it.

46. Tell your story about a time you dealt with acne, a sunburn, or poison ivy.

47. Tell your story about dealing with your period if you have or have had periods.

48. Write down your personal advice for treating a cold, the flu, period cramps, or a hangover.

49. Write about a health or medical issue that most people don't think about often.

50. Write about a reason why you consider yourself lucky to have the body you have.

50 PROMPTS ABOUT HOME

1. Describe your favorite spot in your home and why you like it.

2. Write about the worst house or apartment you've ever lived in.

3. Describe your dream home in detail.

4. Describe your ideal decorating style—modern, global, country, traditional? Or explain why interior decorating means nothing to you.

5. Write about the one luxurious upgrade you would make to your current home if you could.

6. Write about your garden. If you don't have one, write about what you would grow if you did.

7. Is your home usually neat, or usually messy? Why is that? Does it matter? Why or why not?

8. Write about a household chore you actually enjoy.

9. Write about a household chore you *hate* doing.

10. Tell your story about the time you had damage, a big mess, or a minor disaster in your home.

11. Is your home your sanctuary, or is it a place you need to get away from to feel peace? Why?

12. Would you like to live in your home forever, or do you think about moving soon? Why?

13. Write about whether you think you could be happy living in a tiny house or a studio apartment. If you already live in one, write about whether you like it, and why or why not.

14. Describe the contents of your desk drawer or junk drawer and write about the thoughts or memories that the objects in there inspire.

15. Write about your favorite mugs.

16. Write about something you collect...or something you would enjoy collecting.

17. Write a list of things that your kitchen must *always* be stocked with, and explain why.

18. Write about something in your house that you should probably throw out, but you just can't bring yourself to do it.

19. Write about something you "inherited" from a family member, friend, or your home's previous occupant.

20. Write about a "house rule" you have.

21. What does your home smell like? Write about some of the common or recurring odors, good and bad.

22. When you go to sleep at night, what sounds can you hear from outside?

23. Do you have visitors often, or rarely? Why is that? Would you like to have more? Fewer?

24. Tell your story about when you had a delightful guest in your home.

25. Tell your story about when you had an unwelcome visitor in your home—human or animal.

26. Describe the view outside one of your windows.

27. Write about something you would hide or something you would pull out of storage and display prominently if your mom came to visit.

28. Describe the time you were a guest in an unusual household.

29. Imagine that several video cameras were set up in your home to film a reality TV show about you. Would your behavior change, and if so, how?

30. If your house or building were on fire, what three things would you grab before you ran outside?

31. Write about your experience of moving from one place to another.

32. If you had your choice, would you live in a very old house or a brand-new one?

33. Tell your story about a day when you moved from one place to another.

34. Why did you choose to live in your current home? What seemed good about it at the time, if anything?

35. If you live alone, do you think it would be difficult to adjust to living with others?

36. If you live with others, do you think you could have been happy living alone?

37. Do you know any of your neighbors? If so, what are they like? If not, would you like to, or do you not really care?

38. Describe a piece of artwork, a photograph, or a handcrafted item displayed in your home.

39. If you could afford it, would you hire a cleaning service? Why or why not? If you already have a cleaning service, write about the experience of using one.

40. When someone knocks on your door and you're not expecting company, what do you do? Answer the door, find out who it is first, or pretend you're not home? Why?

41. Tell your story about a terrible roommate or someone else who was very difficult to live with.

42. Tell your story about a fun roommate or someone you enjoyed living with.

43. Write about something in your home that might surprise or interest first-time visitors.

44. If you've ever been homeless or unsure of where you would live next, write about that experience.

45. On a Friday night, would you rather stay at home, or do you think staying in would be a waste?

46. Would you rather live in a big house in a small town, or a small apartment in a big city?

47. Do you get rid of possessions you don't need? Or do you hang on to them in case you need them again?

48. Do you feel safe where you live? Why or why not?

49. Is owning a home an important life goal for you, or would you just as soon rent? How come?

50. Do you think you would enjoy working from home? Why or why not?

50 PROMPTS ABOUT YOUR TOWN AND YOUR COUNTRY

1. Write about how you're a typical resident of your city or town...or about how you're different from most people there.

2. Write about how you fit the stereotype of people from your country...or about how you don't fit it at all.

3. Write about a common misconception about your city, region, or country.

4. Do you think your hometown is a good place to live? Why or why not?

5. Write about the benefits of living in a big city (or a small town, depending on where you live).

6. Write about the drawbacks of living in a big city (or a small town, depending on where you live).

7. Describe what it's like to take a walk in your neighborhood.

8. Describe a food, or a few kinds of food, that your city, region, or country is famous for.

9. Write about your favorite restaurant in your town...or the only restaurant in your town.

10. Write about a place that you would take out-of-town guests for entertainment.

11. Write about one of your favorite places to go in town, just to relax and enjoy yourself.

12. Write about some of the main industries in your hometown, or the main ways in which people make a living.

13. Describe the landscape, some of the wildlife, and/or the trees and plants in your part of the country.

14. Discuss something you love about the people in your country.

15. Discuss something you wish you could change about the people in your country.

16. Discuss a group you are involved with and what their meeting times are like. For instance, it could be a church, an organization like the Girl Scouts or Boy Scouts, or some kind of club.

17. Do you live in the city you grew up in? Why or why not?

18. Write about the ways that your hometown has changed over the years.

19. Write about a way your country is changing for the better.

20. What do you think is one of the biggest political issues in your country, and what's your opinion on it?

21. Do you believe there is a lot of bigotry in your country, or do most people treat everyone equally?

22. Describe a lovely place in your town or city.

23. Write about an ugly place in your town or city.

24. Tell your story about a time when the weather in your hometown was extreme.

25. If you can vote in elections in your country, do you do it? Why or why not?

26. Do you think you would be a good president, prime minister, or leader of your country? Why or why not?

27. Propose a sensible law you would like to implement in your country, and explain your reasoning.

28. Propose a frivolous or ridiculous law you would like to implement in your country, and explain your reasoning.

29. Discuss why you believe something that's currently illegal in your state or country should be legal or should at least carry a much less hefty penalty.

30. Tell your story about a time when you were in an unfamiliar part of town or at an unusual establishment or gathering in your town.

31. Write about a place—or several places—that you want to go to and have never been, even though they're right in your own town.

32. Tell your story about attending a sporting event in your town, and why you enjoyed it (or didn't).

33. Write about a celebration that happened (or that happens every year) in your hometown.

34. Write about a controversy or scandal that happened or is happening in your hometown.

35. Write about a time that you were in the newspaper or on the local news...or a time when someone you knew was.

36. Write about a time when your hometown was in the national news.

37. Write about a famous or infamous person who's from your hometown.

38. Propose one improvement that would make your hometown a better place to be.

39. Is there a haunted house or other haunted place near you? Write down the story you've heard about it. Or if there's just a place that seems creepy, write about that.

40. Describe one of the cemeteries in your hometown. (If you haven't been to one, consider a field trip.)

41. Do you feel 100% loyal to your country, or could you imagine moving to another country and becoming a citizen there?

42. Do you have a lot of independent stores and restaurants in your hometown or a lot of retail chain stores? Either way, do you like this, or not?

43. Write about a kind of restaurant or store that your town doesn't have but that you think would be a real hit.

44. Describe a quirky place in your hometown.

45. Write about the diversity where you grew up—or about the lack of diversity. Did it affect how you saw the world?

46. Do you feel safe as a citizen in your country? Why or why not?

47. If it were up to you to choose an official state animal or an animal to represent your country, what would you choose, and why?

48. If it were up to you to design a new flag for your city, state, or country, what would it look like?

49. Do you think your country is going to improve in the next several years, or will it get worse? Why do you think this?

50. If you've lived in another town besides the one you're in now, what's one thing—or a bunch of things—you miss about it?

50 PROMPTS ABOUT SCHOOL AND/OR WORK

1. Write about one of the most admirable classmates or coworkers you've ever had.

2. Write about one of the worst classmates or coworkers you've ever had.

3. Describe a part of your job or everyday work that you love.

4. Describe a part of your job or everyday work that you loathe.

5. Write about what you wish people knew about your job, profession, or calling in life.

6. What advice would you give to someone who was just starting out at your school or place of work?

7. Tell your story about how a teacher, coach, or boss supported or inspired you.

8. Tell your story about how a teacher, coach, or boss was so awful, they didn't deserve to have their job.

9. Tell your story about a time when, rightly or wrongly, you got in trouble at school or at work.

10. What was the strangest course or class you ever took?

11. Describe the way you get to school or to work every day.

12. Write about the first day of school.

13. Write about the last day of school.

14. What is one thing you would change about the rules at your school or workplace, or the rules at your child's school?

15. Tell your story about a time you were a babysitter, a pet sitter, or some other kind of caretaker.

16. Tell your story about having ridiculous or inappropriate fun at work or at school.

17. Do you consider yourself to be underpaid, overpaid, or paid a reasonable salary? Why?

18. Describe an interaction you've had at work with a guest at a restaurant, a customer, a patient, or a client.

19. Write about a time that you felt proud at your workplace or at school.

20. Write about a time you gave a speech or presentation.

21. Write about a time you worked on a group project.

22. Write about a classmate or coworker who was a bully.

23. Write about an eccentric coworker or classmate.

24. Tell your story about a time when someone was very inappropriate at school or work.

25. Write about a job you think you would be terrible at, and why.

26. Describe your dream job.

27. Tell your story about a time you had trouble adjusting to a new school or a new job.

28. If it were up to you, what hours would you go to school or work? (Assume it has to be the same number of hours overall.) Why?

29. If you didn't have to or you didn't need the money, would you still work or go to school at all? Why or why not?

30. Write about a time you were a volunteer for a nonprofit organization or a church.

31. What's one of the biggest challenges you face as a student or in the work you do every day? Why is it a challenge?

32. What's one of the biggest advantages you face as a student or in the work you do every day? Why is it an advantage?

33. Describe what it's like for you to get ready for work or for school in the morning—or what it's like to get your family ready for their day.

34. Write about a time you dropped out of a class, quit an after-school activity, or quit a job.

35. Write about something that stresses you out about your school or your everyday work.

36. Tell your story about a time you helped a fellow student, employee, or parent.

37. Write about some of the perks of the job you have now or have had in the past.

38. Write about an interview—or several—that you've had.

39. Tell your story about getting fired or laid off from a job, or cut from a team or a school activity.

40. Tell your story about something funny that happened at school or at work.

41. Would you move to another city where you didn't know anybody for a job or an education? Why or why not? (If you've done this, write about it.)

42. If you have a job now, could you see yourself doing this job for the rest of your life? Why or why not?

43. If someone gave you $500,000 to start your own business, what business would you start?

44. What is your trip to and from your school or your job like? Do you walk, drive, take a bus, or get there in another way? What do you always see along the way? Do you talk to someone, listen to music or the radio, or do something else? What do you think about?

45. What is your lunch hour like at your school or workplace? Do you bring your lunch, buy lunch on the premises, or go out to a restaurant? Do you eat with others or work through lunch?

46. Describe your workspace, your classroom, or the inside of your locker.

47. Describe something you deal with at your job or at school that might surprise some people.

48. Do you consider yourself a workaholic, lazy, or somewhere in between?

49. Do you think school uniforms are a good idea? Why or why not?

50. What's something about you that nobody at your workplace or school knows about? If everyone knows everything about you, write about that.

50 PROMPTS ABOUT MUSIC, MOVIES, BOOKS, TV, AND THE INTERNET

Songs, stories, and the Internet make great subject matter. They bring people together and help them express who they are. Many blogs and websites are completely devoted to entertainment and culture. Here are prompts to get you writing about the things you've watched, listened to, and read.

1. Write about the first concert you ever attended...or the best concert you ever attended.

2. What song would you want people to play at your funeral, and why?

3. Write about a book that changed your life.

4. Write about a book you couldn't stand...even though you read the whole thing, or at least most of it.

5. Do you think it's sweet when people gush about their spouses or kids on social media, or do you find it annoying? Why?

6. Do you share a lot of photos of yourself on social media? Why or why not?

7. Do you mind other people sharing a lot of photos of themselves on social media...or posting photos of you on social media? Why or why not?

8. Tell your story about a time when you kept on checking

someone's updates on social media, such as a crush, a celebrity, an unusual acquaintance, or an ex.

9. Tell your story about a time you unfriended or unfollowed someone, or someone unfriended or unfollowed you.

10. Write about a time you sang or played a musical instrument.

11. What are some songs that you have to sing along to when you hear them, and maybe even dance to them...or at least, you have to turn them up when they come on the radio?

12. Write about a TV show, movie, band, or book that you're always trying to get other people to watch, listen to, or read.

13. Write a list of seven reasons why you like a certain musician, actor, or author.

14. Write about a fictional character from a book, movie, or TV show who you have a crush on.

15. Write about a series of books, a TV show, or a genre of music that lots of people like...and you don't understand why.

16. Write about a song or music that brings a lot of memories flooding back to you.

17. Write about a song or music that motivates you to do your best.

18. If you could see any band in concert...in any year...who would you see and when?

19. If you were getting married today, what song would you choose for a first dance?

20. Write about the scariest or most disturbing book or books you've ever read.

21. Do you think writers, filmmakers, and game developers are ever somewhat responsible for encouraging violence or other bad behavior? Why or why not?

22. What is a type of story that you're a sucker for?

23. Tell your story about a time when being a fan of a singer or band, a movie, a book, or a TV show brought you closer together with someone else (or many other people).

24. Write about a favorite quote from a book, song, TV show, or movie and why you like it so much.

25. Tell your story about how a book, movie, TV show, or music got you through a hard time.

26. What's something that you wish they would stop doing in books and/or movies?

27. What's something you wish they would have more of in books and/or movies?

28. Write about a TV show or movie that is "comfort food" for your spirit.

29. If you could recommend one animated film, what would it be and why?

30. Write about something you know about that books, TV, or movies *always* portray inaccurately.

31. If you had a year off to write a book from scratch, what kind of book would you write?

32. Do you think you are your "real self" on social media, or do you think you're playing a part?

33. Do you think most other people are their "real selves" on social media? Does it matter?

34. Write about a time you were the victim of online bullying or participated in bullying someone online.

35. Do you get into heated debates online? If so, do you prefer it that way, or do you wish you could refrain? If not, do you consciously avoid them, and if so, why?

36. Tell your story about a memorable experience that took place in a movie theater.

37. Would you say you're addicted to TV or the Internet? If so, is it a problem? If not, is it a problem for other people you know?

38. What's your favorite videogame, computer game, or mobile game? Why do you like it so much?

39. Write about a time when you were mesmerized by a story in the news. Why were you so riveted?

40. What's better: old-fashioned vinyl records or digital files of music?

41. Write about one or more great villains in books, TV, or movies, explaining what makes them so great.

42. What character or characters from TV, movies, or books reminds you a lot of you?

43. If they made a movie of your life, what actor would do a good job of playing you and why? What would they have to do to nail the performance?

44. Write about a character or characters you really wanted to be like. Explain how and why.

45. Write about the worst movie or TV show you've ever seen. What made it so bad?

46. Write about where you get your news from and whether you think it's a particularly good source.

47. Do you ever refuse to watch a filmmaker's or actor's movies, or buy someone's music or books, because of their personal bad behavior? Or do you separate the person from their work?

48. Write about a fictional character you think is a great role model for young people, and explain why they're great.

49. If you could spend a year living in a fictional world, where would you choose and what would you do there?

50. Write about a scene or scenes from a book, movie, or TV show that made you cry.

500 BLOG POST IDEAS

As a longtime blogger, I know all too well that it's easy to fall into a rut. Here are ideas for fifty opinion-based posts, fifty advice-based posts, fifty image-based posts, fifty link roundup posts, fifty food and drink-themed posts, fifty one-word subject matter ideas, one hundred travel-based posts, and one hundred list-based posts (my personal favorite at bryndonovan.com!) Admittedly, there's a lot of overlap between these categories.

All of the autobiographical posts in the previous section, of course, are also potential blog posts, depending on how much you like to reveal about yourself.

I hope these ideas inspire you...and I hope they spark even more great content for your blog. And if you've always considered starting a blog but you weren't sure what to write about, maybe these lists will give you that little extra push you need.

OPINION POSTS

For each of these, you can write a post supporting or arguing against the statement. Please note that many of these statements do not reflect the personal views of the author! Some of these are specific, while others are more open.

Writing about controversial issues can get you a lot of attention... including negative attention. They can affect your reputation, so think carefully about what you truly believe and about the tone you take. Outrage often leads to clicks and shares, and your spontaneous angry rant is very likely to be the one post that goes viral. The Internet is forever. Even if you regret a post and delete it, it may live on and show up whenever people Google your name.

That being said, if you've been blogging a while, you know that there's no way to avoid argument and controversy. Even the most

seemingly benign subjects can sometimes stir up strong objections.
Some people get on the Internet looking for a fight, and you can't take
that too personally.

1. Private religious schools should receive tax dollars.

2. All schools should require students to wear uniforms.

3. No book should ever be banned.

4. Children should go to school year-round.

5. A vegan diet is the most ethical choice.

6. Social media has had a mostly positive effect on society.

7. Things in this country are worse than they were ten years ago.

8. It's wiser to spend money on travel than on home ownership.

9. Graduate school is rarely a sound investment.

10. Here's something that would make our city better.

11. Here's something that would make our country better.

12. Space travel is a high priority for humanity.

13. Sex education should not be taught in schools.

14. Giving a child an unusual name is a terrible idea.

15. This politician or celebrity is getting unfairly criticized.

16. This politician or celebrity was really out of line, and I'll explain why.

17. If your significant other does this, you should break up with them.

18. This product or service is worth the money.

19. Most arguments are not worth having.

20. Lots of people who get divorced just don't take commitment seriously.

21. Marriage is an outdated institution.

22. No one should get dogs from breeders. Adopt, don't shop!

23. Christmas is too stressful.

24. Fruitcake is unfairly maligned.

25. New Year's resolutions are a waste of time.

26. Being child-free is amazing.

27. People who choose not to have children are selfish.

28. It's fine for adult children to live with their parents.

29. Online dating services are a necessity for single people who want to date.

30. Valentine's Day is a dumb holiday.

31. People should dress their age.

32. You're as young as you feel.

33. It's okay to brag about the good deeds you do.

34. Euthanasia should never be legalized.

35. Kids should spend more time outdoors.

36. "The great outdoors" is overrated.

37. This book, TV show, movie, or band is overrated.

38. This coach or general manager isn't as bad as everyone says.

39. This is the most boring sport of all the sports.

40. This sports team would do better if they made this one change.

41. Churches today need to make this one change.

42. Corporations need to make this one change.

43. This particular company needs to do better.

44. People should never try to sell things to their friends and family members.

45. People would enjoy better mental health if they exercised more.

46. Attending church every Sunday is more important these days than ever.

47. Not everybody needs a college degree.

48. It's okay to abstain from voting if you don't like any of the candidates.

49. Women don't need to wear makeup.

50. More people need to understand what it's like to go through life with _____.

ADVICE POSTS

We go to the Internet for practical help in dealing with challenges and making our relationships, families, work, and life better. Sometimes I write advice posts because I believe I have good tips or insight to share. Even if I think I know a lot, I often learn more from my readers via the comments section, so I try not to sound like a know-it-all in the original post (though I'm sure that sometimes I do, anyway!) In most cases, the same advice doesn't work for everyone, but it can still be helpful to share what worked for you.

Here are a bunch of sample blog post titles to inspire you to write advice posts. Obviously, some of these could turn into list posts if you give a lot of examples.

51. Why You Should Get Back Into the Habit of Reading

52. How to Deal With Bullying

53. Don't Make This Personal Finance Mistake I Made

54. Don't Make These Blogging Mistakes I Made

55. Don't Make These Wedding Planning Mistakes We Made

56. Our Secrets to a Happy Marriage

57. How to Make Friends as an Introvert

58. How to Survive the Moving Process

59. How to Survive the Adoption Process

60. My Best Advice to a New Mom

61. How to Write Better Professional Emails

62. How to Ace a Job Interview

63. How to Handle Difficult Coworkers

64. How to Get More People to Read Your Blog

65. How to Get Your House (Pretty) Clean in 30 Minutes

66. How I Overcame Procrastination

67. How I Broke This Bad Habit

68. How to Make Your Home More Welcoming

69. How to Listen to Your Intuition

70. How to Make Spirituality a Part of Everyday Life

71. Why You Should Always Be Yourself

72. Why You Should Volunteer

73. How to Create a Morning Routine

74. Ways to Have More Energy

75. How to Respond to Rude Questions and Comments

76. Ways to Flirt

77. How to Write a Love Letter

78. How to Help a Friend Who's Depressed

79. Public Speaking Tips

80. Running Tips

81. Tips for Growing Out Bangs

82. How I Coped With Losing My Job

83. How I Got Over a Breakup

84. How I Got Over Being Cheated On

85. Advice for Adults Going Back to School

86. Advice for Empty Nesters

87. How to Housetrain Your Pet

88. How to Potty Train Your Child

89. How to Take Better Care of Your Skin

90. How to Not Get Your Feelings Hurt So Easily

91. How to Mingle at a Party

92. How to Take Better Selfies

93. How to Say No...Politely

94. How to Survive a Midlife Crisis...or a Quarterlife Crisis...or a Latelife Crisis

95. How I Finally Lost 10 Pounds

96. What to Do If You Are Hacked

97. What to Do If You're Arrested

98. 98 How to Help Kids Learn About Money and Saving

99. Why You Should Be an Organ Donor

100. Why You Should Forgive

IMAGE-BASED POSTS

A blog post may center around your own images or artwork or around images you've curated. Avoid using other people's creative work without their permission, or at least without giving credit and a link back to the original website.

If you're going to share a lot of images online, make sure you understand best practices regarding file format and size so they don't make your blog take a long time to load. And make sure you have the rights to the images! There are sources for copyright-free images online, but if you use a lot of images, you might also want to get a subscription to a large stock house.

Many people are shy about sharing pictures of themselves, either because they want to guard their privacy or because they're self-conscious. However, sharing photos of yourself is a great way to help blog readers feel like they really know you.

101. Share a picture of your outfit of the day.

102. Share pictures of your favorite outfits for the season... spring, summer, fall, or winter.

103. Share pictures of outfits you *wish* you owned for the season.

104. Post photos of your Halloween costume, or your kids' costumes.

105. Share pictures of amazing historical costumes.

106. Post a picture of your office or studio and write a little about it.

107. Post a "before" and an "after" of a room you've decorated...

108. Or post a "before" and an "after" of a room or closet you've decluttered.

109. Share a bunch of pictures of your dream houses...

110. Or share pictures of your dream cars.

111. Post pictures and descriptions of what you did over the weekend.

112. Share old photos of your ancestors and write about what you know about them.

113. Share pictures of you as a baby, a toddler, a child, and a teenager, and write about what you were like in different stages of your life.

114. If you've been married to or committed to the same person for a while, share pictures of you both over the years and tell your love story.

115. Post pictures of the most beautiful animals you've ever seen in your life.

116. Share your most ridiculous photos of your dogs.

117. Post photo(s) of your rescue pet and tell their story.

118. Share pictures of decorating eggs at Easter.

119. Share photos of your baby or child in different moods: happy, sad, angry, sleepy.

120. Post pictures from your garden.

121. Take a picture of the contents of your backpack or purse, and write about them.

122. If you love your planner, share pictures of your weekly spreads or to-do lists.

123. Share pictures of your favorite famous pieces of art, and link to the museums where they're displayed.

124. Share photos of amazing graffiti.

125. Post a picture of all the books you got from a bookstore or a library.

126. Post a picture of the beauty products you bought on a shopping spree.

127. Create a "vision board" and share it with your readers.

128. Make homemade soaps, sugar scrubs, or bath bombs and share pictures.

129. Share pictures of your kids' favorite toys...

130. Or toys you want for yourself, even if you're an adult.

131. Share pictures of gifts you gave for Christmas (or the

ones you're planning to give, if your friends and family rarely look at your blog).

132. Share pictures of your tattoos...or beautiful tattoo designs that inspire you.

133. Share photos of how you've decorated your home for Christmas.

134. Share pictures of amazing holiday decorations from other sites.

135. Share pictures of displays in store windows.

136. Share your photos of sunsets.

137. Create a blog post with pictures of sunrises and a few uplifting words.

138. Create a blog post with romantic black and white photography.

139. Create a blog post with images that celebrate feeling snuggly and cozy.

140. Create a blog post with images that celebrate the beauty of rain.

141. Share pictures of your child's notes or drawings.

142. Share pictures of your handwritten notes or poems, or your drawings. You don't have to be a professional to inspire people with what you create!

143. Share pictures that make you go "awww."

144. Post photos of the most interesting houses or buildings in your town.

145. Create a blog post with images of very old books.

146. Create a blog post with images of amazing gems and minerals.

147. Create a blog post with images of remarkable butterflies and other insects.

148. Share pictures from the farmer's market.

149. Share pictures from the fair.

150. If you collect something, share pictures of items in your collection.

LINK ROUNDUP POSTS

In the early days of blogging, bloggers focused a lot on sharing links. In fact, "blog" is a shortened version of "weblog," or a log of interesting places on the web.

When you share a collection of links about a certain topic or subject, you make it easy for your blog readers to find great information and content, you make it easy on yourself, and you help out other bloggers and websites.

151. Share links to your favorite blogs or websites in general...

152. Or share links to all your favorite Instagram accounts.

153. Is there a craft or hobby you like? Share links to several free patterns or tutorials...

154. Or share links to several gorgeous finished projects that inspire you.

155. Gather up links for easy craft ideas for kids.

156. Direct people to great posts about learning to draw.

157. In April (National Poetry Month), link to resources for reading and writing poetry.

158. In November (National Novel Writing Month), link to resources for writing fiction.

159. Are your readers stressed out? Direct people to guided meditation videos.

160. Share a bunch of beautiful computer desktop wallpapers, with links.

161. If you're a writer, link to your favorite books, software, pens, journals, and websites to help with writing.

162. Share links to websites and online universities where people can learn for free.

163. Share links to free yoga and other fitness videos.

164. Compile links for DIY home improvement projects.

165. Compile links for color palettes for painting rooms in one's home.

166. Gather up links to history blogs and websites for writers researching a certain era.

167. Gather up links to blogs and websites to help people understand a current issue.

168. Share links to gripping, dramatic stories.

169. Share links to sweet, heartwarming stories.

170. Share links to stories about the paranormal and unexplained.

171. Round up posts that offer great insight into parenting.

172. Round up posts that provide great inspiration about love and relationships.

173. Share links to advice about gardening.

174. Share links to advice about improving one's professional image.

175. Everyone could use a little more laughter in their lives. Point people to videos that crack you up.

176. Share links to various personality tests, and tell people what "type" you are.

177. Share your favorite religious or spiritual sites.

178. Do you have groggy readers? Share resources for overcoming insomnia.

179. Round up posts with a fun and frivolous theme, like unicorns or pirates.

180. Round up posts about mind-blowing new science and technology.

181. Round up all your favorite fanfics for a certain TV show, movie, or game.

182. Share links to beauty or makeup tutorials you'd like to try.

183. Share links to positive articles and posts about aging.

184. Share links to helpful blogging resources.

185. Round up posts to help people learn about typography and combining fonts.

186. Share links to the most interesting sports articles of the month.

187. Share links to the most interesting articles about gaming you've come across lately.

188. Share links to the articles on all kinds of different topics that interested you most in the past week. This gives your readers some insight into what you read and how you think.

189. Share links to homeschooling resources...

190. Or back-to-school resources.

191. Share links to posts that celebrate the season: winter, spring, summer, or fall.

192. At Halloween, share links to great pumpkin-carving tutorials.

193. Before the holidays, or at any time, share links to the best personalizable gifts online.

194. Share links to shopping on fair trade and nonprofit sites.

195. Provide links to news happening in other parts of the world that your readers might have missed.

196. Provide links to uplifting and positive news stories that your readers might have missed.

197. Round up links for instructions on how to clean absolutely everything.

198. Round up links for living with a certain illness or condition.

199. Share links about becoming a better conversationalist and learning social graces.

200. Share links to all the best TED talks.

FOOD AND DRINK-THEMED POSTS

This part of the list is aimed at food bloggers, of course, but you don't have to have a dedicated food blog in order to do the occasional food or drink-related post. Everyone is interested in food! You may even be able to tie recipes into the theme of your blog.

201. Share a recipe that a parent or grandparent made a lot when you were growing up.

202. Invent a cocktail inspired by your favorite sports team and share the recipe.

203. Invent a cocktail (or two or three) using an unusual ingredient and share the recipe.

204. Share recipes for mocktails—festive non-alcoholic drinks.

205. Review a new local restaurant.

206. Write about your favorite restaurant and what makes it so great.

207. Share an idea for a holiday food gift that's actually pretty healthy.

208. Write about a few cookbooks, kitchen gadgets, or whatever else you'd love to have in your kitchen.

209. Review a new cookbook.

210. Write about your favorite cookbook of all time and why you go back to it again and again.

211. Share a recipe in honor of an obscure holiday. For example, January the 5th is Whipped Cream Day, and February the 13th is National Tortellini Day...there are food "holidays" like this for almost every day of the year. This could be the theme of a whole blog!

212. Give directions and recipes for a super easy, virtually foolproof dinner party.

213. Share a recipe that's designed for someone with a particular allergy.

214. Share a recipe that's designed for someone with a particular disease or illness.

215. Post your best dirt-cheap recipe.

216. Design a great sandwich and give it a name.

217. Share three attempts at making the ultimate grilled cheese sandwich and declare a winner.

218. Show people how to have a fondue party.

219. Review a few different local craft beers or barbecue sauces...or types of chocolate.

220. Share your favorite ten-minute meal.

221. Share your favorite slow, painstaking recipe that is truly worth the effort.

222. Write about unusual foods you'd like to try someday.

223. Interview a local chef. (Then make sure the restaurant's social media page shares the post with their followers.)

224. Try out a vintage or historic recipe and report on the results.

225. Share your favorite quotes about cooking or food.

226. Write about your favorite healthy snacks.

227. Share your favorite recipe to bring to someone else's party.

228. Come up with Oscar party appetizers that tie into the nominated movies.

229. Share a cheat sheet of common recipe substitutions. Consider making an infographic.

230. Or share a cheat sheet of common seasonings for various world cuisines...

231. Or a cheat sheet for pairing wine with desserts...

232. Or a cheat sheet for pairing fruit with cheese.

233. Write about a food that's very trendy...that you can't stand.

234. Show how to pack a lunch that isn't boring.

235. Share tips for packing a perfect picnic.

236. Share a campfire cooking recipe.

237. Share a vegetable recipe that even picky people will like.

238. Share a recipe for a less popular vegetable.

239. Tell people about about your biggest cooking disaster.

240. Tell people about your biggest cooking triumph...so far.

241. Tell people about the first thing you ever learned how to make.

242. Share a recipe that's fun for an adult and a child to make together.

243. Post instructions for the ultimate make-your-own-sundae bar...

244. Or the ultimate make-your-own-pizza party.

245. Tell people about must-buy items at a national chain grocery store.

246. Tell people about your favorite food items to order online.

247. Share a Taco Tuesday recipe...

248. Or a Waffle Wednesday recipe...

249. Or a Fish Friday recipe, or any other weekly tradition you'd like to invent.

ONE-WORD SUBJECT MATTER IDEAS

You could take any of these about a thousand different ways.

250. jealousy

251. soulmates

252. rules

253. shopping

254. popularity

255. medications

256. distance

257. hair

258. gym

259. texting

260. patience

261. hugging

262. surprise

263. femininity

264. masculinity

265. military

266. lying

267. luck

268. grudges

269. Facebook

270. positivity

271. predictions

272. diets

273. roommates

274. dreams

275. genealogy

276. recovery

277. etiquette

278. reunion

279. phones

280. gambling

281. mythology

282. networking

283. pregnancy

284. fairness

285. the Bible

286. crushes

287. tests

288. censorship

289. personality

290. rejection

291. attention

292. burial

293. driving

294. millennials

295. magic

296. disability

297. mirrors

298. debt

299. courage

TRAVEL-BASED POSTS

Even if you don't have a blog that's specific to travel, you can do a travel post now and again. If you do have a travel blog, maybe one of these ideas will give you a fresh angle. Either way, for many of these, you don't even have to leave your bedroom: these can be based on research.

300. Write about a few things you never like to travel without.

301. Tell people about a good day trip from your town or city.

302. Tell people about the best places to visit in your town.

303. Write a post about motels with a retro vibe.

304. Write a post about hotels with a futuristic feel.

305. Share your favorite road trip snacks...

306. Or a perfect road trip playlist.

307. Give people suggestions for great beach reads...

308. Or great books to read on the airplane.

309. Write about ways to survive a cross-country drive...

310. Or deal with a long, cramped flight.

311. Share pictures of waterfalls around the world.

312. Tell people about quirky little museums in your country.

313. Write about an awful travel experience.

314. Write about a travel experience that was a pleasant surprise.

315. Tell people the reasons why you're dying to visit a certain city or country.

316. Tell people about your three favorite experiences on a certain vacation.

317. Interview someone in a foreign country about the sights and experiences in their country they recommend. Also ask them to share things that not everybody knows about their country. (If you're good at international networking, this would be a great theme for a whole blog.)

318. Research free attractions and things to do in a city and share them with your readers.

319. Share research on money-saving tips for traveling abroad.

320. Share research about visiting a country that doesn't get a lot of tourists.

321. Write about a national park that doesn't get many visitors.

322. Write about an unusual or amazing annual festival.

323. Suggest a fun three-day itinerary in a city.

324. Share tips for traveling with children.

325. Write about movies that take place in a certain city: Paris, London, Cairo, etc.

326. Write about places where people can go into ice caves.

327. Write about the best bookstores in the world.

328. Write about the best bazaars and street fairs in the world.

329. Tell your readers about how to avoid making a faux pas in foreign countries.

330. Share your favorite travel outfits.

331. Share advice for packing light.

332. Write about an extreme adventure.

333. Write about gorgeous but easy hiking trails.

334. Write about factories that have been converted into hotels.

335. Write about churches that have been converted into inns.

336. Share recommendations for not-too-busy beaches.

337. Share recommendations for fun things to do at the beach.

338. Write about cities with undergrounds you'd like to explore.

339. Write about the places you'd most love to visit in winter.

340. Write about the places you'd most love to visit in spring.

341. Share safety tips for travelers.

342. Share travel opportunities available only to students.

343. Share travel deals available only to seniors.

344. Write about what surprised you most about visiting another country.

345. Write about what you miss from home when you're traveling abroad.

346. Write about a custom in another country that you wish your country would adopt.

347. Write about a little-known side trip from a much-visited city.

348. Interview a tour guide or tour bus driver.

349. Blog about interesting abandoned places.

350. Write about the most haunted places to visit.

351. Write about the most romantic places to visit.

352. Tell people about the world's oldest wineries.

353. Tell people about the world's newest amusement parks.

354. Share charming farm tours.

355. Share fascinating factory tours.

356. Write about places where the water is naturally blue.

357. Share tips on packing for travel to a very cold country.

358. Share tips on packing for travel to a very hot country.

359. Share "6 Vacation-Saving Products to Pack in Your Carry-On."

360. Share inexpensive railway itineraries.

361. Write a post on the world's prettiest currency.

362. Tell people how they can participate in an archeological dig.

363. Write about not-so-famous places to enjoy spring blossoms and blooms.

364. Give people tips for airline travel with their pets.

365. Give people tips for road trips with their pets.

366. Tell people about some of the best places in your state, your country, or the world to see holiday light displays.

367. Blog about unique coffee shops in a certain city.

368. Blog about an important holiday in other parts of the world that isn't celebrated much in your country.

369. Blog about unusual holidays around the world...

370. Or about unusual Christmas traditions around the world.

371. Write about the best souvenirs and gifts to bring home from a city or country.

372. Write about hotels with great rooftop bars.

373. Write about restaurants with stunning lake or ocean views.

374. Share tips for getting better photographs of nature.

375. Share tips for fun couple and family vacation photos.

376. Share a week-long road trip itinerary.

377. Write about eco-friendly hotels and lodges in your area, your country, or another country.

378. Write about the most amazing zip lining adventures.

379. Write about a great birdwatching destination.

380. Blog about places where people can swim with the dolphins.

381. Share camping tips for beginners.

382. Write about gorgeous fountains.

383. Write about striking city statues.

384. Blog about overlooked honeymoon destinations.

385. Blog about a great place to vacation with small children.

386. Blog about a great place to vacation with teenagers.

387. Write about travel experiences that are for extroverts only.

388. Write about vacation ideas that introverts will love.

389. Share a guide to London or New York City for lovers of literature.

390. Share a music lovers' guide to a city that isn't well-known for its music.

391. Blog about beautiful destinations for people who love the snow.

392. Blog about destinations you suspect (or know!) are overrated.

393. Write about ways to deal with fear or anxiety when traveling.

394. Write about ways to deal with jet lag.

395. Blog about the oldest trees in the world.

396. Blog about how to learn another language…for free.

397. Blog about the world's most colorful cities.

398. Share your favorite quotes about travel.

399. Share your travel bucket list.

LIST-BASED POSTS

Obviously, I love to make lists, and I have lots of them on my blog. Blog posts with numbers in the title ("20 Ways to…" "10 Reasons Why…") have a natural appeal to people browsing on social media.

400. Post a list of ten weird facts about yourself. (This one's a classic. It's great for a new blog *or* one that's been around for a while!)

401. Share a bunch of your favorite inspiring quotes…

402. Or a bunch of your favorite funny quotes. (Give credit where credit is due!)

403. Put together a gift guide for dads, or men in general—they

can be hard to buy for! (This is a good opportunity to use affiliate links.)

404. Or put together a list of great gifts for teachers…

405. Or a list of gifts under $10…

406. Or a big list of Christmas stocking stuffers.

407. Share a list of what you believe are the top ten songs of all time.

408. Share a list of the songs you're listening to now.

409. Post a list of all the TV shows you've ever binge-watched on Netflix.

410. Post a list of ten little things that annoy you more than they should. (People will love to chime in and share their own pet peeves.)

411. Share a list of twenty little things that never fail to lift your spirits.

412. Tell people everything you learned in college…

413. Or learned from your current job.

414. Or: on Mother's Day or Father's Day, talk about the things you learned from your mom or dad.

415. Or talk about the things you've learned from your children.

416. Share a list of ways to get more organized.

417. List all your favorite things about Christmas…

418. Or about summer, fall, or spring.

419. If you hate winter...or summer...post a list of products, foods, etc. that help you survive it.

420. Share your list of lifetime goals!

421. Or list your New Year resolutions...

422. Or list your goals for the month.

423. List ways to become more environmentally friendly.

424. List movies that made you cry like a baby.

425. List movies that always make you smile.

426. List twenty-five ways to be more frugal.

427. Support small business owners: share a list of your favorite local independent stores.

428. Or share a list of your favorite big chain stores, if you prefer.

429. List individuals, living or dead, who inspire you.

430. Make a list of your guilty pleasures...or guiltless pleasures.

431. List all of your favorite smartphone apps.

432. List your favorite ways to relax and unwind after a long, hard day.

433. List all of the best picture books for kids.

434. List all of the books on your "to be read" pile.

435. List unusual words and their meanings.

436. List your favorite actors and/or actresses.

437. If you're a teacher, list themes for lessons plans...

438. Or list ways to cut down on your grading time.

439. If you're a business person, list ways to improve PowerPoint presentations...

440. Or list ways to have more effective and/or less boring meetings.

441. If you're an entrepreneur, list ways to increase your social media following...

442. Or list cost-effective ways to promote a product or service.

443. If you're a writer, share a list of ways to beat writer's block...

444. Or a list of good places to pitch articles...

445. Or a list of agents or publishers in your genre.

446. If you're a retail associate, list the most common annoyances of your job...

447. Or your best tips for being successful.

448. List ways that a person can ruin their marriage.

449. List ways that a person can ruin their life.

450. List ways that a person can transform their life.

451. List small ways to reward or treat yourself.

452. List the best compliments you've ever gotten.

453. List lots of great ways to compliment others!

454. List ways to make a little extra cash on the side.

455. Feeling morbid? Share a list of some of the weirdest ways to die.

456. Feeling silly? Share a list of your favorite dumb jokes.

457. Tell readers about your top ten proudest accomplishments. Invite them to share their own!

458. List your regrets, big and small. (But remember...we *all* make mistakes.)

459. List all the worst pieces of advice you've ever received.

460. List ways to improve your backyard.

461. List ways to improve your bedroom.

462. List ways to decorate your cubicle at work.

463. List ten things you should have in your cubicle at work.

464. List ten things you should have in an "emergency bag" at home in case of a fire or natural disaster.

465. List ways to tell if someone is a good person.

466. List ways to tell if you should stay clear of a person.

467. List ways to deal with stress.

468. List ways to become more politically active.

469. List ways to get more people to read a blog.

470. List ways to be more persuasive.

471. List ways to be more romantic.

472. List ways to feel more confident.

473. Share a list of ideas for spring, summer, fall, or winter dates.

474. Share a list of ideas for "family night."

475. Your readers might be looking for a new passion in life! Share a big list of hobbies.

476. For writers or for people focused on self-esteem or self-improvement, share a list of positive traits or positive adjectives describing people. Maybe ask readers to share which five of the words describe them best.

477. Share a list of things to never, ever say to people. (This is almost guaranteed to prompt a lively comments section.)

478. This is *kind* of a list: put together your own thirty-day writing challenge...

479. Or a thirty-day photography challenge...

480. Or a thirty-day fitness challenge...

481. Or a thirty-day cleaning challenge.

482. Post a list of ten things you simply cannot live without. You can actually do this for every season or every month.

483. Make a list of specific things that you're *done* worrying about.

484. Share a list of things that can help you study.

485. Share a big list of ideas for Instagram pictures.

486. List the absolute best Christmas albums...

487. Or the absolute worst Christmas songs.

488. Help your readers celebrate life more! List your favorite weird or obscure holidays. There are several sites online where you can find more than one holiday for every single day of the year.

489. List things you miss from a certain decade.

490. List people you miss.

491. List the best times of your life...so far.

492. List the worst times of your life...and congratulate yourself for being a survivor.

493. List the seven kinds of friends every person should have.

494. List the eight reasons why everyone should own a cat.

495. Share a list of questions for family members at the dinner table at Thanksgiving. (Avoid things that are likely to start a fight!)

496. List great themes for children's birthday parties.

497. List great themes for grownups' parties.

498. List other great ways for adults to celebrate their birthdays. No more of this "oh, it's no big deal"!

499. List ways to be even more awesome.

500. Everyone could use more gratitude in their lives! Share a long list of things you're grateful for to encourage your readers to count their own blessings.

I hope you've enjoyed perusing *5,000 Writing Prompts*. If you found it useful, please help others discover it by writing an online review!

For more writing resources, be sure to check out my blog, bryndonovan.com. And for news and giveaways, go to subscribepage.com/bryn to subscribe to my newsletter.

With creativity, the possibilities are truly limitless. In all your projects and endeavors, I wish you joy and success.

ABOUT THE AUTHOR

Bryn Donovan writes romance novels both as Bryn and as Stacey Donovan, and she blogs about writing and positivity at bryndonovan.com. Her favorite things include French roast coffee, hot sauce, rescue dogs, bubble baths, and adventures. She has an MFA in Creative Writing from the University of Arizona and she works in publishing. A writer, optimist, and geek, she believes in being your true self, expressing yourself creatively, and not letting anyone else set limits for you. She lives in Los Angeles.

Made in the USA
San Bernardino, CA
15 June 2019